*Russia, the Soviet Union,
and the United States:*

An Interpretive History

AMERICA AND THE WORLD

EDITOR: Robert A. Divine

Russia, the Soviet Union, and the
United States: An Interpretive History
JOHN LEWIS GADDIS

America's Response to China:
An Interpretative History of Sino-American Relations
WARREN I. COHEN

The Troubled Encounter:
The United States and Japan
CHARLES E. NEU

America and the Arab States:
An Uneasy Encounter
ROBERT W. STOOKEY

The Uncertain Friendship:
American-French Diplomatic Relations Through the Cold War
MARVIN ZAHNISER

795932   10/80   8 95

Russia, the Soviet Union, and the United States:

An Interpretive History

JOHN LEWIS GADDIS
Ohio University

John Wiley and Sons, Inc.
New York ● *Chichester* ● *Brisbane* ● *Toronto*

Library of Congress Cataloging in Publication Data:

Gaddis, John Lewis.
    Russia, the Soviet Union, and the United States.

    (America and the world)
    Includes bibliographical references.
        1.   United States—Foreign relations—Russia.
2.   Russia—Foreign relations—United States.   3.   United
States—Foreign relations—20th century.   I.   Title.
E183.8.R9G24   327.73'047   77-12763
ISBN 0-471-28910-8
ISBN 0-471-28911-6 pbk.

Printed in the United States of America

10 9 8 7 6 5 4

*For the Grandparents
of Michael and David*

Foreword

It is difficult to conceive of a more significant topic in twentieth-century American diplomacy than our relations with the Soviet Union. Ever since Lenin's accession to power in 1917, Russian leaders and their enigmatic behavior, from Stalin's brutal purges and sphinxlike demeanor to Khrushchev's peasant charm and outrageous tirades to Brezhnev's businesslike habits and conventional joviality, have engrossed American policymakers and the American public alike. Yet, as John Gaddis makes clear in these pages, our relationship with Russia goes back yet another century. Since the American Revolution, United States diplomats have borne the indignities that Russians have heaped on foreigners, have searched for ways to permit mutual interests to triumph over conflicting ideologies, and have sought to win the favor of such capricious rulers as Catherine the Great and Tsar Alexander I. The stakes became much greater in the Cold War years, but the essential outline of Russian-American relations remained unchanged—oscillation between friendship and enmity as diplomats succeeded only occasionally in balancing interests against principles.

Against the backdrop of these nineteenth-century beginnings, Professor Gaddis focuses his attention on the more recent experience with the Soviet regime, tracing the uneven course of relations from the Bolshevik Revolution to the emergence of detente. He treats the varied aspects of Soviet-American diplomacy: repeated efforts to stimulate trade, attempts to lessen Soviet internal repression, negotiations to ease the arms race, and, above all, the constant search for stability in Europe. The continental balance of power remains the focal point from the time Russia leaves

World War I in 1918 through the Helsinki accords that ratified the de facto post-World War II division of Germany, and thus of all Europe, between the East and the West. The result is a comprehensive account that transcends the historiographical disputes over the Cold War to achieve a balanced and perceptive understanding of how these two great nations, so alike in some ways and so different in others, have survived nearly two centuries of mutual distrust.

This book is one in a series of volumes tracing the history of American foreign policy toward those nations with which the United States has had significant relations over a long period of time. By stressing the continuity of diplomatic themes through the decades, each author seeks to identify the distinctive character of America's international relationships. It is hoped that this country-by-country approach will not only enable readers to understand more deeply the diplomatic history of their nation but that it will also make them aware that past events and patterns of behavior exert a continuous influence on American foreign policy.

ROBERT A. DIVINE

Preface

"There are now two great nations in the world which, starting from different points, seem to be advancing toward the same goal: the Russians and the Anglo-Americans. . . . Each seems called by some secret design of Providence one day to hold in its hands the destinies of half the world."[1] It is almost obligatory to begin any history of Russian-American relations with a reference to this famous prophecy, put forward by Alexis de Tocqueville in 1835. In fact, however, there was nothing foreordained about the circumstances which nearly brought its fulfillment more than a century later. The division of most of the post-1945 world into Russian and American spheres was not the result of those two countries' expanding population and territory, as Tocqueville had thought it would be, but rather of the suicidal instincts of the Europeans, whose wars opened opportunities for the simultaneous extension of influence by the United States and the Soviet Union. Nor was this bipolar configuration of power either as absolute or as lasting as Tocqueville had anticipated: the ability of Russians and Americans to control their respective halves of the world was never complete and has, in recent years, substantially declined.

A more fruitful approach to the history of Russian-American relations is to examine the interplay, in the foreign policies of both countries, between interests and ideologies. "Interests" are here understood to mean those conditions a state considers necessary in order to maintain its authority in the world;

---

[1] Alexis de Tocqueville, *Democracy in America*, J. P. Mayer and Max Lerner, eds., translated by George Lawrence (New York: 1966), pp. 378–379.

"ideologies" are the justifications advanced for the exercise of that authority. These admittedly oversimplified definitions are not mutually exclusive: ideologies can become interests, and interests can become ideologies. Even so, this interpretive framework contributes more to an understanding of the topic at hand than does Tocqueville's doctrine of "inevitability," and, for this reason, I have chosen to employ it in the discussion to follow.

This is a work of both synthesis and original scholarship. Where satisfactory secondary accounts exist, I have generally followed them and hereby express my indebtedness to their authors. Where they do not (and there are a surprising number of areas in the history of Russian-American relations where this is the case), I have had recourse to such primary sources as are available. Detailed examinations of historiographical disputes seemed inappropriate in a book of this nature; my accounts of such controversial subjects as the Bolshevik Revolution and the origins of the Cold War should be taken as reflecting my own best judgment, and nothing more.

I should like to express my appreciation to Robert A. Divine for suggesting that I undertake this volume and for the helpful advice he provided while it was being written. Wayne Anderson of John Wiley and Sons has shown great patience in awaiting what is now a long-overdue book. For reading and commenting on preliminary drafts, I am grateful to James A. Field, Jr., Alonzo L. Hamby, David Schoenbaum, Thomas H. Etzold, Alan T. Isaacson, and Akira Iriye. Thomas R. Maddux generously allowed me to consult his unpublished manuscript on Soviet-American relations during the 1930s. An Ohio University Research Council fellowship helped to defray photoduplication expenses. My wife, Barbara, calmly tolerated the tantrums, scowls, and brooding silences which go with authorship. My sons, Michael and David, kindly refrained (most of the time) from scribbling on their father's manuscript.

Portions of Chapters VI and VII appeared originally as an essay in Frank Merli and Theodore A. Wilson, eds., *Makers of American Diplomacy* (New York: 1974), and are reprinted by permission of Charles Scribner's Sons. Before it was abolished in 1918, the Russian calendar was thirteen days behind that of the West for the twentieth century, twelve days for the nineteenth, and eleven days for the eighteenth. All dates cited in this book are according to the Western, or "New Style" calendar.

Newport, Rhode Island,   JOHN LEWIS GADDIS
March 1977

Contents

*Russia, the Soviet Union,
and the United States:*

An Interpretive History

CHAPTER I

A Heritage of Harmony: 1781–1867

"IT WOULD BE BEST FOR US TO WAIVE ALL DISCUSSION upon abstract principles. . . . we must endeavor to settle the differences between our Governments on the basis [of] our *mutual interests*."[1] It was the kind of statement which might have been made at any one of the Nixon-Brezhnev summits of 1972–1974, but in fact it dates from 1824, when Count Karl Robert Nesselrode, foreign minister of the Tsar Alexander I, opened negotiations with American minister Henry Middleton on boundary problems in the Pacific Northwest. Nesselrode, who served as foreign minister from 1816 to 1856, was more noted for his stamina than his sagacity, but in this statement he neatly characterized the early Russian-American relationship. Profound ideological differences existed between the young American republic, in many ways the most revolutionary government of its day, and the ancient tsarist autocracy, which had sworn hostility to revolutions everywhere. But they also shared common interests, and because both states, at this time, gave more weight to interests than ideology in their diplomacy, the basis was established for the most consistently friendly relationship the United States would have with a major European power in the nineteenth century.

I

Americans knew from the beginning that their struggle for independence from Great Britain could not succeed without

---

[1] Henry Middleton to John Quincy Adams, April 19, 1824, in U. S. Congress, Senate (58th Cong., 2nd Sess.), *Alaska Boundary Tribunal, Appendix* (Washington: 1903), pp. 71–72.

foreign assistance. Such aid would not be difficult to obtain, they believed, because independence would open the hitherto-forbidden North American trade to Britain's rivals.[2] In holding this view, the colonists exaggerated the importance of economic considerations in the minds of Old World diplomats, a mistake they would repeat frequently in the next two centuries. France, Spain, and several other powers were prepared to grant the colonists varying degrees of help—and to risk war with Britain in order to do so. But they acted from considerations of power politics; the lure of trade was, for them, a distinctly secondary consideration.

Catherine the Great's Russia was no exception. The chief goal of the Russian monarch at the time of the American Revolution was to maintain a balance of power on the European continent. Her principal instrument for doing this was the so-called "Northern system," a loose alignment with Britain, the Scandinavian and Baltic countries designed to balance the land power of France and Austria. At the same time, Catherine was wary of Britain's becoming too powerful, because that nation could control, through its domination of trade in the Baltic, much of Russia's commerce with the rest of the world.[3] It is within this context that Catherine's response to the American Revolution must be viewed.

Catherine seemed, at first, sympathetic. She made clear her opinion that the British could not suppress the revolt in North America and refused requests from George III for military assistance. In 1780, Catherine formed a League of Armed Neutrality, based on the principle, dear to the Americans, that "free ships make free goods." Her foreign minister, Nikita Panin, originated a plan for mediating the Anglo-French war sparked by the Revolution on a basis which would have confirmed the independence of most, if not all, of the American colonies.[4] These hopeful signs encouraged the Continental Congress, late in 1780, to send Francis Dana, a Massachusetts lawyer then in

---

[2] Felix Gilbert, *To the Farewell Address: Ideas of Early American Foreign Policy* (Princeton: 1961), pp. 54–56.

[3] David M. Griffiths, "Nikita Panin, Russian Diplomacy, and the American Revolution," *Slavic Review*, XXVIII (March, 1969), 4–7.

[4] Ibid., pp. 1–24.

Europe as John Adams' secretary, to St. Petersburg in an effort "to engage Her Imperial Majesty to favor and support the sovereignty and independence of the United States, and to lay a foundation for a good understanding and friendly intercourse between the subjects of Her Imperial Majesty and the citizens of these United States, to the mutual advantage of both nations."[5]

Dana's reception in Russia was, to say the least, disappointing. Catherine studiously ignored the American envoy's presence, on the grounds that she could not acknowledge American independence until the British had done so. When Dana, following the Congress' instructions, tried to associate the United States with the League of Armed Neutrality, Catherine's ministers rebuffed him on the irrefutable ground that the United States could not qualify as a neutral in the existing conflict. Efforts to hold out trade as an inducement to recognition proved equally futile: nonrecognition did not preclude such trade as did exist, nor were the Russians, at that time, very interested in expanding it.[6] Embittered by his treatment, Dana left the Russian capital after two ineffectual and frustrating years. It was not an auspicious beginning for the Russian-American relationship.

The failure of Dana's mission has been variously explained as the result of Catherine's ideological antipathy for the American revolutionaries, the inability of a stuffy Puritan diplomat to engage in boudoir politics, and France's cynical attempts to undercut its American ally.[7] None of these explanations has much merit. In fact, both the Russian government's initial sympathy for the American Revolution and its subsequent indifference to it can best be understood as the product of realistic considerations, on the part of Catherine and her ministers, of Russian national interests.

Neither Catherine nor her advisers saw any particular ideological challenge in the Americans' revolt against Britain: George III, the empress believed, had brought on his own difficulties through inept administration. She did see a threat to

---

[5] Worthington C. Ford, et al., eds., *Journals of the Continental Congress* (Washington: 1904–1937), XVIII, 1168–1169.

[6] David M. Griffiths, "American Commercial Diplomacy in Russia, 1780 to 1783," *William and Mary Quarterly,* XXVII (July, 1970), 390–400.

[7] Ibid., pp. 379–380.

the European balance of power, though, if Britain, an important counterweight to France and Austria, should get bogged down in a lengthy colonial war in North America. It was this consideration which caused Catherine to reject British requests for troops and naval supplies to help put down the rebellion. The eruption of war between Britain and France in 1778, and between Britain and Spain in 1779, lent urgency to the situation: these events moved Panin to propose mediation. Russian interest in American independence stemmed, therefore, from a calculated assessment of what was necessary to maintain equilibrium in Europe, not from any abstract infatuation on the part of the empress or her ministers for republican principles.[8]

Catherine's views on maritime rights, proclaimed in the Declaration on Armed Neutrality, also paralleled those of the Americans, but again for different reasons. The Americans had quite consciously repudiated the mercantilist concept that trade should be the instrument of politics; rather, in their view, the unrestricted flow of commerce throughout the world would provide the means by which a new international order, transcending traditional political rivalries, could be created.[9] Catherine would have none of this. Her support for the "free ships, free goods" principle arose, not out of any rejection of mercantilism, but from a belief that the League of Armed Neutrality would enhance Russian prestige in Europe while freeing Russian commerce from exclusive dependence on British bottoms in time of war.[10] Neither the Continental Congress nor Dana, its representative, understood this point.

Nor did they understand the distinction between mediation and recognition—the first did not necessarily imply the second. Catherine's chief interest was to settle the war between Britain and its enemies. Recognition of American independence before the British had acknowledged it would have impaired her ability

---

[8] Griffiths, "Panin, Russian Diplomacy, and the American Revolution," pp. 1–18; Frank A. Golder, "Catherine II and the American Revolution," *American Historical Review*, XXI(1915), 92–96; N. N. Bolkhovitinov, "Russkaia diplomatiia i voina SShA za nezavisimost' 1775–1783 godov," *Novaia i noveishaia istoriia*, 1964, #1, 73–88.

[9] Gilbert, *To the Farewell Address*, pp. 66–75.

[10] Isabel de Madariaga, *Britain, Russia and the Armed Neutrality of 1780* (New Haven: 1961), p. 440.

to achieve such a settlement. And, by the end of 1781, even mediation had become a remote prospect: the Americans had defeated Cornwallis at Yorktown and were insisting on direct negotiations with the British. Catherine, meanwhile, had turned her attention toward the Turkish Empire, a move requiring reconciliation with Austria and, more than in the past, the benevolent sympathy of Great Britain. The congruence of interests which caused the Continental Congress to send Dana to St. Petersburg was deceptive, therefore; although Russians and Americans took similar positions on several of the great issues of the day, they arrived at those positions from wholly different perspectives which provided little basis for mutual cooperation.

II

A firmer basis for cooperation developed as a result of trade between Russia and the United States during the first decade of the nineteenth century. Commerical contacts between Russians and Americans were nothing new. Virginia tobacco had found its way to Russia, by way of England, in the late seventeenth century, and by 1763 Boston merchants had begun a profitable direct trade with St. Petersburg, in violation of British maritime regulations. It was not until after 1800, however, that the volume of commerce became considerable. Carried on almost exclusively in American ships, it involved the sale of such commodities as sugar, rice, indigo, and, later, cotton, from the United States and the West Indies, in return for Russian hemp, iron, and sailcloth, all highly prized for their use on sailing vessels. Britain remained, of course, Russia's largest trading partner during this period, but the Russian government did attach sufficient importance to direct commerce with the United States to encourage it as a means of escaping London's domination of trade in the Baltic.[11]

---

[11] Norman E. Saul, "The Beginnings of American-Russian Trade, 1763–1766," *William and Mary Quarterly*, XXVI(October, 1969), 596–600; Alfred W. Crosby, Jr., *America, Russia, Hemp and Napoleon: American Trade with Russia and the Baltic, 1783–1812* (Columbus: 1965), pp. 14–39; Aa. Rasch, "American Trade in the Baltic, 1783–1807," *Scandinavian Economic History Review,* XIII(1965), 63–64; N.N. Bolkhovitinov, "Novye raboty o russko-amerikanskoi torgovle v XVII-nachale XIX veka," *Novaia i noveishaia istoriia,* 1967, #4, 122–126.

But commerce could not be kept aloof from politics: by 1807 the Napoleonic wars had seriously constricted Russian-American trade. The British, through their Orders in Council, severely limited neutral trade with the Continent, while Napoleon responded by threatening to confiscate ships found complying with the British regulations. This "damned if you do, damned if you don't" situation led President Jefferson, late that year, to impose an embargo on all American trade with foreign countries. The embargo hit Russia especially hard because she had just gone to war with her major commercial partner, Britain, following the reconciliation with Napoleon at Tilsit. It was this common predicament of being denied access to trade which caused Alexander I and Jefferson, apparently independently of each other, to decide in 1808 to establish formal diplomatic relations between their two countries.[12]

"It cannot be unimportant to have, in a party so powerful and influential as Russia, a good will and wakeful attention to the just rights and interests of the United States," wrote Secretary of State James Madison to William Short, the new minister-designate to St. Petersburg. Alexander I was more blunt. "I seek in the United States a kind of rival to England," he told his new minister to Washington, Count Pahlen. "I believe that it is in their own interest . . . at least to moderate, if not to limit, the baneful despotism which Great Britain exerts over the sea."[13]

When the Senate refused to confirm Short, Madison, who by then had become president, nominated in his place John Quincy Adams. It was not Adams' first exposure to Russia: as a boy, he had spent two years in the Russian capital serving as Francis Dana's secretary. An astute diplomat and an accomplished linguist (in French—Russian was little used at the emperor's court), the crusty New Englander was an excellent choice. The four years he spent in St. Petersburg laid the foundation for

[12] Nikolai N. Bolkhovitinov, *The Beginnings of Russian-American Relations, 1775–1815*, translated by Elena Levin (Cambridge, Massachusetts: 1975), pp. 187–193; John C. Hildt, *Early Diplomatic Relations of the United States with Russia* (Baltimore: 1906), pp. 35–43.

[13] Madison to Short, September 8, 1808, U. S. Department of State Records, National Archives [hereafter DSR], microfilm M-77, roll 2; Alexander to Pahlen, January 8, 1810, Ministerstvo inostrannykh del SSSR, *Vneshniaia politika Rossii XIX i nachala XX veka* (Moscow: 1967), V, 338.

what became a tradition of good relations between the United States and Russia.[14]

The common interest the two countries had in asserting maritime rights led both into war in June 1812, although with different enemies. The alliance between France and Russia had, from the first, rested on a fragile base. It was stretched even further when the British, in 1809, agreed to allow neutral trade with Russia. This action stimulated a great increase in American commerce, freed by repeal of the embargo that same year, to the point that by 1810, American vessels were carrying 20% of all exports out of St. Petersburg.[15] Napoleon's efforts to stop this trade, which he rightly suspected the British of using to undercut his Continental System, contributed in part to the worsening of Franco-Russian relations and to the French invasion of Russia in the summer of 1812.

Meanwhile, United States relations with Great Britain had deteriorated with the refusal of the British to modify their Orders in Council in the face of economic coercion. Both the British and the French violated American neutral rights, but the British violations, involving impressment as well as the searching of ships and the seizure of cargoes, were more humiliating. Furthermore, in Canada the Americans had a convenient place to attack the British; no such contiguous territory under French control existed. As a result, Congress on June 18, 1812, declared war, not knowing that only two days earlier the British government had announced its intention to repeal the offending Orders in Council.

Britain's involvement in war with the Americans posed problems for the Russians, just as some three and a half decades earlier, George III's determination to crush the American Revolution had worried Catherine II. Alexander's response was much the same as his grandmother's: he sought to arrange mediation of the Anglo-American war so that Britain would be free to concentrate its resources against the French in Europe. The tsar proposed mediation in September 1812, and by April of

---

[14] Samuel Flagg Bemis, *John Quincy Adams and the Foundations of American Foreign Policy* (New York: 1949), pp. 156–189.

[15] Norman E. Saul, "Jonathan Russell, *President Adams,* and Europe in 1810," *American Neptune,* XXX(October, 1970), 287–289.

the following year President Madison, without waiting to see whether the British would accept, had dispatched Albert Gallatin and James A. Bayard to join Adams in St. Petersburg for the purpose of negotiating a peace under the benevolent supervision of the Russian emperor.

This proved to be a mistake, for the British refused to discuss peace under Russian mediation. They did propose separate bilateral negotiations with the Americans, however, and these, after much delay, got underway at Ghent in the summer of 1814. By Christmas of that year, a treaty had been signed ending the conflict on the basis of a return to the status quo before the war. Alexander, who by this time had defeated Napoleon at the head of the victorious Fourth Coalition, took little interest in the talks at Ghent, now overshadowed by more dramatic developments at the Congress of Vienna. But the Russian mediation offer had prodded the British into beginning negotiations, and the Americans could at least be grateful for that.[16]

III

The congruence of interests which developed between Russia and the United States during the Napoleonic wars obscured, for the moment, potential areas of conflict, but the return of peace made it clear that antagonisms did exist. The task of resolving these differences amicably provided the first real test of the habit of cooperation which had grown up between the two nations.

One such conflict was territorial. Early in the eighteenth century Russian explorers had laid claim to what is today Alaska, and in 1799 the Russian-America Company had been organized to exploit this area. Almost immediately the company's remote possessions became subject to incursions from American trappers and traders; one reason why the Russians were anxious to establish diplomatic relations in 1803 was their desire to lodge an official protest.[17] Not until 1821, however, did the matter become serious: in September of that year, Alexander I issued a *ukase* denying foreigners access to Russian-America and assert-

---

[16] Frank A. Golder, "The Russian Offer of Mediation in the War of 1812," *Political Science Quarterly*, XXXI(1916), 380–391; Bradford Perkins, *Castlereagh and Adams: England and the United States, 1812–1823* (Berkeley: 1965), pp. 20–24.

[17] Rumiantsev to Levett Harris, May 29, 1808, *Vneshniaia politika Rossii*, IV, 267;

ing control of its adjoining seas for a distance of more than one hundred miles from the shore.

This order, signed at the instigation of the Russian-America Company, aroused concern in Washington not only because of its restrictions on maritime commerce, but also because the conviction had begun to form in the minds of many Americans that the United States was destined to dominate the Western Hemisphere and should therefore oppose further attempts by European powers to establish colonies there. Secretary of State John Quincy Adams put the argument forcefully to the Russian minister in Washington in July 1823:

> I told him specially that we should contest the right of Russia to *any* territorial establishment on this continent, and that we should assume distinctly the principle that the American continents are no longer subjects for *any* new European colonial establishments.[18]

In a somewhat less direct form, this noncolonization principle was incorporated into President Monroe's message to Congress in December of that year, thus forming part of what came to be known as the Monroe Doctrine.

The Emperor Alexander had long since decided not to enforce the 1821 *ukase*, which he had apparently signed without much thought. Confronted with protests from both the American and British ministers, he agreed to initiate joint discussions with them in an effort to establish, once and for all, territorial limits in the Pacific Northwest. These talks resulted, in 1824, in separate Russian-American and Anglo-Russian treaties setting the southern boundary of Russian-America at the latitude fifty-four degrees, forty minutes.[19]

More serious than the territorial question in the Pacific Northwest was the issue of whether Spanish rule was to be restored in Latin America. Independence movements in that

---

Howard I. Kushner, *Conflict on the Northwest Coast: American-Russian Rivalry in the Pacific Northwest, 1790–1867* (Westport, Connecticut: 1975), pp. 11–12.

[18] Charles Francis Adams, ed., *The Memoirs of John Quincy Adams* (Philadelphia: 1875), VI, 163.

[19] Irby C. Nichols, Jr., "The Russian Ukase and the Monroe Doctrine: A Re-Evaluation," *Pacific Historical Review*, XXXVI(February, 1967), 23–25; N. N. Bolkhovitinov, "Russia and the Declaration of the Non-Colonization Principle: New Archival Evidence," *Oregon Historical Quarterly*, LXXII(June, 1971), 110–114.

part of the world had grown out of Spain's weakness resulting largely from the Napoleonic wars, but it was not until after Napoleon's defeat that the European powers were able to give serious thought to what should be done about these insurgencies. Except for the British, who saw trade opportunities in an independent Latin America, the European monarchies could hardly welcome the establishment of republics throughout most of Spain's New World empire. But without the cooperation of the British navy there was little the European monarchs could do to suppress these movements and restore Spanish authority.

Alexander I made clear his antipathy for the Latin American rebels and gave official support to the Spanish government's efforts to suppress them. At the same time, he was realistic enough to recognize that he could do little in the absence of British support and that, by pressing the point too hard, he might alienate the Americans, to whom he still looked as a counterweight to London. And in 1820, revolution broke out in Spain itself, forcing plans for the reestablishment of Spanish control in the New World to be put off. Accordingly, when the United States announced its intention to recognize the Latin American republics in 1822, the Russian government expressed no immediate objections.[20]

The events of 1823, however, altered the situation. That year saw the successful suppression by the French of the Spanish uprising and the development of so strong a fear that the European monarchs might now try to send troops to Latin America that the British foreign secretary, George Canning, proposed to the Americans a joint declaration opposing any such action. Just as the Monroe administration was debating this suggestion, two messages arrived from the Russian government expressing its determination not to recognize the Latin American republics and celebrating the crushing of revolutions in Europe.[21] These messages provoked the statement of the other two principles of

---

[20] Dexter Perkins, "Russia and the Spanish Colonies, 1817–1818," *American Historical Review,* XXVIII(July, 1923), 671–672; William Spence Robertson, "Russia and the Emancipation of Spanish America, 1816–1826," *Hispanic American Historical Review,* XXI(May, 1941), 207–211.

[21] Worthington C. Ford, "John Quincy Adams and the Monroe Doctrine," *American Historical Review,* VII(July, 1902), 685–686, and VIII(October, 1902), 30–32.

the Monroe Doctrine: that while the United States would abstain from interference in European affairs, it would oppose any effort by a European power to extend its political system to the Western Hemisphere.

Because Russian activities in the Pacific Northwest and in Latin America provided the occasion for the Monroe Doctrine, that proclamation has often been interpreted as an anti-Russian measure. This is an inaccurate view. At no point were United States officials seriously worried about Russian intervention in the Western Hemisphere; their concern was directed toward Britain and France.[22] The Russians simply had the bad luck to provide the excuse, through several carelessly worded pronouncements, for a declaration which was really directed against their continental rivals. Indeed, the decision to proclaim the Monroe Doctrine independently of Great Britain was made, at least in part, to avoid giving the Russians the impression that London and Washington were acting together.[23]

It cannot be said that Russian foreign policy during this period was noninterventionist: as one historian has noted, the tsarist government "allowed little distinction or discrimination between international relations proper and the internal affairs of . . . states."[24] But this was true only in Europe; in both Latin America and the Pacific Northwest, the Russians showed a realistic sense of their own limitations and a cautious deference to the power of others. "It may be that our frank & consistent conduct impresses respect," American minister Henry Middleton commented in 1824, "but our *maritime force*, & the consequent *impossibility of dictation* towards us must also be taken into account."[25] If one amends this statement to include British as well as American maritime force, it is not an inaccurate assessment of the situation.

---

[22] Bolkhovitinov, "Russia and the Non-Colonization Principle," pp. 125–126; Nichols, "The Russian Ukase and the Monroe Doctrine," pp. 18–21; Irby C. Nichols, Jr., and Richard A. Ward, "Anglo-American Relations and the Russian Ukase: A Reassessment," *Pacific Historical Review* XLI(November, 1972), 458–459.
[23] On this point, see James Monroe to Thomas Jefferson, December, 1823, printed in Ford, "Adams and the Monroe Doctrine," p. 51.
[24] Nicholas V. Riasanovsky, *Nicholas I and Official Nationality in Russia, 1825–1855* (Berkeley: 1959), p. 236.
[25] Middleton to Adams, March 8, 1824, DSR, M-35: 10.

IV

One of the more puzzling aspects of early Russian–American relations is how two such ideologically disparate states could get along with each other as well as they did. The United States, since independence, had been strongly and self-consciously committed to republicanism: to the right of each nation, as John Quincy Adams put it, to have a government "founded upon the consent, and by the agreement of those that are governed." Russia, after 1815, seemed pledged to precisely the opposite principle. Sworn to uphold legitimacy everywhere, its implacable opposition to revolutions had earned it, by mid-century, the epithet "gendarme of Europe." "Russia occupies, and will continue to occupy, a commanding position in every struggle against popular rights," the American minister in St. Petersburg noted in 1852. "[It is] impelled by a hostility to free institutions, that admits of no compromise and yields to no relaxation."[26]

Certainly Americans were aware of the ideological gulf which separated them from the Russians. The reactionary nature of the tsarist government was the subject of frequent comment in the press and in dispatches from American ministers in St. Petersburg. "In the direction of public affairs here," George Washington Campbell observed in 1819, "the Emperor is, in fact, *everything*, and his Ministers *nothing*." James Buchanan reported to President Jackson in 1832 that "here there is no freedom of the Press, no public opinion, . . . but little political conversation, and that very much guarded. In short, we live in the calm of despotism." The Emperor Nicholas I might be "one of the best of despots," Buchanan added, *"but he is still a despot."*[27]

Moreover, the difficulties of serving in St. Petersburg furnished constant irritants. The climate was harsh—"this Hyperborean Prison," William Pinkney called it. George Washington Campbell lost three of his children to illness there within a week in 1819. John Randolph fumed about "innumerable flies gigan-

---

[26] Ford, "Adams and the Monroe Doctrine," p. 41; Neill Brown to Daniel Webster, January 28, 1852, DSR, M-35: 15.

[27] Campbell to John Quincy Adams, February 18, 1819, DSR, M-35: 7; Buchanan to Jackson, June 22, 1832, John Bassett Moore, ed., *The Works of James Buchanan* (New York: 1908–1911), II, 199. See also Thomas A. Bailey, *America Faces Russia: Russian-American Relations from Early Times to Our Own Day* (Ithaca: 1954), pp. 8–11, 20–21, 27–31, 39–44, and 52–55.

tick as the Empire they inhabit." The diplomatic establishment was expensive to keep up; bribery seemed required to get any information of value. "I am certain," John Randolph Clay wrote in 1831, "that with a little tact and more bribery, I could at this time buy nearly every thing which has taken place with regard to these affairs." Interference with the mails was a constant problem, which the Russians' clumsy efforts to forge the American official seal could not conceal. "The Post Office American eagle here is a sorry bird," Buchanan noted in 1833. Neill Brown summed up the feelings of a steady procession of ministers, past and future, when he observed in 1852 that "this government possesses in an exquisite degree, the art of worrying a foreign representative, without giving him the consolation of an insult."[28]

But there were mitigating factors. One was the belief that Russia was too backward to be governed by anything other than despotism. Henry Middleton commented in 1826 that "the opinion is perhaps not erroneous which holds [absolutism] to be the only principle which can bind together so heterogeneous a mass as is aggregated under the Sceptre of the Russian autocrat." James Buchanan wrote Andrew Jackson in 1833: "The most ardent republican, after having resided here for one year, would be clearly convinced that the mass of the people, composed as it is of ignorant and superstitious barbarians who are also slaves, is not fit for political freedom. Besides they are perfectly contented." Because they saw autocracy as the only form of government suited to Russia, American representatives could even rationalize it into a crude form of self-determination. Charles Todd noted in 1841:

It is a gratifying fact to see the Imperial Autocrat frequently walking the Streets as a private citizen altogether unattended . . . ; and it is rather a singular coincidence that the most absolute Monarch ruling the most powerful Empire, of Europe should be the only Chief Magistrate in Europe or America, with the exception of the President of the United

---

[28] Pinckney to Adams, October 9, 1817, DSR, M-35: 6; Campbell to Adams, May 3, 1819, ibid., M-35: 7; Randolph to Martin Van Buren, August 19, 1830, ibid., M-35: 12; Clay to Edward Livingston, October 7, 1831, ibid.; Buchanan to Livingston, February 22, 1833, ibid.; Brown to Webster, May 27, 1852, ibid., M-35: 15.

States, who can thus mingle with his fellow citizens or subjects. . . . The fact affords curious matter for the contemplation of the political philosopher.[29]

Even if Americans had viewed Russia as ripe for republicanism, they would have felt serious inhibitions about trying to propagate that ideology there. While Americans believed as firmly in the eventual triumph of their system as Lenin and Trotsky did in theirs a century later, they were sensitive to the fragility of republican institutions and to the danger that they might be corrupted by constant involvement in war. Hence, it was perfectly possible for John Quincy Adams to proclaim, on the one hand, that

The influence of our example has unsettled all the ancient governments of Europe. It will overthrow them all without a single exception. I hold this revolution to be as infallible as that the earth will perform a revolution around the sun in a year.

and to state, with equal fervor, on the other, that there would be an "inevitable tendency of a direct interference in foreign wars, even wars for freedom, to change the very foundations of our own government from *liberty* to *power*." Therefore, "though Republican to the last drop of blood in their veins, [Americans] have thought it no sacrifice of their principles to cultivate with sincerity and assiduity Peace and Friendship even with the most absolute Monarchies and their Sovereigns."[30]

The Russians too were well aware of the ideological differences which separated them from the Americans. Count Pahlen, the first Russian minister to the United States, commented upon his arrival in Washington in 1810: "The republican

---

[29] Middleton to Clay, February 11, 1826, ibid., M-35: 10; Buchanan to Jackson, May 29,1833, Moore, ed., *Buchanan Works*, II, 339; Todd to Webster, December 22, 1841, DSR, M-35: 14. See also Marc Raeff, "An American View of the Decembrist Revolt," *Journal of Modern History*, XXV(September, 1953), 286–293.

[30] Adams to Charles Jared Ingersoll, June 19, 1823, W. C. Ford, ed., *The Writings of John Quincy Adams* (New York: 1913–1917), VII, 488; Adams to Edward Everett, January 31, 1822, ibid., p. 201; Adams draft, Monroe presidential address, November 27, 1823, quoted in Ford, "Adams and the Monroe Doctrine," p. 42. See also Adams' famous Independence Day address, July 4, 1821, quoted in E. H. Tatum, *The United States and Europe, 1815–1823: A Study in the Background of the Monroe Doctrine* (Berkeley: 1936), pp. 241–245.

simplicity makes a considerable impression on one accustomed to the pomp of European courts." Count Nesselrode, the Russian foreign minister, found it necessary to warn Pahlen's successor in 1818 that in the United States, "governed by democratic institutions, the political prejudices of the government are all the more difficult to eradicate as those usually common. And however plausible the argument, . . . it always ends by reinforcing the opinions which it sought to reverse." The Russians viewed the Americans as avaricious, contentious, violent, and, above all, saddled with an inefficient form of government. The Russian *chargé* in 1854 described it as the "principle of anarchy, which prevails here under the pseudonym of 'self-government.' " "What can be expected," Russian minister Edouard de Stoeckl complained at the height of the Civil War,

from a country where men of humble origin are elevated to the highest positions, where honest men refuse to vote and dishonest ones cast their ballots at the bidding of shameless politicians? This is democracy in practice, the democracy that European theorists rave about. If they could only see it at work they would cease their agitation and thank God for the government which they are enjoying.[31]

Extremely sensitive to revolution, the Russian government had reason to fear the ideological precedent the Americans had set. As Alexander I noted in 1823, "Too many examples demonstrate that the contagion of revolutionary principles is arrested neither by distance nor by physical obstacles." Moreover, the influence of the American Revolution was not lost on Russian radicals—it played an important part in the Decembrist revolt of 1825, as if in confirmation of Alexander's fears. "I do not mean to state that the Russian government are unfriendly to the people of the United States," Buchanan wrote in 1832, "but yet they

[31] Pahlen to Rumiantsev, June 30, 1810, *Vneshniaia politika Rossii*, V, 472; Nesselrode to Poletica, November 21, 1818, "Correspondence of the Russian Ministers in Washington, 1818–1825," *American Historical Review*, XVIII(April, 1913), 316; Frank A. Golder, *Guide to Materials for American History in Russian Archives* (Washington: 1917, 1937), I, 37, 46, 52, 68, 74, II, 1; Dexter Perkins, *The Monroe Doctrine, 1823–1826* (Cambridge, Massachusetts: 1927), pp. 172–173; Frank A. Golder, "The American Civil War Through the Eyes of a Russian Diplomat," *American Historical Review*, XXVI(April, 1921), 457.

must attribute to our example the existence of those liberal principles in Europe which give them so much trouble."[32]

But the Russian government generally made a distinction
between the American Revolution and its more violent French
and Latin American successors. Catherine the Great took strong
ideological exception to the French Revolution; she did not to
the American. Alexander I, in 1809, could refer to the United
States, "so wise and so well-governed," and in 1823 asked,
"Where are the Franklins, the Washingtons, and the Jeffersons
of southern [Latin] America?" The Russians were well aware of
the American noninterventionist tradition: "Our rule of not in-
terfering with the affairs of other Powers has certainly contributed much towards rendering us acceptable to Russia," John
Randolph Clay noted in 1833. Neill Brown observed in 1851 that
"Americans rank as high here, if not more so [,] than any other
people; and though republicans, they are known and acknowledged not to be propagandists." Finally, Russians tended to
distinguish between the American nation, whose potential
power they respected, and its government, which they could
view as a transitory phenomenon.[33] As a result, what seemed
on the surface to be a fundamental ideological antipathy did not
seriously affect relations between the two countries during the
first half of the nineteenth century.

---

[32] Alexander I to Chateaubriand, quoted in Perkins, *The Monroe Doctrine,
1823–1826*, p. 131; Buchanan to Jackson, June 22, 1832, Moore, ed., *Buchanan
Works*, II, 200. See also Max Laserson, *The American Impact on Russia: Diplomatic
and Ideological, 1784–1917* (New York: 1950), pp. 115–138; George Vernadsky, "Reforms Under Alexander I: French and American Influence," *Review of Politics*,
IX(January, 1947), 47–64; and N. N. Bolkhovitinov, "Dekabristy i Amerika,"
Voprosy istorii, 1974, #4, 91–104.

[33] Bolkhovitinov, *Beginnings of Russian-American Relations*, p. 30; Alexander I to P.
K. Sukhtelen, November 9, 1809, *Vneshniaia politika Rossii*, V, 278; Golder, *Guide
to Russian Archives*, I, 22; Patricia Kennedy Grimsted, *The Foreign Ministers of
Alexander I: Political Attitudes and the Conduct of Russian Diplomacy, 1801–1825*
(Berkeley: 1969), p. 51; Alexander I conversation with La Ferronays, November
28, 1823, quoted in Robertson, "Russia and the Emancipation of Spanish
America," p. 215; Clay to Louis McLane, August 16, 1833, DSR, M-35: 12; Brown
to Webster, November 6, 1851, ibid., M-35: 15; E. A. Adamov, "Russia and the
United States at the Time of the Civil War," *Journal of Modern History*,
II(December, 1930), 593.

V

A mutual interest in preserving the European balance of power also contributed to the amicable nature of the nineteenth century Russian-American relationship. Russia's stake in maintaining the delicate equilibrium established at Vienna in 1815 against nationalism and liberalism is well known. Less well known is the fact that the United States, though committed to a policy of nonintervention in European affairs, did not expect to be able to keep the Western Hemisphere wholly insulated from European quarrels: the balance of power in the New World depended, in part, on what happened in the Old.[34] Thus, Americans looked to Russia, during the first half of the nineteenth century, as a counterweight to those powers most capable of upsetting the New World balance—Great Britain and France.

Francis Dana's mission to St. Petersburg in 1781 can be seen in that context, as can the decision to establish diplomatic relations with Russia in 1808 and acceptance of the tsar's mediation during the War of 1812. Even after proclamation of the Monroe Doctrine, there remained a pervasive fear that Britain and France might try to establish new centers of power in the Western Hemisphere, thereby impairing what Americans saw as their God-given right to dominate the continent.[35] The crushing of the revolutions of 1848 seemed to increase this danger, as did the revolution in naval technology brought about by the use of steam power. "Those who believe . . . that the United States can long escape difficulties with Europe have more faith in the future than I have," United States minister Neill Brown noted in 1852. Ten years later another American minister in St. Petersburg, Cassius M. Clay, made the same point:

It is useless to deceive ourselves with the idea that we can isolate ourselves from European interventions. We become in spite of

---

[34] On this point, see the analysis in Alan Dowty, *The Limits of American Isolation: The United States and the Crimean War* (New York: 1971), pp. 18–27.

[35] Frederick Merk, *The Monroe Doctrine and American Expansionism, 1843–1849* (New York: 1966); David M. Pletcher, *The Diplomacy of Annexation: Texas, Oregon, and the Mexican War* (Columbia, Missouri: 1973); and Dowty, *Limits of American Isloation*, all emphasize this sense of vulnerability.

ourselves—the Monroe Doctrine—Washington's Farewell Address —and all that—a part of the "balance of power."[36]

Since Russia had fewer bases for conflict with the United States than any other European power, Americans saw it throughout the early nineteenth century as a country worth cultivating good relations with, to the end that Britain and France not become too powerful in Europe and hence capable of threatening the balance of power in the New World.

The Russians were, if anything, more interested in maintaining this relationship than the Americans. It was not that they expected military assistance if war broke out in Europe; Alexander I's abortive effort to recruit the United States into the Holy Alliance had taught the Russians something about the Americans' aversion to formal commitments.[37] But they did see good relations with the United States as a means of avoiding excessive reliance on Great Britain in the two crucial areas of trade and technology. Having no substantial merchant fleet of their own, the Russians had looked, since the turn of the century, to trade in American bottoms as a way to ensure access to world markets should the Empire's much larger commerce through Great Britain be cut off.[38] Later, under Nicholas I, Americans were enlisted to build railways, telegraph lines, and naval vessels, again to avoid too much dependence on the British.[39] The theme of seeking good relations with Washington as a counterweight to London recurred frequently in Russian diplomatic correspondence from the 1820s through the 1850s.[40] The idea bore fruit, for both sides, during the Crimean War and the American Civil War.

---

[36] Brown to Webster, May 27, 1852, DSR, M-35: 15; Clay to William H. Seward, April 13, 1862, ibid., M-35: 19.

[37] Benjamin Platt Thomas, *Russo-American Relations, 1815–1867* (Baltimore: 1930, pp. 27–33.

[38] Tatum, *The United States and Europe,* pp. 25, 116–118.

[39] Albert Parry, *Whistler's Father* (New York: 1939), *passim.*; Frederick M. Binder, "American Shipbuilding and Russian Naval Power, 1837–1846," *Military Affairs,* XXI(Summer, 1957), 79–84; Charles Vevier, "The Collins Overland Line and American Continentalism," *Pacific Historical Review,* XXVIII(August, 1959), 237–253.

[40] Golder, *Guide to Russian Archives,* I, 32, 52, 54, 58, 62, 63.

The war in the Crimea brought to an end almost a half-century in which Russia had played a decisive role in maintaining the European balance of power. Involvement in war simultaneously with Britain, France, and Turkey ruined Russia's ability to play off its antagonists against one another. The ignominious defeat the Russians suffered at the hands of the Allies also destroyed the myth of massive and invulnerable Russian armies, poised for intervention in European affairs. Confronted with a hostile Europe, the tsar's government hoped that its friendly relationship with Washington might counterbalance, however modestly, the position of its enemies.

The Russians sought to accomplish this objective in three ways: by encouraging Washington to insist upon the rights of neutrals, in the expectation that such action might bring the Americans into conflict with the British; by securing the right to fit out privateers in American ports to prey on British and French commerce; and by attempting to protect the Pacific Northwest by arranging a fictitious sale of the Russian-America Company's interests to a group of San Francisco businessmen. None of these schemes worked out as planned. The British showed no inclination to interfere with neutral trade. The Russians gave up the effort to fit out privateers for fear of violating American neutrality laws. The sale of Russian–America became unnecessary when the Russian-America Company negotiated its own truce with the Hudson's Bay Company, thereby exempting their respective territories from the war. But the hopes the Russians entertained do indicate the extent to which they saw the United States, in this period, as an element of some significance in the world balance of power.[41]

For Americans, the Crimean War, as United States minister Thomas Seymour put it, presented "no redeeming features. . . . The peace of the world is broken, by the cutthroat nations of Europe, who care infinitely less for 'holy

---

[41] Frank A. Golder, "Russian-American Relations During the Crimean War," *American Historical Review*, XXXI(1926), 462–471; Dowty, *Limits of American Isolation*, pp. 73–83; Norman E. Saul, "Beverly C. Sanders and the Expansion of American Trade with Russia, 1853–1855," *Maryland Historical Magazine*, LXVI(Summer, 1972), 160–168; Eufrosina Dvoichenko-Markov, "Americans in the Crimean War," *Russian Review*, XIII(April, 1954), 137–145.

places' or 'the integrity of the Sultan' than for their own selfish aggrandizement.'' But the war did offer advantages from the point of view of power politics. It tied down Britain and France at a time when relations between the two were close, and when prospects for their intervention in the Caribbean appeared considerable. It provided opportunities for a new definition of neutral rights in wartime and for increased trade with Russia. "Whatever we may think of Russia in its character of a despotic power," Seymour observed, "here is a government which has been uniformly friendly to that of the States, and we can continue our trade with her and improve it if we please, without either endorsing her policy or compromising our republican principles."[42]

Washington's sympathy for the Russians during the Crimean War had no direct effect on the outcome of that struggle. It did demonstrate to the British, though, that Europe and North America could no longer be considered as separate spheres; that events in one could affect the balance of power in the other. The Palmerston government seems to have concluded from this experience that while Britain should not encourage the expansion of United States influence in North America, there was now little it could do to prevent it, since Washington could expect to have friends in Europe in any future conflict with London.[43] This realization would pay important dividends for the Americans in their own Civil War, which was soon to follow.

Within five years of the Crimean War's termination, the United States itself was involved in a bloody civil conflict which involved the prospect of European intervention. Alone among the major European powers, Russia maintained a position of sympathetic neutrality toward the North. There was, at the time, and has been since, much confusion as to why the Russians did this. The half-century tradition of Russian-American friendship was often cited as the explanation, as was the fact that both countries were then going through the process of end-

---

[42] Seymour to William L. Marcy, July 24 and May 8, 1854, DSR, M–35: 16. For the situation in the Caribbean, see Dowty, *Limits of American Isolation*, pp. 133–167; and Kenneth Bourne, *Britain and the Balance of Power in North America, 1815–1908* (Berkeley: 1967), pp. 170–205.

[43] Ibid., pp. 204–205; Charles S. Campbell, *From Revolution to Rapprochement: The United States and Great Britain, 1783–1900* (New York: 1974), pp. 89–90.

ing involuntary servitude. But the real reason was that Russia continued to see the United States as a vital element in the international balance of power. As Prince Gorchakov, the Russian foreign minister, put it in 1861, the United States was "the only commercial counterpoise in the world . . . to Great Britain, and Russia would do nothing, therefore, to diminish its just power and influence."[44]

Russian sympathy for the North played a larger role in the diplomacy of the war than is often realized. Late in 1862 France proposed joint mediation, with Britain and Russia, on a basis which probably would have confirmed Southern independence. Timely Union military victories and the Emancipation Proclamation usually have been credited with forestalling this move, but recent research indicates that, while not without their long-range effects, these events had little immediate impact in Europe. The mediation proposal failed mainly because Britain was unwilling to go to war to enforce it, and because the Russians, whose cooperation was deemed vital to secure the Union's acquiescence without war, refused to go along. It was not that the Russians opposed a negotiated settlement; indeed, they repeatedly urged this course upon Union leaders. But the tsar's government was willing to let Washington choose the proper time for negotiations, and this policy, given the intransigence of both sides, ensured that they would never take place.[45]

Failure of the 1862 mediation proposal by no means removed the danger of European intervention; British and French recognition of the Confederacy remained a possibility throughout the first half of 1863. Once again, though, the interrelation of events in Europe with those in America worked to Washington's advantage. An uprising against Russian rule in Poland broke out in January, and as prospects of British and French intervention

---

[44] John Appleton to Seward, April 20, 1861, U. S. Department of State, *Foreign Relations of the United States*, [hereafter *FR*] *1861*, p. 299. See also Edouard de Stoeckl to Gorchakov, February 24, 1862, and Gorchakov to Stoeckl, October 22, 1863, both quoted in Adamov, "Russia and the United States at the Time of the Civil War," pp. 595, 601–602.

[45] D. P. Crook, *The North, the South, and the Powers, 1861–1865* (New York: 1974), pp. 221–225; Daniel B. Carroll, *Henri Mercier and the American Civil War* (Princeton: 1971), pp. 234–241.

in that crisis increased, chances diminished that Paris and London would seek to impose a settlement in America. Secretary of State William H. Seward, though sympathetic to the Poles, quickly rejected a French invitation to join in remonstrances on their behalf on the grounds that such a move would be inconsistent with the American noninterventionist tradition. Cassius M. Clay, in a dispatch from St. Petersburg, put the reason more bluntly: "Why should Americans take part against an avowed friend, in behalf of the ally of avowed enemies?"[46]

The Russians, grateful to the Americans for their friendly attitude, sent both their Atlantic and Pacific fleets to winter in United States ports late in 1863. Many in both Europe and America took these unannounced visits as a sign of Russian support for the Union, and they were warmly welcomed in the North. But the real reasons for the visits did not escape sophisticated observers at the time. Concerned about the possibility of war over Poland, the Russian government, perhaps with excessive optimism, hoped to use its ramshackle fleet to harass British and French commerce on the high seas. Sending the ships to the United States would keep them from being bottled up in Russian ports and would give them convenient bases from which to operate. The Lincoln administration was well aware of the Russians' motives, but Seward was not above conveying the false impression that a Russian-American defensive alliance had been formed, thereby further discouraging whatever chances still remained of British and French intervention on behalf of the Confederacy.[47]

It is, of course, impossible to say with precision what effect Russian-American cooperation had in inhibiting intervention by those countries, either in Poland or in the American Civil War.

---

[46] Clay to Seward, August 5, 1863, DSR, M-35: 20. See also Carroll, *Henri Mercier*, pp. 315–319; John Kutolowski, "The Effect of the Polish Insurrection of 1863 on American Civil War Diplomacy," *The Historian*, XXVII(August, 1965), 560–577; and Harold E. Blinn, "Seward and the Polish Rebellion of 1863," *American Historical Review*, XLV(July, 1940), 828–833.

[47] Howard I. Kushner, "The Russian Fleet and the American Civil War: Another View," *The Historian*, XXXIV(August, 1972), 633–649. See also Frank A. Golder, "The Russian Fleet and the Civil War," *American Historical Review*, XX(July, 1915), 801–812; Thomas A. Bailey, "The Russian Fleet Myth Re-Examined," *Mississippi Valley Historical Review*, XXXVIII(June, 1951), 81–90; and I. Ia. Levitas, "Russkie eskadry v Amerike," *Istoriia SSSR*, 1968, #5, 135–141.

Certainly it was not the decisive factor in either case. But as early as March 1863, long before the Russian fleet's visit to the United States, Lord John Russell, the British foreign secretary, had speculated privately on the possibility of a Russian-American agreement which might lead to a new balance of power in the world.[48] Given the potential power of these two great states, given the surface appearances of cooperation in their relationship, this possibility could not be without its effect upon the calculations of European statesmen.

VI

An apparent consequence of the cordial relationship between St. Petersburg and Washington during the Civil War was the tsar's decision to sell Alaska, or Russian-America, as it was then known, to the United States in 1867. One needs to be careful in assessing the motives on both sides, though, for what appears on the surface to have been the fruit of an amicable relationship was in fact a sophisticated recognition by the Russians of where power lay along the desolate but strategically important shores of the northern Pacific.

The establishment of mutually recognized boundaries for Russian-America in 1824 had not stopped United States citizens from fishing in its waters or trading with its natives. Despite repeated efforts to achieve self-sufficiency, the Russian-America Company had been forced, by 1854, to arrange with a group of San Francisco businessmen to furnish its forlorn northern outposts with supplies and markets. The company's abortive attempt to "sell" its interests to this group during the Crimean War had not been forgotten, and in succeeding years, California and New England commercial interests pushed energetically for the acquisition of Russian–America, an idea they found consistent with the conveniently malleable principles of Manifest Destiny. Among the most persistent advocates of this point of view was the senator from New York, William H. Seward, who as

---

[48] Russell to Lord Lyons, March 7, 1863, quoted in Kutolowski, "Polish Insurrection," p. 565. See also Crook, *The North, the South and the Powers,* pp. 284–286; and, for evidence that this kind of thinking was widespread in Europe in the mid-ninetenth century, Geoffrey Barraclough, "Europa, Amerika und Russland in Vorstellung und Denken des 19. Jahrhunderts," *Historische Zeitschrift,* CCIII(1966), 280–315.

Secretary of State would later be in an excellent position to realize this vision.[49]

Increasing American interest in Russian-America coincided with a growing conviction among the tsar's advisers that it would be unwise, even futile, to try to retain the territory. Plagued by distance and mismanagement, the Russian-America Company had never made money on its colony. By 1860 the acquisition of Vladivostok and the mouth of the Amur had given Russia a firmer foothold on the Pacific; Russian-America, as a result, became strategically less significant. The most important reason for St. Petersburg's pessimism regarding Russian-America, though, was the belief that if the territory was not soon sold, the Americans would simply take it. As Admiral Ivan Popov, commander of the Russian Pacific fleet, noted in 1860:

> Whatever they may say in Europe about . . . the "Monroe Doctrine," or the doctrine of "manifest destiny," anyone who has lived in [North America] cannot fail to understand instinctively that this principle is entering more and more into the blood of the people, and that new generations are sucking it in with their mothers' milk. . . . [Cede Russian-America, the Aleutians and the islands of the Bering Sea,] . . . but let us retain the Commander Islands so as not to have the Yankees too near us.[50]

The sale of Russian-America might have been arranged as early as 1861 had not the Civil War intervened.[51] By the time that conflict was over, the Russian government was all the more eager to unload its unprofitable colony, and early in 1867, Russian minister Stoeckl, in secret negotiations with Secretary of State Seward, negotiated its sale for $7,200,000, some $2,200,000 more than the price at which Stoeckl had been authorized to sell. Senate approval came quickly, but the House of Representatives delayed appropriating the necessary funds for more than a year.

---

[49] Saul, "Sanders and American Trade with Russia," pp.162–163; Howard I. Kushner, "Visions of the Northwest Coast: Gwin and Seward in the 1850's," *Western Historical Quarterly,* IV(July, 1973), 295–306.

[50] Quoted in Kushner, *Conflict on the Northwest Coast,* p. 138. See also Ronald J. Jensen, *The Alaska Purchase and Russian-American Relations* (Seattle: 1975), pp. 9–22.

[51] Ibid., pp. 23–24.

The history of the Alaskan purchase has become encrusted with more than the usual number of myths unsupported by evidence. Public opinion was not overwhelmingly against the acquisition, and Seward had little difficulty demonstrating that the territory contained more than just walruses and polar bears. Both Russians and Americans were aware of the presence of gold—indeed, one reason the Russians wanted to sell was their fear that the territory would become another California—but fisheries, for the Americans, were probably the more important attraction. It seems likely that the Russian minister did bribe key members of the House of Representatives, but this was done to prevent the attachment of crippling amendments to the appropriations bill; it was not necessary to secure approval of the purchase itself. Finally, the sale of Alaska was the result, not so much of Russian-American friendship, as of a recognition by the Russians of the realities of power. As Stoeckl noted in one of his last dispatches from Washington, if they had not been sold "our possessions, menaced by the proximity of the Americans, would have dragged us into serious disputes with the Federal Government and would have wound up by becoming booty of the Americans."[52]

The cordiality which developed between Russia and the United States during the first half of the nineteenth century was not, therefore, the product of genuine friendship; relations between nations rarely are. It did reflect a peculiar congruence of interests, brought about by the existence of common antagonists, the absence of direct points of conflict, a realistic awareness, particularly on the Russians' part, of the limits of national power, and, probably most important, a determination on the part of both nations to keep diplomacy insulated from ideology. That these components of the early Russian-American relation-

---

[52] Stoeckl to Gorchakov, July 24, 1867, printed in Hunter Miller, "Russian Opinion on the Cession of Alaska," *American Historical Review*, XLVIII(April, 1943), 526–531. See also Thomas A. Bailey, "Why the United States Purchased Alaska," *Pacific Historical Review*, III(March, 1934), 39–48; Anatole G. Mazour, "The Prelude to Russia's Departure from Alaska," ibid., X(September, 1941), 317–318; Jensen, *The Alaska Purchase*, pp. 138–141; Kushner, *Conflict on the Northwest Coast*, pp. 156–158.

ship resulted from the comparatively marginal position which that relationship assumed most of the time in the concerns of Washington and St. Petersburg seems unarguable; events of the late nineteenth and early twentieth centuries would prove that they were decidedly transitory as well.

CHAPTER II

Diverging Interests: 1867–1917

T HE PURCHASE OF ALASKA MARKED A HIGH POINT in Russian-American cordiality. From then on, a gradual deterioration set in, so that when the tsar was overthrown a half-century later, Americans expressed little regret. The good relations which existed in the first half of the ninetenth century had been based on the absence of conflicting interests and, to an extent, on the presence of a mutual antipathy—the suspicion both nations felt toward Great Britain. During the late nineteenth and early twentieth centuries, all this changed: Russia and the United States clashed directly over Manchuria, and a new alignment of powers made Washington a tacit ally of Britain and Japan, another nation whose growing strength the Russians had reason to fear. But this international realignment was not the only reason Russian-American relations worsened. Even before that happened, the United States had begun to take Russia's internal structure as well as external policies into account in shaping its official attitude toward that country. Ideology began to make a difference; questions began to be raised as to whether a democracy could, or should, maintain friendly relations with the most autocratic nation in Europe. This preoccupation with Russian internal conditions was, in the long run, a more lasting cause of tension than Far Eastern rivalries because it made reconciliation dependent upon reform. It is an indication of the resulting bitterness that relations between the two countries remained frigid right up to the onset of the revolution in 1917—despite the development, during the first three years of World War I, of an economic relationship of considerable importance to both countries.

I

"The American eagle should not strain his naturally fine voice by shrill and prolonged screaming on small occasions," Secretary of State Frederick Frelinghuysen commented in 1881.[1] It was an elegant restatement of the nonintervention principle upon which, in large part, the amicable nineteenth-century relationship between Russia and the United States had been based. But nonintervention had never been wholly without challenge. Throughout their history, Americans had reserved and frequently exercised the right to intervene in foreign countries to protect their own citizens. There also existed a proclivity for rhetorical, through rarely actual, intervention on behalf of foreigners for humanitarian reasons.[2] Both traditions began, in the 1870s, to erode traditional noninterventionism as it had been applied to Russia.

Americans long had been aware of the tsarist autocracy's repressive nature, but ideological differences generally had not been seen as an impediment to diplomatic cordiality. This situation changed after the Civil War. The Russian government, under increasing attack from revolutionaries, was becoming more repressive than it had been at a time when Americans, who were traveling more widely and reading more about events in the rest of the world, were becoming more aware than they had been of internal conditions in Russia. Also, adherence to nonintervention in the past had been based on the realistic judgment that, whatever it might think of them, the United States lacked the capacity to influence events in most of the rest of the world. The gradual emergence of the United States as a world power toward the end of the century tended to blur the distinction, in the eyes of many Americans, between what they could only condemn and what they could reasonably expect to change.

Emancipation of the serfs and the other reforms of the 1860s had not solved Russia's problems, and in the following decade the liberalism of Alexander II began to wane. As this happened,

---

[1] Quoted in Milton Plesur, *America's Outward Thrust: Approaches to Foreign Affairs, 1865–1890* (De Kalb, Illinois: 1971), p. 6.

[2] D. A. Graber, *Crisis Diplomacy: A History of U.S. Intervention Policies and Practices* (Washington: 1959), p. 324.

revolutionary activity increased, culminating in the assassination of the tsar in March 1881, after several previously unsuccessful attempts. Americans had little sympathy with the Russian revolutionary movement at this time and certainly none with assassination, but they could not help but object to some of the measures the Russian government took to restore order.

Officially sanctioned anti-Semitism caused the greatest concern. Persecution of Jews in Russia was nothing new, but their suspected involvement in revolutionary activity led, after the tsar's murder, to renewed enforcement of laws forcing Jews to live in the so-called "Pale," a strip of territory along the western border of the Empire, and to pogroms directed against inhabitants of that region which the government made no serious attempt to stop.

These moves offended American sensibilities in two ways. By singling out a whole class for suspicion, the Russian government made American citizens who happened to be Jews subject to discrimination when traveling or residing in Russia. United States diplomats generally succeeded in protecting the interests of American Jews, but only through persistent intervention on a case-by-case basis. Efforts to convince the Russians that an American passport entitled its holder to equal protection regardless of religious belief proved frustratingly futile.[3] But despite the great volume of diplomatic correspondence relating to their affairs, the number of American Jews in Russia was never large. Russian anti-Semitism shocked most Americans, not as a violation of a few of their fellow citizens' rights, but as an outrage against humanity. The problem was to find a basis upon which to protest Russia's treatment of its own citizens without calling into question the generally acknowledged right of a sovereign nation to frame its own laws.

Efforts were made to persuade the Russian government that better treatment of the Jews would be in its own best interests.

---

[3] Cyrus Adler and Aaron M. Margalith, *With Firmness in the Right: American Diplomatic Action Affecting Jews, 1840–1945* (New York: 1946), pp. 171–207; Alice Felt Tyler, *The Foreign Policy of James G. Blaine* (Minneapolis: 1927), pp. 271–277; Edward J. Carroll, "The Foreign Relations of the United States with Tsarist Russia, 1867–1900," (Ph. D. Dissertation, Georgetown University, 1953), pp. 121–159.

"Our experience." Secretary of State Hamilton Fish pointed out gently in 1870, "shows that the removal of restrictions of a sectarian character elevates the class relieved and advances the common good and social organization." Ten years later, his successor, William M. Evarts, told the American minister in St. Petersburg that while the United States could not intervene in Russian internal affairs, his attitude in communications with the Russian government should be "wholly consistent with the theory [of religious freedom] upon which this government is founded." Russian officials politely rejected these suggestions, however, on the grounds that Russian Jews were not of the same character as American Jews, and that since the United States had not seen fit to treat Orientals (not to mention blacks) equally, there seemed little reason why the Russian government should be expected to accord equal treatment to its minorities. Following the 1890 census, American officials were able to show that the emigration of Russian Jews to the United States had greatly increased, thereby demonstrating a direct connection between Russian anti-Semitism and American interests.[4] But the Harrison administration did not press the point, perhaps because of the obvious counterargument that if the United States regarded Russian Jews as undesirable immigrants, it could exclude them, as it did Orientals. There appeared, in short, to be no very effective basis upon which the United States could prevail upon the Russians to improve their treatment of Jews.

But it was not just Jews who suffered in Russia: Americans gradually became aware that arbitrary arrest, imprisonment, and exile to Siberia were common features of life under tsarism. No one did more to impress this view upon the public than George Kennan, indefatigible traveler, writer, and lecturer, whose book, *Siberia and the Exile System,* was published in 1891. Kennan awed audiences all over the country with his vivid accounts of Russian prisons, often delivered in convict garb to the accompaniment of clanking chains. His prolific writings evoked outrage throughout much of the world, including Russia itself,

---

[4] Fish to Curtin, February 4, 1870, DSR, M-77: 137; Evarts to Foster, April 14, 1880, *FR: 1880,* p. 873; Foster to Evarts, December 30, 1880, *FR: 1881,* pp. 996–1004; Blaine to Smith, February 18, 1891, *FR: 1891,* pp. 737–739. See also Adler and Margalith, *With Firmness in the Right,* pp. 215–225.

where they circulated surreptitiously in an early form of *samiz-dat*. Organizations were formed to protest conditions in Russia, and exiled Russian radicals, their way prepared by Kennan's work, toured the United States, attracting large and sympathetic responses.[5]

Kennan's writings had little direct effect on Russian-American diplomatic relations, which remained correct though not as cordial as in the past. But they did do much to change public attitudes toward Russia, and, in an age when public opinion was having an increasingly important influence on diplomacy, this shift eventually had its effect. When famine broke out in Russia in 1891–1892, the response of individual Americans was generous, but a considerable debate broke out in Congress over whether United States citizens should be aiding a repressive autocracy. Two years later, the Senate's approval of a treaty providing for the extradition of Russian political refugees provoked surprisingly widespread criticism. "I am more and more convinced," United States minister Clifton Breckinridge reported from St. Petersburg late in 1895, "that . . . to protect our own sense of dignity and right, we need to let [the Russians] know that, however regretful it may be to us, it is possible to cool our ardor by persistently trampling in matters concerning us, upon principles we hold most dear."[6]

The change in public attitudes toward Russia between 1875 and 1895 marked the end of the friendly relationship which had persisted throughout most of the nineteenth century. It was not that Russia had done anything directly harmful to American interests, though what seemed like a direct challenge would come, soon enough, in the Far East. What had happened was

---

[5] Taylor Stults, "Imperial Russia Through American Eyes, 1894–1904," (Ph. D. Dissertation, University of Missouri, 1970), pp. 10–20, 45–46; Louis J. Budd, "Twain, Howells, and the Boston Nihilists," *New England Quarterly*, XXXII(September, 1959), 351–371; Bailey, *America Faces Russia*, pp. 126–135; Laserson, *American Impact on Russia*, pp. 303–316.

[6] Breckinridge to Olney, December 24, 1895, DSR, M-35: 48. See also Bailey, *America Faces Russia*, pp. 150–160; Carroll, "Foreign Relations of the United States with Tsarist Russia," pp. 196–228; George S. Queen, "American Relief in the Russian Famine of 1891–1892," *Russian Review*, XIV(April, 1955), 140–150; and Harold F. Smith, "Bread for the Russians: William C. Edgar and the Relief Campaign of 1892," *Minnesota History*, XLII(Summer, 1970), 54–62.

that the American people had come to regard ideological differences as important in their relations with the tsarist empire. As a later George Kennan (and distant relative of the first) has noted:

> The rise of the institution of what we might call popular nationalism in the nineteenth century . . . brought new qualities into the conduct of diplomacy everywhere. Not the least of these was a tendency on the part of statesmen to conduct foreign policy histrionically, as on a stage, bearing prominently in mind at all times the reaction of a domestic public opinion, which constituted the audience, rather than the bare requirements of the situation from the standpoint of national interest. What you did, in these circumstances, became less important than how you looked doing it.[7]

The tendency of professional diplomats is to eschew ideology, to base relationships solely on interests. But an aroused public can limit their ability to do this, and, while the attention devoted to Russia was never large in the nineteenth century, it did expand significantly in the late 1880s and the 1890s.[8] This development altered the tone, and eventually the substance, of United States policy.

II

Neither Russian nor American interest in the Far East originated in the 1890s. The tsar's empire had made extensive territorial gains there at China's expense in 1858 and 1860, while the United States had been working during the same period to open Japan and China to trade with the West. But in the mid-nineteenth century, St. Petersburg and Washington had seen each other's activities in the Far East as complementary. Both worried about the pretensions of Great Britain; both had been willing to cooperate to keep London from gaining a dominant position in the Pacific.

The situation in the 1890s was very different. Russia and the United States again were looking to the Far East, but this time they came to see their interests there as mutually antagonistic. Two unrelated events which occurred in 1895 helped to produce

---

[7] George F. Kennan, "Arbitration and Conciliation in American Diplomacy," *Arbitration Journal*, XXVI(1971), 29.
[8] Stults, "Imperial Russia," pp. 8–10.

this change: China's defeat by Japan demonstrated for all to see the extreme vulnerability of the Middle Kingdom and set off a scramble for concessions which quickly appeared to threaten that country's continued existence as an independent state. Meanwhile, the Venezuelan crisis sparked a slow but steady improvement in the long-touchy relationship between the United States and Great Britain. Russian-American cordiality, based as it was on the absence of direct conflicts and the existence of shared antipathies, did not survive these developments. Russia would henceforth see the United States as associating itself with Great Britain in the Far East to the detriment of its own interests. The United States, convinced of Britain's good intentions, would now see Russia as the chief threat to the Far Eastern balance of power, at a time when American interests increasingly demanded that that balance be maintained.

The Russian stake in the Far East was both strategic and economic. Construction of the Trans-Siberian Railroad in the 1890s promised access to the area; with it came opportunities to improve Russia's military position on the Pacific and to exploit the "great China market," a myth as believable to Russians as to Americans.[9] The Russians' immediate problem was to obtain transit rights for the railroad across Manchuria, which, though Chinese territory, offered the easiest and shortest route, and to secure an ice-free port. For this purpose the Russians negotiated a treaty with the Chinese in 1896 giving them permission to build the Trans-Siberian through Manchuria (this section would be known as the Chinese Eastern Railroad). Two years later, following the example Germany had set at Kiaochow, Russia obtained leases from China to the ice-free Manchurian harbors of Port Arthur and Talienwan, together with the right to connect these to existing rail lines by a branch to be known as the South Manchurian Railroad.

Americans did not immediately see Russian activities in Manchuria as a threat. There was as yet no indication that United States trade would be discriminated against, and the Russian government, perhaps seeking to reinforce this impression, placed large orders with American firms for railroad equipment

---

[9] Andrew Malozemoff, *Russian Far Eastern Policy, 1881–1904* (Berkeley: 1958), pp. 20–68.

to be used there. Private American investors in China at this time saw the Russian presence as an asset rather than a liability in extracting concessions from the Chinese government. Nor were the Russians alone in their imperial enterprises: the Germans had preceded them, the British and French were soon to follow, and the United States was on the verge of taking the Philippines, a move to which the Russian government pointedly made no objection.[10]

But concerns were quick to develop. As early as January 1898, Charles Denby, the United States minister in Peking, raised the possibility that Russia might try to shut American influence out of Manchuria. Such an event, Denby thought, might well justify modifying the nonintervention principle which had guided American foreign policy since Washington's Farewell Address. Such worries increased in 1899 when Secretary of State John Hay had difficulty in securing Russian endorsement of the First Open Door Note, designed to ensure equal commercial access within spheres of influence in China. Hay in the end was reduced to announcing the Powers' general acquiescence, knowing full well that the Russians had no intention of applying the Open Door policy in Manchuria but gambling, successfully as it turned out, that they would not publicly say so. Shortly thereafter, Russia took advantage of the Boxer Rebellion to occupy all of Manchuria. Its failure to withdraw led to the formation of the Anglo-Japanese alliance in 1902; although the United States did not formally associate itself with this new alignment, Russian fears that Washington's sympathies lay in that direction were, by this time, correct.[11]

American interests in Manchuria were not large—in retrospect, they hardly seem worth the diplomatic ink spilled over them. But it must be kept in mind that what was at stake were

[10] Marilyn Blatt Young, *The Rhetoric of Empire: American China Policy, 1895–1901* (Cambridge, Massachusetts: 1968), pp. 56, 94–95; Edward H. Zabriskie, *American-Russian Rivalry in the Far East: 1895–1914* (Philadelphia: 1946), pp. 33–34, 37–38, 44; James K. Eyre, Jr., "Russia and the American Acquisition of the Philippines," *Mississippi Valley Historical Review*, XXVIII(March, 1942) 539–562.
[11] Denby to Sherman, January 31, 1898, DSR, M-92: 104; Tyler Dennett, *John Hay: From Poetry to Politics* (New York: 1933), pp. 292–294. See also Theodore Roosevelt to Albert Shaw, June 22, 1903, Elting R. Morison, ed., *The Letters of Theodore Roosevelt* (Cambridge, Massachusetts: 1951), III, 497.

not actual but potential interests: it was this fact which made them capable of indefinite extension in the minds of ambitious politicians, enterprising exporters, aggressive consuls, and gloomy geopoliticians. It is significant that Brooks Adams, Charles Conant, and Alfred Thayer Mahan all published books in 1900 warning that prosperity at home required expansion overseas, that the Far East offered the most fertile fields for such expansion, and that Russia, having gained a foothold in Manchuria, was the nation most likely to resist it.[12] Or, as Henry Miller, the free-spelling United States consul in Manchuria, put it in 1901:

[Russia] will annihilate American trade here, and with her political methods will make industrial slaves of the Chinese race and soon become a serious obsticle [sic] to the extention [sic] of our trade in all the Orient, and eventually a menace to our higher civilization.[13]

Escalating rhetoric of this type could easily transform marginal interests into vital ones; Manchuria quickly became nothing less than a symbolic test of American willingness to wield power in the world. It was a test in which Russia provided the main challenge.

It is not at all clear that the Russians had anything like this in mind; indeed, the tsar's ministers took a surprisingly benign attitude toward the expansion of American influence in the Far East. Slow to see the significance of the Anglo-American rapprochement, they welcomed the annexation of Hawaii as evidence that the United States had resolved to thwart the ambitions of Britain and Japan. Nor did American acquisition of the Philippines concern them, though Russian officials were prepared to object should the islands fall to one of their European rivals. St. Petersburg's dilatory response to the first Open Door note reflected not so much hostility as genuine puzzlement at Washington's intentions, together with the characteristic cau-

---

[12] Brooks Adams, *America's Economic Supremacy* (New York: 1900); Charles A. Conant, *The United States in the Orient* (New York: 1900); Alfred Thayer Mahan, *The Problem of Asia* (Boston: 1900). For an assessment of these works and their influence, see Young, *Rhetoric of Empire*, pp. 219–231; and Michael Hunt, *Frontier Defense and the Open Door: Manchuria in Chinese-American Relations, 1895–1911* (New Haven: 1973), pp. 34–35.

[13] Miller to H. G. Squires, June 27, 1901, quoted in ibid., p. 82.

tiousness and inertia of the Russian bureaucracy. Russian diplomats did betray some irritation at American persistence in defending the Open Door: "If it were not for the Philippines the United States . . . would have been . . . satisfied with a passive relationship to . . . China," one envoy complained during the Boxer Rebellion. "Now, the interference of America is spreading in wider and wider circles."[14] But generally Russian officials saw no reason for American and Russian interests in the Far East to clash: they appear to have been surprised at the hostile response Russian actions in Manchuria provoked.

By 1903 this hostility had reached the highest levels of the Roosevelt administration. President Roosevelt and his secretary of state, John Hay, had not at first seen sinister motives in the Russian occupation of Manchuria. As late as May 1902, Hay could assure Roosevelt that "no matter what happens . . . the United States shall not be placed in any worse position than while the country was under the unquestioned domination of China." But in April 1903, the Russians decided to prolong their occupation of Manchuria indefinitely. Hay regarded this decision as "injurious to our legitimate interests" and complained of the difficulties of dealing "with a government with whom mendacity is a science." Roosevelt agreed, writing in July:

I have not the slightest objection to the Russians knowing that I feel thoroughly aroused and irritated at their conduct in Manchuria; that I don't intend to give way and that I am year by year growing more confident that this country would back me up in going to an extreme in this matter.

That same month he congratulated the Navy on the excellence of its plans developed in anticipation of a possible war with Russia in the Pacific.[15]

---

[14] De Wollant (first secretary, Russian embassy in Washington), to the Ministry of Foreign Affairs, June 7, 1900, quoted in A. Ia. Kantorovich, *Amerika v bor'be za Kitai* (Moscow: 1935), p. 94. See also Ernest R. May, *Imperial Democracy: The Emergence of America as a Great Power* (New York: 1961), pp. 234–236; Eyre, "Russia and the American Acquisition of the Philippines," pp. 550–551; Zabriskie, *American-Russian Rivalry*, pp. 55, 57, 201; and Tower to Hay, December 11 and 28, 1899, DSR, M-35: 55.

[15] Hay to Roosevelt, May 1, 1902, quoted in Tyler Dennett, *Roosevelt and the Russo-Japanese War* (New York: 1925), pp. 135–136; Hay to McCormick, April 25,

The prospect of war was never great, however, because Roosevelt was not in fact sure that the country would back him up. In January 1904, he told a group of luncheon guests, including George Kennan, that while public opinion had coalesced into an anti-Russian attitude, there was not sufficient support for a military confrontation. But then he added, with a laugh, "If everybody regarded this thing as Mr. Kennan and I do, I know where our warships would be." There would be no Russian-American war over Manchuria, but, as Kennan noted, "the sentimental 'friendship' that has long been supposed to exist between the governments of Russia and the United States is at an end—& thank the Lord for it!"[16]

The United States was not willing to fight for its interests in Manchuria, but Japan was, and, in the end, Roosevelt came to rely on Tokyo to contain St. Petersburg's Far Eastern ambitions. The Japanese would have tolerated Russian control of the Manchurian railroads, but when the Russians made it clear that they would keep a permanent military force in Manchuria and refuse to allow the Japanese a comparable sphere of influence in Korea, the Tokyo government responded violently. On the night of February 8–9, 1904, Japanese naval forces suddenly attacked the Russian Far Eastern fleet at Port Arthur, and the Russo-Japanese War was on. Roosevelt could scarcely contain his glee. "For several years Russia has behaved very badly in the Far East," he wrote to his son. "I was thoroughly well pleased with the Japanese victory, for Japan is playing our game."[17]

The Russians were bitter about the attitude of the American government and came to believe that the Japanese would not have acted so freely had they not had the tacit support of Britain and the United States. "How dare you to pretend to be our

---

1903, DSR, M-77: 140; Hay to Roosevelt, May 12, 1903, quoted in Alfred L. P. Dennis, *Adventures in American Diplomacy, 1896–1906* (New York: 1928), p. 357; Roosevelt to Hay, July 18, 1903, Morison, ed., *Roosevelt Letters*, III, 520; Stults, "Imperial Russia," p. 218n. See also Howard K. Beale, *Theodore Roosevelt and the Rise of America to World Power* (Baltimore: 1956), pp. 229–233.

[16]Kennan to Lyman Abbott, January 4, 1904, quoted in Stults, "Imperial Russia," pp. 222–223, 225.

[17] Roosevelt to Theodore Roosevelt, Jr., February 10, 1904, Morison, ed., *Roosevelt Letters*, IV, 724. See also John Albert White, *The Diplomacy of the Russo-Japanese War* (Princeton: 1964), pp. 95–131.

friends while you were knifing us all the time in the back?" the wife of the Russian ambassador in Tokyo complained to her husband's American colleague there. On the day of the Japanese attack, *Novoe Vremiia,* a leading St. Petersburg newspaper, speculated that "were the Panama Canal ready, were the powerful fleet of America in existence, were the Americans and the English in possession of [an] organized army . . . , peace would stand very little chance in general and the Russian in particular." A year later, the same newspaper published a report from its London correspondent charging that "America, uniting the European Powers and Japan by means of the doctrine of 'The Open Door,' commenced to instigate Japan to war with Russia." Another St. Petersburg newspaper, the semiofficial *Journal de St. Petersbourg,* commented self-pityingly on the "painful spectacle of what human inconstancy can do" and ran a long series of documents reminding Americans of the help Russia had provided them during the Civil War.[18]

But, despite his fulminations about "the literally fathomless mendacity of the Russians," Roosevelt did not in fact oppose their continued presence in the Far East. When, by 1905, an unbroken series of Japanese victories appeared to threaten Russia with expulsion from that region, the president began working energetically to arrange a settlement. "While Russia's triumph would have been a blow to civilization," he wrote, "her destruction as an eastern Asiatic power would also in my opinion be unfortunate. It is best that she should be left face to face with Japan so that each may have a moderative action on the other." Through skillful diplomacy, Roosevelt managed to bring Russian and Japanese emissaries together at Portsmouth, New Hampshire, in August 1905. There, under his careful but discreet supervision, they negotiated a settlement which gave

---

[18] Lloyd Griscom, *Diplomatically Speaking* (Boston: 1940), p. 242; *Novoe Vremiia,* February 8, 1904, and April 11, 1905, translations enclosed in McCormick to Hay, February 9, 1904, and Meyer to Hay, April 18, 1905, DSR, M-35: 60, 62; *Journal de St. Petersbourg,* June 17 and 18, 1904, translation enclosed in McCormick to Hay, June 25, 1904, DSR, M-35: 61. Soviet historiography still reflects bitterness over the American attitude in 1904. See, for example, L. I. Zubok, *Ekspansionistskaia politika SShA v nachale XX veka* (Moscow: 1969), especially pp. 211–215.

Japan control of southern Manchuria, but left Russian interests in northern Manchuria substantially intact.[19]

Following successful mediation of the Russo-Japanese War, the crucial question for the United States was whether its interests would better be served by continuing Roosevelt's policy of "balanced antagonisms"—a policy which would keep Manchuria from falling under the domination of any one power but did little to preserve the principle of the Open Door—or by trying to challenge Russian and Japanese influence in Manchuria in the name of the Open Door. Roosevelt's balance of power instincts led him in the first direction, but he did not supervise Far Eastern policy as closely as he might have during his last years in office. Overzealous subordinates in the State Department pushed the idea of challenging both Japan and Russia, in cooperation with China, and during the Taft administration they put this policy into effect.[20]

Taft's secretary of state, Philander C. Knox, hoped to pry open Manchuria by encouraging American investment there. Two approaches were tried: a project to lend China sufficient money to purchase all foreign-owned railroads in Manchuria, thereby neutralizing them, and, failing that, the construction by China of parallel lines there, with Western financing, in hopes of competing with the Russians and the Japanese. Neither project succeeded. American investors were reluctant to risk scarce capital on politically motivated projects whose economic potential seemed questionable. European investors had capital available but were not likely to sink it in projects like this without the approval of their governments. And with Britain allied to Japan, France allied to Russia, and Russo-Japanese and Anglo-French rapprochements well underway, the diplomatic climate was

---

[19] Roosevelt to George Von Lengerke Meyer, December 16, 1904, Morison, ed., *Roosevelt Letters*, IV, 1079; Roosevelt to Henry Cabot Lodge, June 16, 1905, ibid., p. 1230. See also White, *Diplomacy of the Russo-Japanese War*, pp. 206–309; and Eugene P. Trani, *The Treaty of Portsmouth: An Adventure in American Diplomacy* (Lexington: 1969).

[20] Hunt, *Frontier Defense and the Open Door*, pp. 142–178; Raymond A. Esthus, *Theodore Roosevelt and Japan* (Seattle: 1966), pp. 229–245; Charles E. Neu, *An Uncertain Friendship: Theodore Roosevelt and Japan, 1906–1909* (Cambridge, Massachusetts: 1967), pp. 260–268, 319.

distinctly unfavorable to Knox's schemes. "When the United States put the Manchurian proposal forward . . . , it primarily wished to separate Russia and Japan," the Chinese foreign ministry commented with some asperity early in 1910. "Now they have on the contrary joined together. If the United States has some remedy, what then is it?"[21]

The United States in fact had no remedy other than to retreat to pious but impotent invocations of the Open Door. Knox's Manchurian policy had been a classic case of projecting interests beyond capabilities: it sought to break up, through nonforcible means, spheres of influence which both Russians and Japanese were prepared to use force to maintain. Far from balancing antagonisms, it only served to unite them in opposition to Washington's ineffectual intrusions. But the Russians too would soon be cut out of the Manchurian market. World War I, and the turmoil of revolution and civil war which followed, would win Japan dominance in the Far East by default. Russian and American dreams of empire in that part of the world proved, in the end, to be equally illusory.

It is interesting to speculate on why the United States did not make a greater effort to cooperate with the Russians in the Far East. Certainly the Russians, despite lingering suspicions over the role the United States had played in the Russo-Japanese War, considered the idea and even made tentative approaches to Washington at several points.[22] Both nations should have realized, it would seem, that Japan was the real threat to the China market, and that if either of them was to have any significant influence in the Orient in the future, they would have to work together.

There would appear to be several reasons why this cooperation did not take place. Professionalization and bureaucratiza-

---

[21] Wai-w.i Pu to Chang Yin-t'ang, February 7, 1910, quoted in Hunt, *Frontier Defense and the Open Door*, pp. 215–216. See also ibid., pp. 181–244; Zabriskie, *American-Russian Rivalry*, pp. 144–189; and Walter V. and Marie V. Scholes, *The Foreign Policies of the Taft Administration* (Columbia, Missouri: 1970), pp. 109–248.
[22] On this point, see Hunt, *Frontier Defense and the Open Door*, p. 206; Scholes, *Foreign Policies of the Taft Administration*, pp. 151–152; Zabriskie, *American-Russian Rivalry*, pp. 148–153; and William Appleman Williams, *American Russian Relations, 1781–1947* (New York: 1952), pp. 52–80.

tion in the State Department, symbolized by the formation, in 1908, of a separate Division of Far Eastern Affairs, drained authority from the White House, reducing the kind of close control over foreign policy which would have been required to implement Roosevelt's balance of power strategy. Moreover, Taft and his advisers had little understanding of this policy to begin with; their approach placed far more emphasis on the defense of abstract principle than had Roosevelt's. But even Roosevelt would have found it difficult to cooperate with the Russians, not because they were autocratic, but because they were "so corrupt, so treacherous and shifty, and so incompetent."[23] This, in the end, may have been tsarist Russia's greatest sin in the eyes of progressive Americans: not its despotic government, not its imperialism, but its inefficiency.

III

The Far East was not the only area of controversy in Russian-American relations; by the turn of the century the Jewish question had again begun to attract attention. This time, Jewish organizations within the United States succeeded in applying sufficient pressure on the White House to bring about official protests to St. Petersburg and, in 1911, unilateral abrogation of a seventy-nine-year-old Russian-American commercial treaty. The United States thus took its stand on behalf of suffering humanity; unfortunately, as in the Far East, American concern was projected into an area beyond the influence of American power. The result was a further deterioration in relations between Russia and the United States, with no discernible improvement in the situation of the protested persecution's victims.

It was news of the Kishinev pogrom of April 1903, in which some 45 Jews were killed, between 400 and 600 injured, and at

---

[23] Roosevelt to Lodge, June 16, 1905, Morison, ed., *Roosevelt Letters*, IV, 1230. See also Jerry Israel, "A Diplomatic Machine: Scientific Management in the Department of State, 1906–1924," in Israel, ed., *Building the Organizational Society* (New York: 1972), pp. 185–187.

least 10,000 made homeless,[24] which again brought the issue of Russian anti-Semitism into the public eye. Neither the State Department nor President Roosevelt condoned this outrage, of course, but their initial inclination, upon being assured that Americans had not been involved, was to do nothing. This approach was consistent with the policy of the past thirty years, in which protests against Russian anti-Semitism had been confined to cases directly involving American interests. As Secretary of State John Hay wrote to Jacob Schiff, the wealthy Jewish financier, "What possible advantage would it be to the United States, and what possible advantage to the Jews of Russia, if we should make a protest against these fiendish cruelties and be told that it was none of our business?"[25]

But when public protests continued to mount, Roosevelt reversed himself, received a delegation of Jewish leaders, and promised to forward to St. Petersburg a petition which the group was putting together. The Russian government refused to receive this document on the grounds that "the Emperor whose will is the sole law of this land had no need of information from outside sources as to what is taking place within his dominions." It was not the kind of reply likely to improve Russian-American relations, especially since it came just as Roosevelt was threatening to "go to extremes" over Manchuria. "What inept asses they are, these Kalmucks!" Hay fumed, in a letter to the Chief Executive. "They would have scored by receiving the petition & pigeonholing it. I think *you* have scored, as it is!"[26] But Roosevelt's action in transmitting the appeal had been significant: for the first time the United States government had associated itself with a protest against Russian anti-Semitism, not on the grounds that American interests were directly involved, but in the name of humanity at large.

---

[24] Taylor Stults, "Roosevelt, Russian Persecution of Jews, and American Public Opinion," *Jewish Social Studies*, XXXIII(January, 1971), 14; Philip Ernest Schoenberg, "The American Reaction to the Kishinev Pogrom of 1903," *American Jewish Historical Quarterly*, LXIII(March, 1974), 262–263.

[25] Hay to Schiff, May 10, 1903, quoted in Stults, "Roosevelt, Russian Persecution," pp. 17.

[26] Riddle to Hay, July 16, 1903, DSR, M-35: 60; Hay to Roosevelt, July 16, 1903, quoted in Dennett, *John Hay*, p. 400.

It is ironic that this happened in the administration of Theodore Roosevelt, one of the few American presidents in recent history to recognize the need to keep rhetoric in line with capabilities. There is no doubt that the plight of the Jews genuinely moved Roosevelt, and that the way the Russians treated them confirmed his view of the tsarist empire as an incompetent, reactionary autocracy. But Roosevelt's political interests were also involved: leading Jews such as Schiff and Oscar Straus had called his attention to the favorable impact this protest would have on his reelection prospects, and Roosevelt himself suggested that "it will be a good thing to recite [in the campaign literature] what has been done in the Kishineff matter." It is only fair to note that Roosevelt continued his efforts on behalf of Russian Jews after the election: during the Portsmouth peace negotiations in 1905 he approached the Russian delegate, Count Witte, on the subject, at Straus's request. But he retained reservations about the effectiveness of this kind of diplomacy. "For the Jews in Russia," he acknowledged, "we were able to accomplish a little, a *very* little, toward temporarily ameliorating their conditions." But he added that "out in the west we always used to consider it a cardinal crime to draw a revolver and brandish it about unless the man meant to shoot. And it is apt to turn out to be sheer cruelty to encourage men by words and then not back up the words by deeds."[27]

The Russian government's treatment of the Jews had a direct effect on its ability to finance the Russo-Japanese War. Schiff, senior partner in the firm of Kuhn, Loeb & Company, had been one of the leaders in the protest against the Kishinev pogrom. Unlike many other Jews, he was in a position to do something about Russian anti-Semitism. Schiff worked to discourage loans to Russia by the Rothschilds and other European banking firms and, once the Russo-Japanese War got underway, helped arrange the extremely successful Japanese financing effort.

---

[27] Roosevelt to Elihu Root, June 2, 1904, Morison, ed., *Roosevelt Letters,* IV, 810; Roosevelt to George Otto Trevelyan, May 13, 1905, ibid., pp. 1174–1175. See also Stults, "Roosevelt, Russian Persecution," pp. 21–22; and Naomi W. Cohen, "The Abrogation of the Russo-American Treaty of 1832," *Jewish Social Studies,* XXV(January, 1963), 5.

Schiff's motives were quite frankly those of the Russian revolutionaries of 1905: to work for a Russian defeat at the hands
of Japan, in the belief that this would hasten the revolution
which, Schiff thought, would improve the condition of the
Jews.[28]

But, as it turned out, the revolutionary violence of 1905 resulted, in November, in the worst pogroms yet. These attacks
attracted considerable attention in the United States, and again
protest meetings were held and relief campaigns organized. But
this time, despite persistent efforts, Straus and Schiff were unable to secure an official protest from the White House. Though
privately sympathetic to the plight of Russian Jews, Secretary of
State Elihu Root opposed public action on the grounds that this
would only worsen their conditions. Roosevelt agreed, telling
Schiff with some irritation that "we could do nothing, and
where we can do nothing I have a horror of saying anything. We
have never taken—and while I am President we will never
take—any action which we cannot make good." But of course
the United States had done precisely that two years earlier, at
the time of Kishinev. It may be uncharitable, but probably not
inaccurate, to suggest that what was different this time was the
fact that Roosevelt was not running for reelection.[29]

When, in spite of everything, the Russian government remained adamant on the Jewish question, pressure began to develop among Jewish groups in the United States for direct retaliation through abrogation of a commercial treaty James Buchanan had negotiated with Russia almost eight decades earlier.
This 1832 treaty provided that Russians and Americans should

mutually have liberty to enter the ports, places and rivers of the ter-

---

[28] Gary Dean Best, "Financing A Foreign War: Jacob H. Schiff and Japan,
1904–1905," *American Jewish Historical Quarterly*, LXI(June, 1972), 313–324; C. C.
Aronsfield, "Jewish Bankers and the Tsar," *Jewish Social Studies*, XXXV(April,
1973), 99–102; Cyrus Adler, *Jacob Schiff: His Life and Letters* (Garden City, New York:
1928), II, 120–128; White, *Diplomacy of the Russo-Japanese War*, pp. 169–170, 260–261,
290.

[29] Roosevelt to Schiff, December 14, 1905, Morison, ed., *Roosevelt Letters*, V, 113.
See also Arthur W. Thompson and Robert W. Hart, *The Uncertain Crusade: American and the Russian Revolution of 1905* (Amherst, Massachusetts: 1970), pp. 103–117;
Philip C. Jessup, *Elihu Root* (New York: 1938), II, 65–66; Dennett, *John Hay*, p.401;
and Adler, *Jacob Schiff*, II, 133–140.

ritories of each party, wherever foreign commerce is permitted. They shall be at liberty to sojourn and reside in all parts whatsoever of said territories, in order to attend to their affairs, and they shall enjoy, to that effect, the same security and protection as natives of the country wherein they reside, on condition of their submitting to the laws and ordinances there prevailing, and particularly to the regulations in force concerning commerce.

The Russians had violated this treaty, the argument ran, by refusing to honor passports to Russia held by American Jews and by prohibiting American Jews residing in Russia from living where they wanted. United States officials as early as 1873 had seen such discrimination as contrary to the treaty, but the clause conditioning freedom of residence on adherence to domestic laws complicated the matter, since there could be no denying that a large body of laws existed in Russia imposing restrictions on Jews.[30]

As far as American Jewish organizations were concerned, though, the issue was not simply those few Jews who wanted to travel to or reside in Russia. Their concern was the treatment of Russian Jews generally; their belief was that by forcing the Russians to abandon discrimination against American Jews, they would soon have to do the same thing for all Jews. Hence, following the Russo-Japanese War, these groups concentrated on having the United States threaten to abrogate the 1832 commercial treaty—a threat which, it was thought, would carry weight with the Russians because of the increasing volume of Russian-American trade.[31]

These arguments did not impress the Taft administration, which considered the legal reasoning dubious (the United States itself still reserved the right to deny citizenship to Japanese and Chinese) and believed that abrogation would have no effect. Moreover, State Department officials argued that making an issue of the treaty would harm growing commercial ties with Russia and endanger American efforts to maintain a balance against increasing Japanese influence in the Far East. Undeter-

---

[30] Hamilton Fish to Marshall Jewell, November 20, 1873, and May 22, 1874, DSR, M-77: 137. For the 1832 treaty, see Hunter Miller, ed., *Treaties and Other International Acts of the United States of America* (Washington: 1931–1948), III, 723–734.
[31] Cohen, "Abrogation of the Russo-American Treaty," pp. 7–8.

red by these arguments, the Jewish organizations launched a
public campaign for abrogation, and by the end of 1911 had
succeeded in getting through the House of Representatives, by a
301–1 vote, a resolution unilaterally abrogating the treaty. Confronted with the likelihood of a similar vote in the Senate, the
administration quickly gave the Russians notice of termination
in a year's time; shortly thereafter the Senate unanimously approved this action.[32]

Abrogation of the commercial treaty failed to have the effect
its supporters had anticipated. St. Petersburg officials saw it as
an attempt to interfere in Russian internal affairs, and a strong
anti-American backlash developed, especially among right-
wing elements in the capital. The Jews' condition actually worsened as the government subjected them to new reprisals.
United States diplomats, who had opposed abrogation, quickly
worked out an informal *modus vivendi* with the Russians which
prevented any significant disruption of trade relations. The action of Congress accomplished little other than to increase the
already considerable sense of bitterness educated Russians felt
toward the United States. The joke, Taft is said to have chuck-
led, was on the Jews.[33]

The treaty episode was important, however, because it indicated a growing susceptibility on the part of Washington officials to the influence of pressure groups on foreign policy—Taft,
like Roosevelt in 1903, had not been unmindful of the fact that
an election was coming up. It is significant that although the
United States was in no way unique in having its Jewish citizens
discriminated against in Russia, no other country followed the
American example in launching a protest.[34] The American peo-

[32] Ibid., pp. 8–37; Clifford L. Egan, "Pressure Groups, the Department of State,
and the Abrogation of the Russian-American Treaty of 1832," American
Philosophical Society *Proceedings*, CXV(August, 1971), 329–333; Gilbert C.
Kohlenberg, "Russian-American Economic Relations, 1906–1917," (Ph. D. Dissertation, University of Illinois, 1951), pp. 182–188.

[33] Cohen, "Abrogation of the Russo-American Treaty," pp. 38–41; Egan, "Pressure Groups," pp. 333–334; Laserson, *American Impact on Russia*, pp. 359–361;
Kohlenberg, "Russian-American Economic Relations," pp. 75–82.

[34] Zosa Szajkowski, "The European Aspect of the American-Russian Passport
Question," *Publications of the American Jewish Historical Society*, XLVI(December,
1956), 86–100.

ple, Ambassador Curtis Guild explained to the Russian foreign minister, were "more easily appealed to by questions of sentiment when the appeal was made on the ground of humanity and civilization than any other nation in the world."[35] Unfortunately in this case, as in the case of Knox's Manchurian policy, Americans lost sight of the relationship between objectives and capabilities; economic diplomacy, in both situations, had little effect in altering policies the Russian government considered to be in its vital national interests.

IV

Economic relations between the United States and Russia had, until 1911, remained more or less insulated from political difficulties. Although by no means oblivious to the advantages of increased economic ties with the rest of the world, government officials generally refrained, until the Taft administration, from trying to direct foreign trade and investment in such a way as to reinforce diplomatic policies.[36] Nor did American businessmen depend on government to keep economic opportunities open; while the government could furnish useful information and, occasionally, help in times of crisis, those businessmen who sought trade and investment opportunities overseas—and this was by no means the majority of them[37]—normally did so on their own.[38] As a result, deteriorating political relations had surprisingly little effect on economic contacts between Russia and the United States.

Trade between the United States and Russia had never been very extensive because of the similarity of exportable products produced in each country, the existence of tariff barriers, the lack of direct shipping facilities, European competition, and the persistent reluctance of American exporters to adapt their pro-

---

[35] Guild to Knox, December 16, 1911, FR: 1911, pp. 696–697.

[36] Mira Wilkins, The Emergence of Multinational Enterprise: American Business Abroad from the Colonial Era to 1914, (Cambridge, Massachusetts: 1970), p. 67.

[37] William H. Becker, "American Manufacturers and Foreign Markets, 1870–1900," Business History Review, XLVII(Winter, 1973), 466–481; Paul S. Holbo, "Economics, Emotion and Expansion: An Emerging Foreign Policy," in H. Wayne Morgan, ed., The Gilded Age, Revised Edition (Syracuse: 1970), pp. 199–221.

[38] Wilkins, Multinational Enterprise, pp. 74–75.

ducts to foreign tastes and needs.[39] Official statistics show an unremarkable increase in trade volume during the three decades preceding World War I, with exports rising from an annual average of $13 million for 1881–1885 to $20 million for 1907–1911, and imports from $2.6 million to $14.1 million during the same period. These figures do not reflect trade through third countries, however, and since most Russian-American commerce went by way of Germany, they are almost certainly too low. Reputable estimates place the actual volume of American exports to Russia in 1911 at between $65 and $70 million, or around 3.3% of total exports, and imports at $17.0 million, or 0.8% of the total. American imports as a percentage of total Russian imports were about 9% in 1911, making the United States Russia's third largest source of imports, after Germany and Great Britain.[40]

Until around the turn of the century, cotton made up the bulk of American exports to Russia. Geography and climate made it difficult for the Russians to produce this commodity, and despite official efforts to encourage its cultivation, almost half the raw cotton used in Russian mills still came from the United States as late as 1905. Agricultural equipment constituted another large portion of American exports: in 1911 Russia took more than one-third of all agricultural implements and machinery produced for export in the United States. Other popular American products included rails and rolling stock, mining and milling equipment, machine tools, typewriters, cash registers, and probably the most ubiquitous American export of all during this period, Singer sewing machines. Imports from Russia, con-

---

[39] Kohlenberg, "Russian-American Economic Relations," pp. 61–69; George S. Queen, "The United States and the Material Advance in Russia, 1881–1906," (Ph. D. Dissertation, University of Illinois, 1942), p.98.

[40] Based on statistics in U. S. Treasury Department, Bureau of Statistics, *Statistical Tables Exhibiting the Commerce of the United States with European Countries from 1790 to 1890* (Washington: 1893), p. xxxviii; U.S. Department of Commerce, *Statistical Abstract, 1913* (Washington: 1914), pp. 327, 363; Gail L. Owen, "Dollar Diplomacy in Default: The Economics of Russian-American Relations, 1910–1917," *Historical Journal,* XIII(1970), 265; John V. Hogan, "Russian-American Commercial Relations," *Political Science Quarterly,* XXVII(December, 1912), 641; Margaret Miller, *The Economic Development of Russia, 1905–1914,* Second Edition (New York: 1967), pp. 66, 77.

sisting mainly of animal hides and raw wool, fell far behind exports, so that by 1911 the United States was running an annual credit balance of around $50 million on a total trade of approximately $85 million.[41]

American investment in Russia took two forms: investment in government securities and in privately owned businesses. Government bonds were sold on the New York Stock Exchange from time to time, but they were not popular, probably in part because of the activities of Jacob Schiff. American insurance companies operating in Russia were required to put capital generated by their Russian policies into government securities, though, so that the two major American companies active there, New York Life and Equitable, did have extensive holdings. Most American investment, however, went into private enterprises operating within the Russian Empire. Many of these were branch factories set up to produce popular export items without having to pay tariffs. Thus, by 1911, the Singer, International Harvester, Westinghouse, and New York Air Brake companies all had factories in Russia. Other investment capital went into oil, mining, chemical, tobacco, and pharmaceutical enterprises. Estimates of total American investments in Russia are difficult to make, but a rough approximation places it at around $160 million by 1911, or about 8% of total American investment overseas at that time.[42]

The Russian government welcomed American trade and investment. Finance Minister Sergei Witte, whose industrialization program required the importation of foreign capital, had tried, unsuccessfully, to float Russian government bonds on the New York money market in 1898 and again in 1905. He also

[41] Queen, "Material Advance," pp. 112–173; Kohlenberg, "Russian-American Economic Relations," pp. 99–129; Hogan, "Russian-American Commercial Relations," pp. 638–641; M. K. Kuz'min, "K istorii russko-amerikanskoi torgovli," *Istoricheskii Arkhiv*, 1956, #6, p. 88. See also George S. Queen, "The McCormick Harvesting Machine Company in Russia," *Russian Review*, XXIII(April, 1964), 164–181.

[42] Richard B. Fisher, "American Investments in Pre-Soviet Russia," *American Slavic and East European Review*, VIII(1949), 90–105; Barbara Jackson Gaddis, "American Economic Interests in Russia, August, 1914-March, 1917," (M. A. Thesis, University of Texas, 1966), pp. 8–11; Queen, "Material Advance," pp. 176–221; Wilkins, *Multinational Enterprise*, pp. 102–105, 212–213.

encouraged American imports on the grounds that Americans were "honest and single-minded . . . not as in the case of certain other people we have to deal with, who make a treaty of commerce with us today and tomorrow we find a cannon hidden behind it!" After the Russo-Japanese War, the Russian government made several unsuccessful attempts to draw American capital into Manchurian railroad investments in hopes of creating a counterweight to growing Japanese influence there. In 1910, it invited American financier John Hays Hammond to visit Russia in an effort to facilitate the flow of American and British capital into that country. Hammond was personally welcomed by the tsar and other top officials, and left "convinced [that] I had with me the most important packet of commercial opportunities ever to be of such prospective benefit to two nations."[43]

But, by this time, deteriorating political relations had begun to affect economic ties. The Russians welcomed American investment in Manchuria only if it would strengthen their sphere of influence there; the Taft administration's encouragement of investment in Manchurian railroads seemed designed to undercut that position and hence was unacceptable. While abrogation of the commercial treaty in 1911 had no significant effect on trade, the anti-American outbursts it provoked probably did inhibit investment prospects. Hammond claimed, in retrospect, that abrogation "utterly destroyed any hope of carrying out my plan of obtaining American capital for Russia."[44] Economics, for the moment, had fallen victim to politics, but only for the moment, for an unforeseen event—the outbreak of war in Europe—would soon drive Russian-American economic contacts to unprecedented heights.

When Russia went to war against Germany in August 1914, it did so against a country which, in the previous year, had supplied 47.4% of its imports and had taken 31.8% of its exports.

---

[43] Tower to Hay, July 3, 1901, DSR, M-35: 58; *The Autobiography of John Hays Hammond* (New York: 1935), II, 467–474. See also Theodore H. Von Laue, *Sergei Iu. Witte and the Industrialization of Russia* (New York: 1963), pp. 105–107; Paul A. Varg, *Open Door Diplomat: The Life of W. W. Rockhill* (Urbana: 1952), pp. 101–103; Zabriskie, *American-Russian Rivalry*, pp. 148–153; and the documents relating to Hammond's visit in DSR, 711.61/4–18 (M-333: 2).

[44] Hammond, *Autobiography*, II, 475.

Germany had long dominated Russian foreign trade, but now, with commercial access cut off, Russia had to look elsewhere for the war supplies its own poorly developed industries could not provide. Like its allies, Britain and France, Russia soon had to turn to the United States for these materials. American businessmen were not at all hesitant to take advantage of the opportunity.[45]

During the year ending June 30, 1914, just on the eve of the war, United States exports to Russia amounted to $31.3 million, or 1.3% of total exports. Three years later, for the year ending June 30, 1917, United States exports had risen to $558.9 million, or 8.9% of total exports. These figures do not appear particularly impressive when compared to the percentage of American exports going to Great Britain during the latter year (32.5%) or to France (16.1%). But the rate of increase was striking: exports to Russia in fiscal 1917 were 1785% of what they had been in fiscal 1914, as compared with a 334% rise for exports to Britain and a 632% rise for exports to France. Exports to Germany during the same period declined from 14.6% of total exports to virtually nothing three years later. Russian-American trade had achieved such importance that by 1917 one-fourth of all American profits on foreign trade and two-thirds of all outside Russian military assistance were deriving from it.[46]

Financing these exports caused problems. Even after the Wilson administration overcame its objections against private loans to belligerents, American bankers remained reluctant to arrange direct loans to Russia, partly because of the absence of Russian collateral in the United States, the inadequacy of direct banking facilities, the continued objections of the Schiff group, and the general deterioration in political relations which had followed abrogation of the commercial treaty. In the end, the Russians financed their American purchases principally by borrowing from their Anglo-French allies, who in turn arranged loans in

---

[45] Boris E. Nolde, *Russia in the Economic War* (New Haven: 1928), pp. 125–127; Miller, *Economic Development of Russia,* pp. 63–65; Gaddis, "American Economic Interests," pp. 16, 20–25, 39–40, 51–52.

[46] U. S. Department of Commerce, *Statistical Abstract, 1918,* (Washington: 1919), pp. 383, 416; Gaddis, "American Economic Interests," pp. 51–52, 115; Owen, "Dollar Diplomacy," p. 266.

the United States to cover their resulting indebtedness. Direct American advances to Russia from August 1914 through March 1917 totaled $233 million; indirect advances to Russia through Britain and France, all arranged by J. P. Morgan and Company, came to $1480 million during the same period. Since total advances to Britain and France during this period totaled $2112 million, it is apparent that approximately 70% of the loans extended to Britain and France during the period of American neutrality went to cover Russian war orders.[47]

Hence, despite decidedly cool official relations, American financial resources played a crucial role in supporting tsarist Russia's war effort. As in the case of relations with Britain and France, the Wilson administration's political neutrality did not extend to economics. *Laissez-faire* still prevailed; "dollar diplomacy," if by this is meant efforts by government to channel private trade and investment in directions consistent with its political objectives, had proven to be a distinctly transitory phenomenon.[48]

V

Growing economic ties between Russia and the United States did little to improve political relations, which remained, in the words of a Russian newspaper, in a state of "cold indifference." Woodrow Wilson had described the Russian government in 1889 as "a belated example of those crude forms of politics which the rest of Europe has outgrown," and there is little evidence that he had modified his views significantly in the intervening years. Fully conscious of the political advantages of doing so, he had publicly supported abrogation of the commercial treaty in 1911 on the grounds that economic interests ought not to take precedence over "the maintenance of those rights of manhood which [the United States] government was set up to vindicate." Upon becoming president, Wilson demonstrated the relative unimportance he attached to Russian affairs by naming to the St. Petersburg embassy a succession of political appointees whose

---

[47] Ibid., pp. 258–267; Cleona Lewis, *America's Stake in International Investments* (Washington: 1938), p. 355.
[48] Owen, "Dollar Diplomacy," pp. 271–272.

qualifications, even by the relaxed standards of his administration, were minimal—so much so, indeed, that the Russian government rejected the first two of them. When Wilson finally did come up with an acceptable ambassador, George Marye, in the summer of 1914, the Russians made it clear that, despite the outbreak of war, they were in no hurry for him to proceed to his post.[49]

Efforts to negotiate a new commercial treaty with Russia had met with no success. "The [Russian] Government has the firm intention," Foreign Minister Sazonov had told the Imperial Duma in 1912, "not to allow any infringements from abroad of the inalienable rights of Russia, as a sovereign state, to regulate its internal legislation." President-elect Wilson had written, several months later, "I feel it is absolutely inconsistent with either the dignity or the principles of our government to enter into any treaty relations with the government of Russia which would permit the treatment of one class of our citizens in one way and all other classes in another." The Russians did show some interest in a new treaty late in 1914, when it became apparent that the war was going to require a large volume of supplies from the United States, but the indirect financing arrangement for Russian war orders which the British and the French worked out through J. P. Morgan removed any need to deal directly with the United States government, and Russian interest in a new commercial treaty quickly waned. Neither Ambassador Marye nor his successor, David R. Francis, had any success in pursuing the matter.[50]

---

[49] *Novoe Vremiia,* January 14, 1914, translation enclosed in Charles S. Wilson to William Jennings Bryan, January 16, 1914, DSR, 711.61/29, M-333: 2; Arthur S. Link, et al., eds., *The Papers of Woodrow Wilson* (Princeton: 1966–), VI, 259–260; R. S. Baker and W. E. Dodd, eds., *The Public Papers of Woodrow Wilson* (New York: 1925), II, 318–322; Arthur S. Link, *Wilson* (Princeton: 1947–), I, 338, II, 102–103; George Thomas Marye, *Nearing the End in Imperial Russia* (Philadelphia: 1929), pp. 17–22.

[50] Sazonov speech to the Imperial Duma, April, 1912, quoted in Laserson, *American Impact on Russia,* p. 366; Wilson to Curtis Guild, November 30, 1912, quoted in Ray Stannard Baker, *Woodrow Wilson: His Life and Letters: Governor, 1910–1913* (Garden City, New York: 1931), p. 417; Owen, "Dollar Diplomacy," p. 260; Kohlenberg, "Russian-American Economic Relations," pp. 189–195.

Wilson and his advisers reflected considerable ambivalence in thinking about Russia and the war. The president initially sympathized with Russian territorial aspirations on the grounds that Russia deserved better access to the sea—in January 1915, he even endorsed the Russian acquisition of Constantinople. But Wilson shared the fear of his confidant, Colonel Edward M. House, that a complete German defeat might only substitute Russian despotism for Prussian militarism in Europe. Through his intermediary, House, Wilson was not above holding out the possibility of a separate German-Russian peace as a means of frightening the British and French into accepting less than total victory. But Russian experts like George Kennan and Samuel Harper, the nation's only academic specialist in Slavic affairs, argued that Russian autocracy was not a danger: the war, they believed, would provoke either reform or revolution in Russia. By 1917, Wilson and House had come to accept this argument. When the possibility of a postwar German-Russian-Japanese alliance was raised at a February 1917 cabinet meeting, Wilson dismissed it with the observation that "the Russian peasant might save the world this misfortune." The overthrow of the tsar, which occurred a month later, therefore came as no great surprise to Washington officials.[51]

The March Revolution (February by the old Russian calendar, still in effect at this time) has often been seen as having facilitated an ideological justification for American entry into World War I. Wilson could not credibly have portrayed that struggle as a "fight to make the world safe for democracy," the argument runs, had he been forced to ally himself with the Russian tsar.[52] There is reason to believe, though, that Wilson would have justified the war in much the same way even if the Revolution

---

[51] Harley Notter, *The Origins of the Foreign Policy of Woodrow Wilson* (Baltimore: 1937), pp. 373, 614; Ernest R. May, *The World War and American Isolation, 1914–1917* (Cambridge, Massachusetts: 1959), pp. 77, 85; Charles Seymour, *The Intimate Papers of Colonel House* (Boston: 1926), II, 121, 129, 258; Christopher Lasch, *The American Liberals and the Russian Revolution* (New York: 1962), pp. 1–26.

[52] See, for example, George F. Kennan, *Russia and the West Under Lenin and Stalin* (Boston: 1961), p. 18; Peter G. Filene, *Americans and the Soviet Experiment, 1917–1933* (Cambridge, Massachusetts: 1967), pp. 12–13; Bailey, *America Faces Russia*, p. 232.

had not occurred at the fortunate time that it did. His commitment to the international diffusion of democratic institutions
predated the Revolution, having been most notably expressed
in his "peace without victory" speech in January 1917. Nor, as
that very phrase implied, was universal democracy necessarily a
prerequisite for ending the war; that goal reflected rather the
kind of international structure Wilson thought most likely to
sustain peace once the war was over. Nor did Wilson see
ideological consistency as a requirement for joint military action:
he carefully depicted the United States as an "associated," not
an "allied" power, and presumably could have operated on this
basis even with tsarist Russia. The Revolution probably did
allow Wilson to use more sweeping rhetoric than would otherwise have been the case; it also doubtless encouraged his belief
in the feasibility of a league of democratic states which would
integrate order with justice in the postwar world.[53] It would be a
mistake, though, to see the gap between promises and performance which came to characterize Wilsonian diplomacy as
necessarily, or even primarily, the result of the portentous
events which occurred in St. Petersburg in March 1917.

The deterioration of Russian-American relations which took
place in the fifty years separating the Alaska Purchase from the
Russian Revolution occurred primarily as a result of American,
not Russian, initiatives. The traditional concerns of Russian
foreign policy—secure frontiers, access to open seas, ethnic and
religious solidarity, and maintenance of a balance of power in
Europe[54] —remained largely constant. American diplomatic objectives, however, changed drastically. The cautious noninterventionist tradition of the nineteenth century had given way to
the belief that American institutions could be made secure only
through their maximum possible diffusion in the world. The
consequent proliferation of interests brought the United States

[53] Notter, *Origins of the Foreign Policy of Woodrow Wilson,* pp. 648–649; Harry H.
Savage, "Official Policies and Relations of the United States with the Provisional
Government of Russia, March-November, 1917," (Ph. D. Dissertation, Univer-
sity of Minnesota, 1971), pp. 31–56.
[54] Cyril E. Black, "The Pattern of Russian Objectives," in Ivo J. Lederer, ed.,
Russian Foreign Policy: Essays in Historical Perspective (New Haven: 1962), pp. 6–22.

into conflict with Russia over economic-strategic rivalries in the Far East and, on humanitarian grounds, over the very internal structure of the Russian state. Under the pressures of revolution that structure would now change, but not in a manner to the Americans' liking. The events of 1917 would produce, in the end, a government more committed to ideological imperialism than the United States had ever been. The result would be to frustrate the hopes so widely held in the United States for the improvement in relations the Russian Revolution had been expected to bring.

CHAPTER III

The Russian Revolution: 1917–1920

T HE YEAR 1917 SAW THE UNITED STATES ENTER WORLD WAR I and Russia, for all practical purposes, leave it. Wholly unrelated sets of circumstances produced these developments, but their cumulative effects upon the course of history would be profound. These would include the eventual migration of international political power from the center of Europe, where it had been concentrated for several hundred years, to its periphery. They would also include proclamation of two rival ideologies, Wilson's versus Lenin's, which, though selective in application, were sufficiently universal in their appeal to make them powerful influences on the behavior of men and nations for decades to come. Finally, though somewhat anticlimactically, the events of 1917 would, for the first time in their long history of contacts, make the policies of Russia and the United States matters of major concern to statesmen in each country.

I

On the night of April 2, 1917, Woodrow Wilson stood before the Congress of the United States and asked it to declare war on Germany. In the course of his address, the president referred to "the wonderful and heartening things that have been happening within the last few weeks in Russia." That country, Wilson continued,

was always known by those who knew it best to have been always in fact democratic at heart. . . . The autocracy that crowned the summit of her political structure, long as it had stood and terrible as was the reality of its power, was not in fact Russian in origin, character, or purpose; and now it has been shaken off and the great, generous Russian people have been added in all their naive majesty and might to the forces that are fighting for freedom in the world, for justice and for peace.[1]

It has been pointed out that none of the assumptions which lay behind this statement were correct: Russia had no democratic tradition; the tsarist autocracy had hardly been an alien regime; the Russian people did not see the war's objectives in the same way that Americans did.[2] Wilson's statement, it seems clear, reflected more what he wanted to believe than what was, in fact, the case.

It is significant, though, that Wilson made these remarks, not in relation to prosecuting the war, but in the context of what would be necessary to keep war from breaking out in the future. "A steadfast concern for peace can never be maintained except by a partnership of democratic nations," the president had proclaimed, immediately before making his observations on Russia: "No autocratic government could be trusted to keep faith with it or observe its covenants." This, for Wilson, was the chief significance of the March Revolution: not so much its effect on the war as its long-range implications for the postwar international structure. Lasting peace would require both order and justice; only a coalition of democratic states could achieve these goals. Overthrowing its autocracy made Russia a "fit partner" in this postwar "league of honor."[3]

But this very conviction that peace and autocracy were incompatible had the ironic effect of rendering Wilson insensitive to the requirements for democracy's survival in Russia. It is clear in retrospect, though admittedly it was not at the time, that three years of bloody and mismanaged conflict had so demoralized that country as to render its new government capable of remaining in authority only by ending active participation in the war. But Wilson, by this time, had accepted the view of his Anglo-French allies: that the only guarantee of lasting peace would be vigorous prosecution of the war to total victory, an

---

[1] R. S. Baker and W. E. Dodd, eds., *The Public Papers of Woodrow Wilson: War and Peace* (New York: 1927), I, 12–13.
[2] Kennan, *Russia and the West*, p. 19.
[3] Savage, "Official Policies," pp. 35–39.

enterprise in which continued Russian belligerency would be essential.[4] Hence, the short-range problem of keeping Russia in the war came to overshadow Wilson's long-range hopes for the March Revolution.

Most American experts on Russia (and the number who qualified in this respect could have been counted on the fingers of one hand) expected that the overthrow of the tsar would enable Russia to fight more effectively. The upheaval in Petrograd had been a political, not a social, phenomenon, they believed; while discontented elements doubtless existed in Russia, the Provisional Government would, it was thought, be able to keep them well in hand. Wilson, interestingly, was one of the few Americans to question this judgment. He is said to have suggested, in a conversation on April 14, that "in setting up their new form of Government and in working out domestic reforms [the Russians might] find the war an intolerable evil and would desire to get out of it on any reasonable terms. It would be a serious blow to the Allies if that took place."[5]

Events soon confirmed Wilson's fears. Although the Provisional Government formally assured its allies of Russia's continued commitment to the war, that government, it quickly became clear, possessed only the trappings of political authority. Real power rested with the Petrograd Soviet, or council, an amorphous and unruly body of several thousand elected workers' and soldiers' representatives which, through its Executive Committee, controlled the factories and garrisons of Petrograd. This confused situation gave the Soviet, made up of Social Revolutionaries and the two mutually antagonistic factions of the Social Democratic Party, the Mensheviks and the Bolsheviks, a veto over the Provisional Government's policies. Similar Soviets were formed in urban centers and military units throughout the country. The Soviets did not, it is important to note, call for a separate peace. They did view the war as an "imperialist"

---

[4] Arno J. Mayer, *Political Origins of the New Diplomacy, 1917–1918* (New Haven: 1958), pp. 182–183.

[5] Link, *Wilson*, V, 410n. See also Savage, "Official Policies," pp. 30–31; and R. Sh. Ganelin, *Rossiia i SShA, 1914–1917: Ocherki istorii russko-amerikanskich otnoshenii* (Leningrad: 1969), pp. 160–161.

struggle, though, and appealed to "all the peoples, in our Allies' countries as well as in the countries at war with Russia, to exert pressure on their governments to renounce their programs of conquest."[6]

On the surface, this formula was not all that different from Wilson's "peace without victory" concept, enunciated several months earlier. But there were important incongruities. The Soviet's peace appeal proclaimed the war to be unjust almost exactly at the time Wilson had convinced himself of its justice. It implied revolutionary action to end the war if diplomatic negotiations failed, a prospect no established government could welcome. It threatened, by increasing the disarray which already existed within the Russian Army, to bring an end to military operations on the eastern front, thereby permitting Germany to transfer large numbers of troops to the west. For these reasons, the Soviet's call for a peace based on "no annexations, no indemnities" met with as little sympathy in Washington as it did in London and Paris.[7]

The appeal of the Petrograd formula might have been neutralized by clarifying the objectives for which the Allies were fighting, but Wilson adamantly refused to allow public discussion of war aims at this time. When the Soviet called for an international conference of socialists to meet at Stockholm to discuss peace prospects, Wilson denied passports to the American delegates who wanted to attend and encouraged the British and French to do the same. Shortly thereafter, he dismissed Pope Benedict's appeal for a statement of war aims on the grounds that there could be no negotiation with "the present rulers of Germany." Requirements of coalition warfare dictated these positions: although Wilson himself did not object to the "no annexations, no indemnities" formula, he knew that his allies did. Public discussion of war aims would only provoke disagreements, thereby weakening the war effort. "When the war is over we can force them [Britain and France] to our way of thinking," Wilson wrote House, "because by that time they will, among other things, be financially in our hands; but we cannot

[6] Robert Paul Browder and Alexander F. Kerensky, eds., *The Russian Provisional Government, 1917* (Stanford: 1961), II, 1084.

[7] Mayer, *Political Origins,* pp. 182–183.

force them now."[8] Maintenance of Allied unity took precedence, in the White House view, over satisfying the demands of the Petrograd Soviet.

There would thus be no revision of war aims, but there were other means of trying to keep Russia in the war, and the Wilson administration was quick to use them. Official expressions of sympathy for the Revolution had been generous, and widely publicized, from the beginning; indeed, the United States had been the first nation to extend formal recognition to the Provisional Government, on March 22. Economic assistance would be more useful, though, and on this the Wilson administration held back until it had clear assurances from Petrograd that Russia would not quit the war. In the end some $450 million was set aside for Russia, but only $188 million had actually been used by the time the Provisional Government was overthrown in November.[9] The Wilson administration's chief initiative, however, involved the dispatch of a series of official "missions" to Russia, designed to welcome that country into the ranks of democratic states and to investigate ways in which the United States could aid the Russian war effort.

The most elaborate of these was the delegation headed by Elihu Root, staunch conservative Republican and former secretary of state, which arrived in Petrograd in June. The Root Mission had been selected in a leisurely manner, with more care being taken to choose members who would reflect the diversity of American life than to find experts on Russia capable of explaining developments there to Washington. To say that the delegation was ill-prepared for what it found would be a considerable understatement. The American warship on which it was traveling sailed into Vladivostok harbor unnoticed, an unusual occurrence, the members noted, in the middle of a war. During the long trip across Siberia the mission frequently encountered loaded troop trains headed away from the front. At

---

[8] Wilson to House, July 21, 1917, quoted in Ray Stannard Baker, *Woodrow Wilson: Life and Letters: War Leader* (New York: 1939), p. 180. See also Mayer, *Political Origins,* pp. 225–229, 233–236; and David F. Trask, *The United States in the Supreme War Council: American War Aims and Inter-Allied Strategy, 1917–1918* (Middletown, Connecticut: 1961), pp. 6–8.

[9] Savage, "Official Policies," pp. 27, 336n.

Novo-Nikolaevsk, Cyrus McCormick, president of the International Harvester Company and a member of the delegation, was disconcerted to learn that despite a 45% wage increase, half his company's employees in the area had quit. One customer had written that since he "supposed all machines belonged to the government . . . that would release him from paying the note he owed." On arriving in Petrograd, the mission found that political power had shifted dramatically to the left, with the formation of a new coalition government including six members of the Soviet, so that the carefully balanced delegation put together in Washington now bore little relevance to the actual configuration of power in the Russian capital.[10]

Despite all of this, the delegation remained surprisingly optimistic. Root confined himself to contacts with business and government officials, in one case solemnly explaining the advantages of constitutional guarantees of private property to the members of the Moscow bourse. General Hugh L. Scott, chief of staff of the United States Army, managed to visit the front just as the ill-fated July offensive was getting underway. The sight of troops advancing convinced him that the Russian army would be able to hold its own; news of their disastrous reverses several days later did little to shake his optimism. Admiral James H. Glennon, the Navy's representative, twice encountered situations in which local Soviets had superseded the authority of Russian naval officers, but neglected to mention these in his report. Charles Edward Russell, the lone Socialist on the delegation, did address the All-Russian Congress of Soviets, but his efforts to achieve rapport by wearing a red tie and waving membership cards in the American Socialist Party and the International Typographical Union had little effect. Russell was one of the few members of the mission who perceived the power of the Soviets and the strength of antiwar sentiment in Russia, yet he too made no effort to evaluate these factors in his report to the State Department.[11]

The Root Mission concluded that its visit had materially strengthened the Provisional Government. While the Russians

[10] Alton Earl Ingrams, "The Root Mission to Russia, 1917," (Ph. D. Dissertation, Louisiana State University, 1970), pp. 38–64.

[11] Ibid., pp. 157, 206, 214–216, 220–223, 225–227, 239–241, 251–252.

would need aid, particularly in the area of war supplies and transportation equipment, "we have little doubt that they will be able to establish and maintain successfully free self-government on a grand scale." Almost as an afterthought, the mission recommended that a propaganda agency be set up in Russia to "sell" the war, and that representatives of the Young Men's Christian Association be sent out to help improve morale in the Russian Army. "I am astounded at their optimism," Secretary of State Robert Lansing wrote in his diary after reading the mission's report. "I cannot see upon what it is founded. . . . I hope they are right and I presume they know more about it than I do, and yet in spite of what they say I am very skeptical."[12] Other "missions" soon followed. A group of railroad experts under John F. Stevens arrived in Russia at the same time as the Root Mission for the purpose of recommending improvements in the Russian transportation system, particularly the vital Trans-Siberian Railroad. A Red Cross commission, operating as a military unit but financed largely from private sources, arrived in August. Shortly thereafter the Committee on Public Information opened its propaganda office in Russia, and the YMCA's "morale boosters" arrived. These groups coexisted alongside the regular representatives of the State, War, Navy, and Treasury departments, as well as a considerable number of well-intentioned individuals who came to Russia on their own, often under the impression that they were to "report" their findings directly to the president.[13]

There is no evidence that any of these missions, official or unofficial, had any significant effect on the Russian war effort. Expressions of sympathy were of but limited utility, and the Provisional Government was overthrown before more tangible forms of assistance had begun to arrive. The missions could have been useful in gathering information on conditions in Russia, but their members were rarely selected for this purpose. Instead, the optimism they were supposed to impart to the Rus-

---

[12] Ibid., pp. 288–300.

[13] George F. Kennan, *Russia Leaves the War* (Princeton: 1956), pp. 41–70, 78; Claude E. Fike, "The Influence of the Creel Committee and the American Red Cross on Russian-American Relations, 1917–1919," *Journal of Modern History*, XXXI(June, 1959), 93–109; W. B. Fowler, *British-American Relations, 1917–1918: The Role of Sir William Wiseman* (Princeton: 1969), pp. 108–118.

sians colored their own reporting, particularly on military affairs. Few of the Americans who went to Russia in 1917 understood the importance of the Soviets; confusing legitimacy with authority, they assumed that power resided in the Provisional Government, and, with rare exceptions, confined their attention to it.[14] And, because their activities were not coordinated, there was no mechanism by which the members of one mission could compare their findings with those of the others. The result, as can be imagined, was more confusion than enlightenment.

Meanwhile, the Provisional Government's authority was crumbling. The failure of the July offensive set off rioting in Petrograd which the government managed to suppress only by locking up prominent Bolsheviks and driving others into exile. But less than two months later, the government of Premier Alexander Kerensky had to seek help from the Bolsheviks in order to repel a right-wing coup led by General Lavr Kornilov. Kerensky was successful once more, but the price was a further erosion of his power. The Kornilov affair gave the Bolsheviks a majority in the Soviet, and from this point it was only a matter of time until the Provisional Government fell. The event occurred on the night of November 7, 1917; the next morning Vladimir Ilich Lenin mounted the rostrum of the Congress of Soviets to announce construction of the Socialist order.

There appears to be, in retrospect, painfully little which the Wilson administration, or any of the Allies, for that matter, could have done to alter this course of events. It may be, as a distinguished student of Russian affairs has argued, that the Bolshevik Revolution, and the consequent alienation of Russia from the West, was part of the price the Allies had to pay for insisting on military victory over Germany.[15] But there is little evidence that the German government was prepared to accept anything like reasonable terms in the summer of 1917.[16] Nor is it fair to blame the Provisional Government's suicidal July offensive on the Allies' "no fight, no credits" policy: that ill-

---

[14] Ganelin, *Rossiia i SShA*, pp. 177–178.

[15] Kennan, *Russia and the West*, p. 32.

[16] On this point, see Gordon A. Craig, *The Politics of the Prussian Army, 1640–1945* (New York: 1956), pp. 326–337; and Fritz Fischer, *Germany's Aims in the First World War* (New York: 1967), pp. 327–443.

considered operation was at least as much the product of a strange belief on the part of Kerensky and his associates that the best way to restore army morale and increase Russian influence at the peace table was to launch an attack.[17] The revolution in Russia, like the one in China some thirty years later, grew largely out of internal conditions not susceptible to manipulation or modification from the outside.

What was inexcusable was not Wilson's policy of trying to keep Russia in the war, a matter in which, given the circumstances, he had little choice, but rather his failure to send experts to Russia capable of assessing realistically the prospects for continued belligerency. Nor did Wilson rely as much as he might have on the regular American diplomatic establishment in Russia: while Ambassador David R. Francis was ill-equipped to interpret events there (it was once said of him that he would not have known a Left Social Revolutionary from a potato[18]), subordinates such as Consuls North Winship in Petrograd and Maddin Summers in Moscow regularly forwarded to Washington detailed and, on the whole, perceptive accounts of what was going on. Unfortunately, these usually went by pouch instead of cable, and so arrived from four to six weeks after the events they described. It seems unlikely that Wilson ever saw them, or acted on the basis of the information they contained.[19] Instead, the president relied on the reports of the various "missions" he had dispatched to Russia; these left him with the comfortable but inaccurate impression that time still existed for the Provisional Government to pull itself together. In fact, the events of 1917 had produced an unprecedented acceleration in the process of political evolution.[20] Neither Wilson, nor his Allied counterparts, ever quite caught up.

II

"Extreme socialist or anarchist named Lenin making violent speeches and thereby threatening Government; designedly giv-

---

[17] Savage, "Official Policies," pp. 216–217.

[18] R. H. Bruce Lockhart, *British Agent* (Garden City, New York: 1933), p. 279.

[19] These reports are printed in *FR: 1918: Russia*, I, 1–186. See also Ganelin, *Rossiia i SShA*, pp. 178–179.

[20] See, on this point, Mayer, *Political Origins*, pp. 8–9.

ing him leeway and will deport opportunely."[21] This cryptic and misleading cable from Ambassador Francis gave the State Department the first news it had of the arrival in Russia, in April 1917, of the man who would overthrow the Provisional Government and establish the first Socialist state in history. American observers badly underestimated Lenin and the Bolsheviks in the months that followed, but they were hardly alone in this. Few foreigners perceived the depth of antiwar sentiment in Russia; most assumed that, since Lenin had been forced to seek German help in returning, the Bolsheviks would be seen as agents of the Kaiser and would hence be incapable of winning popular support. But popular support was not the crucial determinant of events at this time. Organization and discipline were, and these the tightly controlled Bolsheviks, who were as far from being anarchists as it is possible to imagine, alone were able to provide.

The sudden overthrow of the Provisional Government in November 1917, thus came as a shock to the Americans and their allies; there was little in their own experience to guide them in dealing with the new regime, which immediately proclaimed its intention of withdrawing from the war and abolishing the private ownership of land. Nonetheless, first reactions in the West were to do nothing, partly because there was nothing that could be done immediately, partly because the Allies still clung to the belief that the Russian people supported the war and would soon rise up in wrath to expel the tiny band of outrageous revolutionaries who had seized power in Petrograd.[22] When this did not happen, when it became clear, as it did by December, that the Bolsheviks were in earnest about taking Russia out of the war, the Allies had to begin thinking seriously about what their response would be.

One thing was clear at the outset: the Allies would not join the Bolshevik government in negotiating a peace settlement with Germany. Lenin and Trotsky had never envisaged making a separate peace; with a degree of naivete wholly inconsistent

---

[21] Francis to Lansing, April 21, 1917, *FR: 1918: Russia*, I, 27.

[22] Isaac Deutscher, *The Prophet Armed: Trotsky, 1879–1921* (New York: 1954), p. 347; Robert D. Warth, *The Allies and the Russian Revolution: From the Fall of the Monarchy to the Peace of Brest-Litovsk* (Durham: 1954), pp. 162–167.

with their usual realism, they had assumed that the simple proclamation of a proletarian government in Russia would spark revolutions elsewhere, forcing bourgeois governments on both sides of the conflict to seek an end to it on the basis of "no annexations, no indemnities." Much to their chagrin, Europe remained as calm as could be expected under the circumstances of total war, and the Bolsheviks found themselves facing Germany alone at the peace table at Brest-Litovsk.[23]

Nor was diplomatic recognition seriously considered. The Bolsheviks, seeking legitimacy, encouraged contacts with foreign governments, but their position on the war inhibited official relations, as did their forcible dissolution of the freely elected Constituent Assembly in January 1918. Moreover, their ideological appeal was characterized, as Secretary of State Lansing noted, by a "determination, frankly avowed, to overthrow all existing governments and establish on the ruins a despotism of the proletariat in every country." The revolutionary proclamations to the masses, which Lenin and Trotsky had hoped would force bourgeois governments into official relations with the Bolsheviks, turned out to be one of the major impediments that prevented them.[24]

In the absence of formal recognition or participation in the peace talks at Brest-Litovsk, there remained three separate courses of action open to the Allies and their American associates in dealing with the Bolshevik Revolution. All were designed to keep Russia in the war, one way or another; all were pursued, at one time or another, during the winter of 1917–1918.

The first of these involved finding some way to aid anti-Bolshevik forces in Russia, in the hope that they would be able to overthrow the Bolsheviks and continue the war. Early in December, President Wilson approved clandestine financial aid through the British and French to General Kaledin in South Russia, but it quickly became apparent that Kaledin's Cossacks did not constitute an effective fighting force, and no aid was

---

[23] Kennan, *Russia Leaves the War*, p. 194; Edward Hallett Carr, *The Bolshevik Revolution, 1917–1923* (New York: 1951–1953), III, 6–7.
[24] Lansing memorandum, early December, 1917, quoted in *The War Memoirs of Robert Lansing* (New York: 1935), p. 340. See also Deutscher, *The Prophet Armed*, pp. 348–352.

actually sent. Another possibility was direct military intervention in Siberia, a course of action strongly supported by the
French and the Japanese, somewhat less so by the British. Wilson firmly rejected intervention, though, partly because he
feared it would only win sympathy for the Bolsheviks, partly
because he distrusted the motives of those proposing intervention, particularly the Japanese. As long as the negotiations at
Brest-Litovsk continued, there remained the possibility, however faint, that the Bolsheviks might yet reject a separate peace
and resume the struggle against Germany. Intervention, or
even aid to opponents of Bolshevism in any quantity, risked
foreclosing that possibility and hence was, for the moment,
rejected.[25]

The second course of action open to the Americans and their
allies involved informal diplomatic contacts with the Bolshevik
authorities in the hope of influencing the peace negotiations.
Allied diplomats had remained in Petrograd following the
November revolution, but had refrained from official relations
with the new Soviet government. On December 1, 1917, however, General William V. Judson, the American military attaché,
saw Trotsky on his own initiative to urge that the Bolsheviks try
to prevent the Germans from transferring troops to the western
front. Somewhat surprisingly, Trotsky agreed, and the Bolsheviks did make energetic, if ultimately futile, efforts at Brest-
Litovsk to prevent German redeployments. Judson was recalled
for breaking the ban on contacts, but Washington officials soon
came to see the advantages of informal relations as a means of
monitoring and possibly influencing the peace negotiations, and
tacitly allowed them to continue.[26]

But there were definite limitations on the effectiveness of this
kind of diplomacy. Ambassador Francis proved wholly unable
to coordinate the activities of his enthusiastic but mutually antagonistic subordinates, notably the dynamic head of the
American Red Cross mission, Raymond Robins, who soon de-

[25] Kennan, *Russia Leaves the War*, pp. 160–190, 291–330; Warth, *The Allies and the
Russian Revolution*, pp. 189–195; Trask, *The United States and the Supreme War
Council*, pp. 101–111; Betty Miller Unterberger, "President Wilson and the Decision to Send American Troops to Siberia," *Pacific Historical Review*, XXIV (February, 1955), 63–68.
[26] Kennan, *Russia Leaves the War*, pp. 107–130, 230–233.

veloped a remarkably cordial working relationship with Lenin and Trotsky. Communications with Washington were poor, leaving the Americans in Petrograd in the dark much of the time regarding the Wilson administration's intentions, and giving officials of that administration only the fuzziest impression of what was going on in the Russian capital. The American diplomatic establishment simply was not equipped, at this relatively early stage in its development, to conduct diplomacy efficiently outside of official channels.[27] Yet the Bolsheviks, conspiracy theorists that they were, assumed a greater degree of coordination among the Americans than actually existed: Robins's sympathetic attitude may well have led them to expect some kind of aid from the United States and its allies in case their negotiations with the Germans at Brest-Litovsk broke down.[28]

Wilson did have aid of sorts in mind, but it was in the form, not of guns and ammunition, but of a belated public reformulation of war aims: this was the third early Allied approach to the Bolshevik Revolution. The events of November had caused Wilson to develop second thoughts about his policy of not discussing war aims while the fighting was going on. Had the Allies made their objectives clear from the outset, the president speculated in a message to Congress in December, then "the sympathy and enthusiasm of the Russian people might have been once for all enlisted on the side of the Allies, [and] . . . the sad reverses which have recently marked the progress of their affairs . . . might have been avoided."[29] Following the start of German-Russian negotiations at Brest-Litovsk, a reconsideration of this question got underway within the Allied camp. Efforts to agree on a joint redefinition of war aims failed, because of the reluctance of the French and Italians to repudiate annexations, but in January 1918, both Wilson and Lloyd George made

[27] Ibid., pp. 32–70, 99–100; Fike, "Influence of the Creel Committee," pp. 108–109.

[28] Soviet historiography still attaches considerable importance to these early informal contacts between Americans in Russia and the new Bolshevik government. See I.M. Krasnov, "Neizvestnye Leninskie dokumenty o Sovetsko-Amerikanskikh otnosheniiakh," *Voprosy istorii*, July, 1969, #7; Liudmila Gvishiani, *Sovetskaia Rossiia i SShA (1917–1920)* (Moscow: 1970), pp. 36–40, 62–71.

[29] Baker and Dodd, eds., *Wilson Public Papers: War and Peace*, I, 134.

important unilateral statements designed largely as a reply to the Bolsheviks.[30]

Wilson's was his famous Fourteen Points address. In it he praised the Russian people, without referring directly to the Bolshevik government, for stating their war aims "with frankness, a largeness of view, a generosity of spirit, and a universal human sympathy which must challenge the admiration of every friend of mankind." Somewhat surprisingly, Wilson argued that the Russians had "refused to compound their ideals or desert others that they themselves would be safe":

They call to us to say what it is that we desire, in what, if anything, our purpose and our spirit differ from theirs; and I believe that the people of the United States would wish me to respond, with utter simplicity and frankness. Whether their present leaders believe it or not, it is our heartfelt desire and hope that some way may be opened whereby we may be privileged to assist the people of Russia to attain their utmost hope of liberty and ordered peace.

Within this context, Wilson went on to outline his fourteen points, the sixth of which called for the "evacuation of all Russian territory and such a settlement of all questions affecting Russia as will . . . [obtain] for her the independent determination of her own political development and national policy." The treatment accorded Russia by her sister nations, Wilson added, would be "the acid test of their goodwill, of their comprehension of her needs as distinguished from their own interest and of their intelligent and unselfish sympathy."[31]

There was much in the Fourteen Points which coincided with the public peace program of the Bolsheviks, notably the emphasis on self-determination, open diplomacy, and a nonpunitive war settlement. Lenin and Trotsky welcomed it with moderate enthusiasm and even facilitated efforts by American officials to have copies distributed widely in Russia and behind the lines in Germany.[32] Yet it seems clear that the Bolsheviks' relatively friendly response reflected certain tactical advantages

---

[30] Kennan, *Russia Leaves the War*, pp. 131–140; Mayer, *Political Origins*, pp. 286–290.

[31] Baker and Dodd, eds., *Wilson Public Papers: War and Peace*, I, 157–160.

[32] Mayer, *Political Origins*, pp. 372–373; Kennan, *Russia Leaves the War*, pp. 260–264.

they saw deriving from the speech, not any fundamental agreement with Wilson on the shape of the postwar world. Wilson's open endorsement of what seemed to be important portions of the Bolshevik peace program could not help but strengthen the Soviet government's position in Russia, nor could Lenin and Trotsky object to Wilson's attempt to sow dissension behind German lines, since they had been trying to do the same thing themselves. The speech may have also further encouraged the Soviet leaders to believe that the United States might send aid should the Brest-Litovsk negotiations break down and Russia be forced to resume the war: indeed Lenin and Trotsky forwarded a written inquiry regarding this possibility through Robins on March 5. Through a bureaucratic mix-up, however, the message did not reach Washington until March 16, the very day the All-Russian Congress of Soviets ratified the peace.[33]

It probably did not make any difference. Lenin was not above giving the Allies the impression that their aid might have kept Russia in the war, but it seems unlikely that he ever counted on getting such assistance in any significant way. Only massive and immediate aid could have sustained the Bolsheviks against the German onslaught in March 1918, and Lenin knew that there was no way to provide this, given transportation difficulties and the priorities of the western front. Moreover, the Bolshevik government depended for its survival on the support, or at least the toleration, of the peasantry: in securing it the promise of peace was at least as important as the promise of land. In the end, Lenin attached the highest importance to remaining in power, no matter how small his power base was.[34] The only way he could realistically expect to accomplish this was to make peace, even if it meant, as it did, the loss of one-third of Russia's population, one-third of its cultivable lands, including the rich Ukraine, and one-half of its heavy industry.[35]

But the Bolsheviks did receive help from the United States in another, less direct way. The conclusion of the Brest-Litovsk negotiations coincided with the launching of the German spring

---

[33] Ibid., pp. 497–498, 516.

[34] Carr, *The Bolshevik Revolution*, III, 33–35, 52.

[35] Warth, *The Allies and the Russian Revolution*, p. 233.

offensive in the west. An almost immediate effect was to weaken German pressure on Russia, a trend which grew far more pronounced in the summer when the Allies, bolstered by the arrival of fresh American troops, began their successful counteroffensive.[36] It is unclear to what extent Lenin had anticipated, in March 1918, the quick impact American participation in the fighting would have in hastening Germany's defeat. Certainly he did not hesitate to take credit for such foresight at the time of the armistice, though characteristically he attributed the German surrender to revolutionary pressures, not battlefield reverses.[37] Yet it seems clear that at least "objectively," to use a term popular with Marxist historians, the United States played a major role in freeing Russia from the onerous terms imposed by the Germans at Brest-Litovsk.

III

The Americans and their allies received no credit, however, because during the spring and summer of 1918 they had reversed their policy on intervention and dispatched troops to Russia. The reasons are both complex and simple: complex in that an involved set of circumstances related to pursuit of the war, compounded by confusion and preoccupation on the part of policymakers, provided the immediate occasion for intervention; simple because behind it all was a loathing for Bolshevism so strong that it could cause honest men to put forward and possibly even believe flimsy excuses for involving themselves in the internal affairs of another nation. At both levels, however, the means employed corrupted the end envisaged. The result was unnecessarily to poison relations between Russia and the West for years to come.

Conclusion of the Brest-Litovsk treaty created a kind of panic in Allied capitals, since it coincided almost exactly with the launching of the final German offensive in the west. Many observers now assumed that Russia had become, to all intents and purposes, a satellite of Germany. Not only would this mean that the Germans could now transfer troops to the western front, but they would also have access to the vast agricultural and industrial facilities of Russia and to the huge stockpiles of un-

---

[36] Carr, *The Bolshevik Revolution*, III, 79–80.
[37] Ibid., p. 54.

used war supplies that had accumulated in and around the ports of Murmansk, Archangel, and Vladivostok. There were, to be sure, certain inconsistencies in this view. How Germany could occupy Russia and still spare troops for transfer to the west was not made clear. Nor was it apparent how the Germans would be able to utilize stockpiled war supplies any more effectively than the Russians had: the problem here was the inefficiency of Russian railroads, a situation which could not be changed overnight.[38] But these considerations were not thought of in the heat of the moment. The chief inhibition which had prevented intervention up to this point had been the fear of driving the Bolsheviks into the hands of the Germans. Now that that seemed to have happened, there appeared to be little reason to hold back.

But Wilson, doubtless recalling his unhappy experiences with Mexico several years earlier,[39] remained skeptical. He would consider intervention in Russia only if some way could be found to reconcile it with the principle of self-determination to which he had committed himself, and the nation, in the Fourteen Points speech several months earlier. As was usually the case in Wilsonian diplomacy, though, there proved to be a surprising number of ways in which this integration of power and ideals could be accomplished.[40]

One way would have been for the Bolsheviks themselves to invite the Allies in. In the spring of 1918, this possibility was not as farfetched as it might sound. The Soviet leaders made no secret of their contempt for the Brest-Litovsk treaty, and had no inhibitions about violating it when they could do so with impunity. Allied representatives in Moscow had been led to believe that the Bolsheviks might yet welcome help against the Germans, and, in a moment of panic during the Brest-Litovsk negotiations, Trotsky had actually authorized the Murmansk Soviet to accept "any and all assistance" from the Allies to forestall a possible German advance against the Murmansk railway. In fact, however, the prospects for intervention by invitation

---

[38] George F. Kennan, *The Decision to Intervene* (Princeton: 1958), pp. 3–4, 97–98; Trask, *The United States in the Supreme War Council*, p. 111.

[39] Fowler, *British-American Relations*, pp. 185, 196.

[40] On this point, see N. Gordon Levin, *Woodrow Wilson and World Politics: America's Response to War and Revolution* (New York: 1968), pp. 43–45, 52.

were never great. Lenin viewed the Allies and the Germans with equal suspicion, half expecting them at any moment to unite in a common crusade against Bolshevism. He was prepared to accept food and military supplies from the Allies in order to play them off against the Germans, but not armed intervention, a move which would only encourage German countermeasures at the expense of the still-vulnerable Soviet state. As it became clear in the months following Brest-Litovsk that the Germans had no intention of occupying Russia or of challenging the existence of the Soviet government, opportunities for Allied intervention by invitation quickly faded.[41]

There remained the possibility of intervention without invitation. This too could be reconciled with the principle of self-determination if it could be shown to be vital for victory over Germany, for without victory, it could be argued, there would be little chance for self-determination anywhere. Wilson was not so naive as to believe that the presence of a few thousand American troops in Siberia or North Russia would make any great difference in the outcome of the war. But any weakening of Allied unity could, and Wilson proved to be very sensitive to this possibility. In March 1918, he almost approved a British-French request for Japanese intervention in Siberia, not from any military advantage he saw deriving from it, but from a reluctance to go against the wishes of the Allies. Several months later, in July, he did in fact authorize the dispatch of a small contingent of American troops to North Russia. The possibility of Germany's seizing the military supplies stockpiled at Murmansk and Archangel was at least credible; moreover, as Secretary of War Newton Baker later recalled, "the British and French were pressing it upon his [Wilson's] attention so hard and he had refused so many of their requests that they were beginning to feel that he was not a good associate, much less a good ally."[42]

---

[41] Ibid., pp. 97–98; Carr, *The Bolshevik Revolution,* III, 72, 79–80; Kennan, *The Decision to Intervene,* pp. 46–48, 123–135.

[42] Baker to Ralph Hayes, December 24, 1929, quoted in R. S. Baker, *Woodrow Wilson: Life and Letters: Armistice* (New York: 1939), p. 284n. See also Kennan, *Russia Leaves the War,* pp. 471–483; Kennan, *The Decision to Intervene,* pp. 376–379; Trask, *The United States in the Supreme War Council,* pp. 118–119; Betty Miller Unterberger, *America's Siberian Expedition, 1918–1920* (Durham: 1956), pp. 30, 64.

Somewhat different considerations caused Wilson, that same month, to reverse his previous policy and sanction limited Japanese-American intervention in Siberia. Here, intervention could in no way credibly affect the course of the war, which was being fought some 5000 miles away. Nor was Allied unity a motive: Wilson decided on intervention in Siberia without telling the British and the French, and had not intended that they participate. The president was concerned about the ambitions of the Japanese in Manchuria and the Russian Far East, though: convinced that eventual Japanese intervention there was inevitable, he resolved to try to control it by turning it into a joint enterprise. Then, too, there had suddenly arisen the problem of the Czech Legion, a force of some 70,000 Czechoslovak exiles and prisoners-of-war who had been fighting on the side of the Russians. The Czechs had chosen to leave Russia by way of the Trans-Siberian Railroad following signing of the Brest-Litovsk treaty. Fighting with the Bolsheviks broke out along the way, however, and Wilson had come to believe by July that only by sending American troops to Siberia could the way be cleared for the Czechs to get out. This proved to be the decisive justification, in the president's mind, for intervention in Siberia.[43]

The decision to send troops to North Russia and Siberia reflects, as well as any decision in modern history, the imperfect control government leaders sometimes have over events which they themselves set in motion. The forces sent to North Russia had strict orders not to fight the Bolsheviks, but they were placed under British command and were in fact ordered to fight. The Siberian intervention, which Wilson justified mainly as an effort to remove the Czechs, turned into something more when the British, Canadians, French, Italians, and Chinese insisted on joining the operation, and when the Japanese sent 70,000 troops instead of the 7000 Wilson had expected. "The other governments are . . . acting upon a plan which is altogether foreign from ours and inconsistent with it," Wilson admitted in August. Nor were the Czechs themselves in any hurry to get out. They had begun fighting the Bolsheviks at the instigation of their

[43] Kennan, *The Decision to Intervene,* pp. 381–404; Unterberger, *America's Siberian Expedition,* pp. 67–88; Levin, *Wilson and World Politics,* pp. 112–119; John Albert White, *The Siberian Intervention* (Princeton: 1950), pp. 227–255.

French advisers; moreover, no one had thought to bring ships to Vladivostok with which to evacuate them should they in fact choose to leave. On top of all of this, these events coincided with the final life and death struggle on the western front, so that American and Allied officials were able to give them only fragmentary attention.[44]

It would be a mistake, though, to see Allied intervention in Russia solely as a result of bureaucratic bungling. The fact is that a fundamental loathing for Bolshevism influenced all of Wilson's actions with regard to Russia and the actions of his Allied counterparts as well. This should hardly be surprising, since the Bolsheviks made no secret of their fundamental loathing for the West. Nor did Wilson see his antipathy for Bolshevism as in any way inconsistent with his belief in self-determination: in his view, as in the view of other Allied leaders, the Bolsheviks were not representative of the Russian people. They had come to power by force, they had dissolved the Constituent Assembly, they had made a separate peace with Germany, and there were even indications, according to documents circulating in the West in the summer of 1918, that they were German agents. Hence the overthrow of Bolshevism could be seen, in Wilson's view, not as a violation of self-determination, but as an action necessary to its attainment.[45]

Wilson was, however, far more sensitive than the other Allied leaders to the counterproductive effects of a direct onslaught against Bolshevism—something which could not be undertaken in any case as long as the war was on.[46] Accordingly, he portrayed intervention variously as designed to bolster the war effort, promote Allied unity, monitor the Japanese, help the

[44] Wilson to Lansing, August 23, 1918, *Foreign Relations: The Lansing Papers, 1914–1920* (Washington: 1940), II, 378–379. See also Kennan, *The Decision to Intervene*, pp. 376–380, 399–429; and Unterberger *America's Siberian Expedition*, pp. 55–59, 72–79.

[45] Levin, *Wilson and World Politics*, p. 109; Christopher Lasch, "American Intervention in Russia: A Reinterpretation," *Political Science Quarterly*, LXVII(June, 1962), 217–223; George F. Kennan, "The Sisson Documents," *Journal of Modern History*, XXVIII (June, 1956), 130–154; Robert James Maddox, "Woodrow Wilson, the Russian Embassy and Siberian Intervention," *Pacific Historical Review*, XXXVI(November, 1967), 435–448.

[46] Maddox, "Wilson, the Russian Embassy, and Siberian Intervention," pp. 436–437.

Czechs—anything, it would seem, but an openly avowed attempt to overthrow Bolshevism. Wilson hoped that the half-measures he had approved, and had sought to justify in such a nonexceptionable manner, would weaken Bolshevism without attracting sympathy for it, whether in Russia itself or among liberals and socialists in the West. It was a subtle strategy, but one dependent on keeping American motives insulated from the franker and less innocent objectives of the Allies. Given the need to cooperate with the Allies in securing sufficient manpower to make intervention effective, such insulation proved difficult to achieve. In the end, Wilson's attempt to "purify" intervention by contributing United States troops had the perverse effect of rendering unconvincing the aura of disinterestedness he considered vital to the success of his Russian policy.

IV

The Paris Peace Conference was held, of course, chiefly for the purpose of agreeing upon and imposing a peace settlement on Germany. But during the six months it took to do this, and for a long time thereafter, the problem of what to do about Russia remained much in the minds of Western leaders. It was, Herbert Hoover later wrote, "the Banquo's ghost sitting at every Council table."[47] In the end, the Allies had no choice but to learn to live with the Bolshevik regime. They did not come to this position gracefully, however; their failure to do so would further intensify the already considerable hostility which existed between Russia and the West.

The United States had sent troops into Russia ostensibly as part of the war effort against Germany, yet those forces remained in place long after the fighting had ended. American troops did not leave North Russia until June 1919; they remained in Siberia until April 1920. Such had not been Woodrow Wilson's wish: still sensitive to the counterproductive effects of intervention, he had wanted to withdraw United States forces from Russia as soon as possible after the armistice.[48] But, as in

---

[47] Quoted in John M. Thompson, *Russia, Bolshevism, and the Versailles Peace* (Princeton: 1966), p. 2.

[48] Ibid., pp. 49–50.

the case of the original decision to intervene, Wilson's long-range objectives fell victim to short-range preoccupations.

At no time during the Paris Peace Conference was Wilson able to give careful and sustained thought to the Russian question. It is true that the prospect of Bolshevism spreading into Europe was a major concern of the Big Four, but they sought to deal with it not so much by confronting the Russian problem directly as by attempting to construct a postwar European order capable of resisting the contagion from the East.[49] Discussions of what to do about Russia therefore had to be fitted in around the larger and more time-consuming questions of making peace with Germany and drafting the League of Nations covenant. When the Russian question did come up, it often did so at bad moments: just as Wilson was leaving for a short visit to the United States in mid-February, for example, or at the time of Clemenceau's attempted assassination a few days later, or of Wilson's sudden illness in early April. Moreover, inadequate information, always a problem in dealing with Russian affairs, was now even more of a difficulty since the Allies no longer had representatives on the Bolshevik side; virtually all of their information came from the White Russians. As a result, distraction, misinformation, and ineptitude marked deliberations at Paris on the Russian question; despite its importance at no point did it receive, either from Wilson or his colleagues, the attention it deserved.[50]

But, distracted as he was, Wilson could not simply "forget" the presence of some 14,000 American troops in Russia. There were other reasons why they remained where they did. One important one involved coalition diplomacy. Intervention had been a joint project from the beginning: Wilson had sent troops to Russia in part to promote Allied unity and in part to control Allied actions there. Both goals precluded independent initiatives. As the American ambassador to Japan noted, in a concise summary of Wilson's policy, "unity of action in Siberia is more

---

[49] Ibid., pp. 240–241; Levin, *Wilson and World Politics,* pp. 168–169, 174–182; Arno J. Mayer, *Politics and Diplomacy of Peacemaking: Containment and Counterrevolution at Versailles, 1918–1919* (New York: 1967), pp. 9–10.
[50] Kennan, *Russia and the West,* pp. 129, 147–148; Thompson, *Russia, Bolshevism, and the Versailles Peace,* pp. 381–382.

important than the character of the action." Allied coordination remained no less vital at the peace table than it had been in war, and Wilson was loath to imperil it by a unilateral decision to withdraw American troops. He was determined to work for withdrawal but only as part of a general settlement between the Allies and the Russians.[51]

But Wilson's attitude made his Russian policy a prisoner of the mixed motives with which the Allies had embarked upon intervention. Neither the French nor the Japanese had any intention of withdrawing their troops from Russia merely because the Germans had surrendered. British policy was more ambivalent, with Lloyd George sharing Wilson's skepticism about intervention but doing little to restrain more activist members of his government like Winston Churchill, secretary of state for war, who pressed for an even more energetic use of force against the Bolsheviks.[52] This lack of agreement among the Allies frustrated two important initiatives Wilson and Lloyd George took to try to arrange a settlement of the Russian question.

The first, proposed in January 1919, involved a conference of all contending elements in Russia, to be held on the Prinkipo Islands in the Sea of Marmara under supervision of the Allies, for the purpose of trying to resolve outstanding differences. The Bolsheviks, anxious for recognition and legitimacy, accepted the invitation, but the Whites, now under at least the nominal authority of Admiral A. V. Kolchak's government at Omsk, refused to go along. Later it became known that the French, who had agreed to the Prinkipo proposal only with the greatest reluctance, had secretly encouraged the Whites to reject participation in the conference. The conversations, had they been held, would likely have accomplished little; differences among Russians by this time were probably too great to be resolved through negotiations. Still, not much would have been lost by

---

[51] Roland S. Morris to the State Department, May 3, 1919, *FR: 1919: Russia*, p. 339. See also Levin, *Wilson and World Politics*, pp. 163, 171; and Betty Miller Unterberger, "The Russian Revolution and Wilson's Far Eastern Policy," *Russian Review*, XVI(April, 1957), 45.

[52] Thompson, *Russia, Bolshevism, and the Versailles Peace*, pp. 50–60; Unterberger, *America's Siberian Expedition*, p. 231.

trying; the inability of the Allies to agree on Russia was the main reason why the effort was not made.[53]

A second major initiative occurred in March 1919, with the dispatch of a young American diplomat, William C. Bullitt, to Moscow for the purpose of sounding out the Bolsheviks on possible bases for a cease-fire. Bullitt was not empowered to negotiate with the Bolsheviks, but he did receive from Lenin a promising offer to accept greatly constricted boundaries, pay off Russian debts, and declare a general amnesty in return for a cease-fire and the withdrawal of foreign troops. Bullitt returned to Paris eager to implement this arrangement but was astonished to find himself repudiated by Wilson and Lloyd George upon his arrival. The reasons for Bullitt's repudiation are still not wholly clear, but among the probable explanations are concern over offending the French, who had not been consulted; fear of an unfavorable public response, certainly on Lloyd George's part but possibly also on Wilson's; preoccupation with negotiations on the German question; and the distraction of Wilson's brief but sudden physical incapacity during the first week in April. Whatever the cause, an opportunity to end the Russian civil war on terms far more favorable to the Whites than would later be available was thereby lost.[54]

But perhaps the main reason for the conspicuous half-heartedness with which Wilson pursued both the Prinkipo and the Bullitt proposals is that both would have implied at least partial recognition of the Bolshevik government. Wilson had never been prepared to go that far. Although he was more sympathetic than his Allied counterparts to the goals of the Russian Revolution, the revolution he had in mind was that of March 1917, not November. He never viewed Bolshevism as any less dangerous than did his colleagues, and at no point was he prepared to acknowledge the legitimacy of the Moscow government.[55] What he sought was a way to undermine Bol-

---

[53] Thompson, *Russia, Bolshevism, and the Versailles Peace*, pp. 82–130; Kennan, *Russia and the West*, pp. 126–130; Mayer, *Politics and Diplomacy of Peacemaking*, pp. 427–449.

[54] Thompson, *Russia, Bolshevism, and the Versailles Peace*, pp. 149–177, 233–247; Mayer, *Politics and Diplomacy of Peacemaking*, pp. 450–487; Beatrice Farnsworth, *William C. Bullitt and the Soviet Union* (Bloomington: 1967), pp. 32–54.

[55] Levin, *Wilson and World Politics*, pp. 204, 210, 212.

shevism peacefully, without damaging the interests of the Russian people, yet without in any way recognizing the Bolshevik regime. Herbert Hoover came up with a similar policy in late March, when he proposed to the president an ambitious scheme for establishing a relief commission in Russia which would provide food impartially to Russians on both sides. The plan's aura of impartiality was deceptive, though: Hoover made it clear privately that its intent was to erode Bolshevik authority. The plan would have required a cease-fire and transfer of the entire Russian transportation network to Allied control, yet it made no provision for the evacuation of foreign troops. Not surprisingly, the Bolsheviks rejected it.[56]

Few options now remained open other than the direct use of force against Bolshevism. At several points during the Paris Peace Conference, Marshall Foch tried to win Anglo-American support for a quick peace with Germany and a subsequent attack on Bolshevik Russia, using Poland and Rumania as staging areas. Both Wilson and Lloyd George rejected this idea, partly because they thought public opinion in their respective countries would not stand for it, partly because of the astronomical expenditures which would have been involved, partly because they feared than an overt attack would only strengthen Bolshevism. But the Allies did, in June 1919, announce partial recognition of the Kolchak government at Omsk and the dispatch of aid to it. In view of the Kolchak regime's authoritarian nature, Wilson had some difficulty squaring this decision with his commitment to self-determination, but when Kolchak promised to move toward a more democratic orientation, the president reluctantly agreed to go along. Once again, though, the Allies' timing was wrong. No sooner had they announced partial recognition than the Bolsheviks began to drive Kolchak back. Within a year, he would be captured and executed, the Bolsheviks would control most of central Russia and Siberia, and the civil war would, to all intents and purposes, be over.[57]

---

[56] Thompson, *Russia, Bolshevism, and the Versailles Peace,* pp. 247–267; Mayer, *Politics and Diplomacy of Peacemaking,* pp. 474–487.
[57] Thompson, *Russia, Bolshevism, and the Versailles Peace,* pp. 178–192, 268–308; John Silverlight, *The Victors' Dilemma: Allied Intervention in the Russian Civil War* (New York: 1970), pp. 340–352.

What Wilson had hoped to do, both in the decision to intervene and in the various initiatives he took at Paris, had been to reconstitute a political arena in Russia in which anti-Bolshevik elements could compete, with some chance of success, for the allegiance of the Russian people. This was, in itself, an ambitious undertaking, since such an arena had never existed in Russia in the first place. Its success was rendered even less likely by the severe limitations which distance and cost imposed upon the Allies' ability to influence events inside that country. Nor were the Allies in agreement among themselves: Wilson and Lloyd George found their policies constantly undercut by the hard-line approach of their French and Japanese associates and sometimes by their own subordinates. Nor was Wilson himself ever completely clear on how best to achieve his objective: as was the case with his German policy, there was in his approach to the Russian question a curious tension between the tactics of repression and reintegration which made him susceptible to appeals from both points of view, but prevented the emergence of any clear and consistent policy of his own.[58]

As a consequence, the Allies fell between stools. They sent enough force to Russia to allow the Bolsheviks credibly to portray themselves as defenders of the besieged Russian fatherland, but nothing near the number of troops which would have been required actually to overthrow that regime. In the end, they were reduced to letting events in Russia take their own course. Commitments had been projected beyond capabilities; as is usually the case in such situations, the only results were bitterness, frustration, and recrimination.

V

It is curious that in both the United States and Russia there should have been in power, in 1917–1919, leaders capable of promulgating ideologies to which much of the world would look, in the decades to come, as guides to action. There were even certain similarities in their respective points of view: both Wilson and Lenin believed in the universal applicability of their

---

[58] Levin, *Wilson and World Politics*, pp. 5–6.

philosophies of government and in the inevitability of their eventual triumph; both sought to alter the traditional structure of international relations in such a way as to end imperialism and war; both, in their own way, looked to democracy as the ultimate objective. But here the similarities end. Where Lenin conceived of democracy only in economic terms, Wilson tended to think of it primarily in political terms; where Lenin endorsed violent social revolution as the only means of attaining this goal, Wilson favored evolution, or, at most, controlled revolution within a liberal-capitalist framework; where Lenin sought to overthrow the existing international order, Wilson sought to alter it from within—to be in it but not of it.[59]

It would appear, at first glance, that the differences between these competing ideologies would have been sufficiently great as to preclude any kind of normal diplomatic relations between the nations which espoused them. But this was not necessarily the case. Ideologies reflect aspirations more often than they shape policies; before ideas can be put into action, practical concessions to reality usually have to be made. The ease with which this can be done in turn determines the possibilities for conventional relations between ideologically disparate states.

There was nothing in Lenin's approach to government which forbade making such concessions; indeed when choices had to be made between the competing claims of ideology and national interest, the latter almost always won out. Brest-Litovsk was the first and in many ways the most striking example, but others would follow, among them acceptance of the Prinkipo summons, the proposals made through Bullitt, and, as will be seen, Lenin's persistent offers of economic cooperation with the capitalist world. None of these initiatives indicated any weakening in the ultimate aims of Leninist ideology, but they did suggest a flexibility in tactics which could tolerate, and even encourage, normal diplomatic contacts with the West.

With Wilson the situation was more complex. He too, was capable of retreating from ideological positions where necessary, as he demonstrated more than once on non-Russian issues at the Paris Peace Conference. But Wilson was also inclined

---

[59] Ibid., p. 8; Thompson, *Russia, Bolshevism, and the Versailles Peace,* p. 43.

toward extreme inflexibility in particular situations, especially where high hopes had, in his view, been betrayed.[60] The Russian Revolution was one such situation: although the president had difficulty in deciding whether force or cooperation would best destroy Bolshevism, he was firm in his belief that, one way or another, it would have to be destroyed. At no point was he prepared, even for tactical purposes, to acknowledge the legitimacy of the Bolshevik regime. In this respect, he showed considerably less flexibility than did Lenin, who at least was willing to deal with capitalist governments while simultaneously plotting their destruction.

But in fairness it should be recognized that Wilson had to contend, to a greater extent than did Lenin, with the problem of placating constituencies, both at home and overseas. While Lenin's government was never a monolith, and while sharp opposition to some of his ideological compromises did at times surface, the Russian leader never had to contend with an aroused public opinion or with the problem of maintaining unity among allies. These factors limited the extent to which Wilson could depart from his public ideological stance in order to arrange accommodations with his ideological rival. Moreover, the problem of Russia could never be wholly separated from the problem of Europe as a whole: Wilson, like most Allied leaders, feared that the contagion of Bolshevism would spread into a Europe which had been left extremely vulnerable to such appeals by the social and physical destruction of war.[61] Recognizing the Bolsheviks, or dealing with them in any way which would acknowledge their legitimacy, might, it was felt, facilitate this process.

For the moment, therefore, the national interest, as Wilson perceived it, coincided with Wilsonian ideology. This would not always be the case in years to come. Such coincidence was even less frequent in the case of the Soviet Union: from the time of Brest-Litovsk on, there would exist in Soviet diplomacy a persistent tension between the competing requirements of ideology

[60] See, on this point, John Morton Blum, *Woodrow Wilson and the Politics of Morality* (Boston: 1956), pp. 23–37, 186; Patrick Devlin, *Too Proud to Fight: Woodrow Wilson's Neutrality* (New York: 1975), pp. 36–41, 50–60.

[61] Mayer, *Politics and Diplomacy of Peacemaking*, pp. 3–30.

and national interest.[62] The future of Russian-American relations would thus be determined, in large measure, by the ease with which each nation could transcend the fundamental ideological polarities which now set them apart, and find, on the firm ground of national self-interest, some mutually acceptable basis for peacefully tolerating each other's existence.

---

[62] Carr, *The Bolshevik Revolution*, III, 57–58; Adam B. Ulam, *Expansion and Coexistence: Soviet Foreign Policy, 1917–73* (New York: 1974), p. 75.

CHAPTER IV

Nonrecognition: 1920–1933

B Y 1920, THE GOVERNMENTS OF BOTH SOVIET RUSSIA AND THE UN-
ITED STATES had begun to grapple with the problem of establishing a permanent relationship toward one another. It had
become clear to the Wilson administration that neither intervention nor integration had succeeded in undermining Bolshevism;
the Leninist regime seemed, for the moment, defiantly en-
trenched. Simultaneously, Lenin and his colleagues had come
to the realistic conclusion that world revolution, upon which
rested their hopes for ultimate survival, was not on the immediate horizon. Normalization of relations would depend
upon the ability of each side to move beyond the deep ideological antagonisms which separated them. Somewhat surprisingly,
it was the highly ideological Soviet state which showed more
flexibility in this area than did the more pluralistic, and presumably nonideological, United States.

I

There was a significant ambiguity in early Bolshevik thought
about relations with the capitalist world. On the one hand, it
stressed the monolithic nature of capitalism and the implacable
hostility states of that persuasion could be expected to direct
toward the young Soviet republic. But, on the other hand, Lenin
attached great importance to playing off the capitalists against
one another—to encouraging "contradictions" within the
capitalist camp which would prevent concerted action against
the revolution and gain time for consolidation and

reorganization.[1] Brest-Litovsk had been an important part of this strategy; so too was the promotion of a "special relationship" with the United States.

The Bolsheviks had, from the earliest days of the revolution, differentiated between the United States and other capitalist countries. Wilson's public sympathy for the revolution's ideals, together with informal contacts with Americans in Petrograd, had led Lenin and Trotsky to believe that they might get help from the United States if they resumed the struggle against Germany. Even after Brest-Litovsk, the Soviet leaders had not been able to bring themselves to believe that the United States would actually intervene against the Bolsheviks, partly for reasons of economic self-interest, partly because of the antagonism Lenin saw developing between Japan and the United States.

These considerations led to a remarkable proposal which Lenin made to Raymond Robins on the eve of the latter's departure from Russia in May 1918. The Soviet leader handed Robins an unsigned paper, with a note that its contents had been approved in the highest councils of the Russian government. The paper called attention to the disastrous condition of the Russian economy and noted the extent to which, in the years preceding the revolution, Russia had been dependent on imports from the West, especially the United States. It then observed that although, under the Brest-Litovsk treaty, Germany would be entitled to most-favored nation treatment in Russia after the war, she would be too exhausted to take advantage of it. The real opportunities would lie with the United States, which could take over a large share of the Russian market if it were willing to advance credits. As security, Lenin proposed granting American businessmen extensive coal, lumber, and railway concessions in eastern Siberia, as well as the opportunity to participate in the construction of power stations and the development of water routes in central Russia.[2]

Lenin made no secret of his motives in making this unusual offer. In a speech to the All-Russian Central Executive Commit-

---

[1] Ulam, *Expansion and Coexistence*, p. 78.

[2] Ministerstvo inostrannykh del SSSR, *Dokumenty vneshnei politiki, SSSR* (Moscow: 1967–   ), I, 286–294. For the circumstances surrounding delivery of this note, see Kennan, *The Decision to Intervene*, pp. 217–220.

tee and the Moscow Soviet on May 14, the same day the note to Robins was delivered, Lenin pointed out that the fledgling Soviet state was "a lone island in the stormy seas of imperialist robbery," and that its future security would depend on encouraging the "contradictions that have arisen out of the frenzied struggle between the imperialist powers." The two most important contradictions, Lenin argued, were those between Britain and Germany on the one hand and Japan and America on the other. Just as the Brest-Litovsk treaty had prevented the German conquest of Russia, so exacerbation of Japanese-American conflict would preserve Siberia from Japanese rapaciousness. "We must not forget," he concluded, "that however solid the imperialist groupings may appear to be, they can be broken up in a few days if the interests of sacred private property, the sacred right of concessions, etc., demand it."[3]

Much to Lenin's surprise, the United States made no response to this offer. Robins' close ties with the Bolsheviks had undermined his credibility, and he was ignored upon his return to Washington. Nor did Japanese-American rivalry, which was real enough, forestall intervention. But even after American troops landed in Russia, the Bolsheviks continued to make distinctions between the United States and its allies. Foreign Minister Georgii Chicherin commented in September 1918 that although the Bolshevik government had been forced to intern British and French citizens inside Russia, "our attitude is entirely different towards American citizens, to whom these measures were not extended, because, although the United States Government also was compelled by its Allies to agree to participate in intervention, . . . its decision is not regarded by us as irrevocable."[4] And as it became clear that the war was ending in an Allied victory, the Russians looked to Washington as the chief agent through whom an end to intervention could be arranged.

Again, the Soviet government held out the lure of trade and concessions as an incentive. "Do the capitalists want some of the timber in the North, part of Siberia?" Lenin asked, in his

---

[3] V. I. Lenin, *Collected Works*, (Moscow: 1960–   ), XXVII, 366–368.

[4] Chicherin speech of September 2, 1918, in Jane Degras, ed., *Soviet Documents on Foreign Policy* (London: 1951–1953), I, 104. For Robins' reception in the United States, see Kennan, *The Decision to Intervene*, pp. 229–232.

instructions to Chicherin. "If so, they won't disguise it anyway. We suggest you say straight out, how much?" Chicherin did indeed make such an appeal in a note to Wilson in October 1918, demanding "precise and businesslike replies" to the following questions:

Will the Governments of the United States, England, and France cease demanding the blood of the Russian people and the lives of Russian citizens, if the Russian people agree to pay a ransom, such as a man who has been suddenly set upon pays to one who attacked him? If so, precisely what tribute do the Governments of the United States, England, and France demand of the Russian people? Do they demand concessions, do they want the railways, mines, gold deposits, etc., to be handed over to them on certain conditions, or do they demand territorial concessions, some part of Siberia, or the Caucasus, or perhaps the Murmansk coast?

The note could not have been better calculated to ensure that it would not be answered, and Maxim Litvinov, the Soviet assistant commissar for foreign affairs, later admitted that its sardonic tone had been a mistake. The strategy it so blatantly expressed, however, remained the basis of early Bolshevik policy toward the United States.[5]

During the Paris Peace Conference the Soviet government continued its policy of holding out promises of economic gain in return for an end to intervention. In an unofficial conversation with an American emissary in Stockholm in January 1919, Litvinov observed that the Bolshevik regime could not survive without foreign technical and financial assistance; he promised protection of foreign enterprises and valuable concessions if intervention ceased. The following month, Foreign Minister Chicherin, in accepting the Prinkipo invitation, announced that "in view of the great inclination which foreign capital has always displayed to exploit Russia's natural resources for its own advantage, the Russian Soviet Government is disposed to grant mining, timber, and other concessions to nationals of the Entente Powers." Wilson considered these offers insulting, and

---

[5] Lenin to Chicherin, October, 1918, quoted in A. Leonidov, "Lenin and the United States: Kremlin Documents," *New Times*, January 22, 1969, pp. 4–5; Chicherin to Wilson, October 24, 1918, Degras., ed., *Soviet Documents*, I, 118–119. See also Thompson, *Russia, Bolshevism, and the Versailles Peace*, p. 88n.

did not respond to them. "I suppose because they know they have no high motives themselves," he complained, "they do not believe that anybody else has."[6]

Undeterred, Lenin continued to push for economic ties with the United States. "We are emphatically in favor of economic arrangements with America, with all countries, but *particularly* with America," he commented, in October 1919. And, in February 1920: "We will need American industrial goods —locomotives, automobiles, etc.—more than those of any other country." Several months later, Lenin gave what must stand as his most comprehensive statement on relations with the United States:

So long as we have not won the entire world, so long as, from the economic and military point of view, we remain weaker that the rest of the capitalist world, we must know how to exploit the contradictions and antagonisms among the imperialists. If we had not kept to that rule, we should long ago have all been hanging from the lampposts.

In Lenin's view, one of the most important of these "contradictions" was that between the United States and the remainder of world capitalism:

America is strong, everybody is now in its debt, everything depends on it, everybody hates America more and more . . . everything indicates that America cannot come to terms with other countries, because the most profound economic differences divide them, because America is richer than the others. Therefore we shall consider all questions about concessions from this angle.

The United States, Lenin argued, could furnish the Soviet Union with the means of production necessary to make possible the transition to socialism. But it would not do this for nothing: "To attract the Americans, we must pay them. They are business people. What shall we pay with? . . . We shall answer this question with the help of concessions."[7]

In October 1920, the Soviet government announced that it had granted an American syndicate headed by Los Angeles engineer

---

[6] Buckler to Lansing, January 18, 1919, FR: 1919: Russia, pp. 15–16; Chicherin to Entente Governments, February 4, 1919, ibid., p. 40; Joseph P. Tumulty, *Woodrow Wilson as I Know Him* (Garden City, New York: 1921), p. 374.

[7] V. I. Lenin, *Polnoe sobranie sochinenii* (Moscow: 1958–1965), XXXIX, 209, XL, 152; Degras, ed., *Soviet Documents*, I, 221–224.

Washington B. Vanderlip exclusive coal, oil, and fisheries rights for 60 years in some 400,000 square miles of northeastern Siberia, including the entire Kamchatka peninsula. Lenin made no secret of his motives in granting this concession. Kamchatka and much of the Russian Far East were under Japanese control at this time, and Lenin hoped to involve the United States, through the lure of economic advantages, in conflict with Tokyo. "When capitalistic thieves sharpen their knives against us," he noted, "our immediate duty is to direct such knives against one another." Lenin's scheme failed to materialize, however, because of a comic-opera series of misapprehensions. First, the Russians had confused Washington Vanderlip with a distant relative, the "billionaire" financier Frank A. Vanderlip, and did not discover their mistake until it was too late. As Lenin noted ruefully, the *Cheka* (the Russian secret police) was not yet as efficiently organized in the United States as it might be. Second, Lenin labored under the misapprehension, which Vanderlip did nothing to dispel, that the syndicate had close ties to President-elect Harding, and that upon the new president's inauguration, diplomatic recognition would be forthcoming. In fact no such ties existed; the Harding administration continued and even strengthened Wilson's nonrecognition policy. The concession never went into operation, and Vanderlip, the self-styled "Khan of Kamchatka," faded into obscurity.[8]

Lenin tried again in 1922, this time with a capitalist whose ties to the Harding administration could not be doubted. Oil magnate Harry F. Sinclair signed a contract with the Far Eastern Republic, a Soviet satellite soon to be absorbed into the USSR, for the exploitation of oil reserves on the northern half of the island of Sakhalin, which, like Kamchatka, was under Japanese control at the time. As had been the case with Vanderlip, Lenin apparently hoped that Sinclair would use his influence with Washington to get the Japanese out. Sinclair tried, but his efforts produced no response from the State Department. In part, this failure resulted from the department's desire to avoid unnecessarily provoking the Japanese. Part of the difficulty also was that Sinclair's ties to the Harding administration were *too*

---

[8] Albert Parry, "Washington B. Vanderlip, the 'Khan of Kamchatka'," *Pacific Historical Review*, XVII(August, 1948), 311–330.

close; after the Teapot Dome scandal broke in 1924, the succeeding Coolidge administration went out of its way to avoid supporting Sinclair's interests. Finally, the State Department resented what it considered a Soviet effort to "buy" recognition through Sinclair. In the absence of official support, Sinclair was never able to exploit his concession; in time the Russians withdrew it and gave it to the Japanese.[9]

The abortive Vanderlip and Sinclair concessions were early expressions of what was to become a persistent theme in Soviet diplomacy: the view that the interests of the Soviet state could be promoted by facilitating "businesslike" dealings with foreign capitalists. Based on what one American termed an "abiding faith in bourgeois venality,"[10] the policy looked to economic self-interest as a means by which the United States government (presumably the tool of capitalist "ruling circles") could be made to oppose foreign, especially Japanese, intervention, accord the new regime the legitimacy of recognition, and provide the technology necessary to build the industrial base which would, in the long run, ensure the survival of the Soviet state. It was a strategy not unlike that of the infant American republic a century and a half earlier, when it sought recognition from European powers by holding out the lure of trade. Oddly, though, of all the major capitalist states to which this appeal was directed, it was the United States, under the impeccably "businesslike" Republican administrations of the 1920s, which proved to be most resistant to it.

II

Traditional American policy would have been to enter into diplomatic relations with the Bolshevik government once it had become clear that it controlled Russia. But Wilson had departed dramatically from normal practice in 1913, when he refused to recognize the Huerta government in Mexico because it had come to power through unconstitutional means. Two years later, in a case not directly involving diplomatic recognition, Secretary of State Bryan had declined to take official cognizance

---

[9] Floyd J. Fithian, "Dollars Without the Flag: The Case of Sinclair and Sakhalin Oil," *Pacific Historical Review,* XXIX(May, 1970), 205–222.

[10] DeWitt Poole to Frank Polk, February 11, 1919, *FR: 1919: Russia,* p. 52.

of any treaty arrangements imposed by Japan on China which might threaten the principle of the Open Door.[11] Hence, by the time of the Bolshevik Revolution, there was precedent for the view that recognition was not a neutral act, that it carried with it the connotation of approval, and that where such approval did not exist, recognition should be withheld.

Nonrecognition was more of a reflex response than a calculated decision during the first two years of Bolshevik rule. Brest-Litovsk killed whatever remote possibility existed that recognition could be used to keep Germany and Russia from making a separate peace; after March 1918, it would have meant endorsement of Russia's withdrawal from the war and was never seriously considered. By the time the war ended, civil conflict and intervention had raised the real possibility that Bolshevism might be overthrown. This circumstance, together with increasing domestic hysteria over the Bolshevik "menace," made recognition an even more remote possiblity. Not until 1920 did it become clear that the Soviet regime was likely to survive; only then did the Wilson administration begin working out a public rationale for nonrecognition.

This took the form of an open letter from Secretary of State Bainbridge Colby to the Italian ambassador. Drafted in large part by the staunchly anti-Bolshevik American socialist John Spargo, it was published partly for the purpose of defining, for the first time, a clear-cut and comprehensive policy toward the Soviet Union, partly also in order to make it difficult for the Republicans to reverse Wilson's policy should they gain the White House in the November election.[12]

The Colby note began with expressions of sympathy for the Russian people, specifically exonerating them of responsibility for "the disastrous surrender at Brest-Litovsk." It viewed with confidence the prospect that "a free and unified Russia will

---

[11] Edward M. Bennett, *Recognition of Russia: An American Foreign Policy Dilemma* (Waltham, Massachusetts: 1970), pp. 1–14; Warren I. Cohen, *America's Response to China: An Interpretative History of Sino-American Relations* (New York: 1971), p. 94.

[12] Ronald Radosh, "John Spargo and Wilson's Russian Policy, 1920," *Journal of American History*, LII(December, 1965), 548–560. See also Daniel M. Smith, *Aftermath of War: Bainbridge Colby and Wilsonian Diplomacy, 1920–1921* (Philadelphia: 1970), pp. 55–74.

again take a leading place in the world." This could not happen, however, as long as the Bolsheviks remained in power:

The existing regime in Russia is based upon the negation of every principle of honor and good faith, and every usage and convention, underlying the whole structure of international law; the negation, in short, of every principle upon which it is possible to base harmonious and trustful relations, whether of nations or of individuals.

Specifically, Colby made three charges against the Bolshevik government: (1) that it had seized power by force and was not representative of the Russian people; (2) that it could not be trusted to carry out its international obligations; and (3) that it had sworn hostility to existing governments throughout the world, convinced that its own position would not be secure until the revolution had spread everywhere. "There cannot be any common ground," Colby noted, "upon which [the United States government] can stand with a Power whose conceptions of international relations are so alien to its own, so utterly repugnant to its moral sense." Colby concluded with an endorsement of prewar Russian territorial integrity, with the exceptions of Finland, Poland, and Armenia. "Thus only can the Bolshevist regime be deprived of its false, but effective, appeal to Russian nationalism and compelled to meet the inevitable challenges of reason and self-respect which the Russian people, secure from invasion and territorial violation, are sure to address to a social philosophy that degrades them and a tyranny that oppresses them."[13]

The interlocking arguments of the Colby note represented an intricate attempt to turn Russian nationalism against the Bolsheviks by picturing Lenin's government as an alien regime, sustained in power at the point of a gun, determined to sacrifice the national interests of the Russian state in favor of an abstract, internationalist, revolutionary ideology. There were several difficulties with this approach. Its emphasis on Bolshevik internationalism neglected Lenin's frequently demonstrated ability, where necessary, to subordinate the interests of the world revolution to those of the Soviet state. It assumed that the Russian people, given the chance to make their views known, would

---

[13] Colby to Avezzana, August 10, 1920, *FR: 1920*, III, 463–468.

have honored the international obligations of the tsarist and Provisional governments, forgetting the extent to which those governments' determination to meet those commitments had contributed to their respective downfalls. Its endorsement of prewar boundaries (except for Finland, Poland, and Armenia) left a considerable number of non-Russian peoples within the Russian state, and allowed the Bolsheviks, with their highly successful nationalities policy, to pose as advocates of self-determination. Finally, it neglected the impact of foreign intervention, which had, more than anything else, conferred upon the Bolsheviks the aura of national legitimacy.

Yet at the same time that Washington was hardening its policy on recognition, it was relaxing its position on trade. Those parts of Russia controlled by the Bolsheviks had been placed under an Allied blockade after Brest-Litovsk, and, while the United States had not officially recognized it, Washington had cooperated by refusing to grant export licenses. As late as August 1919, President Wilson had expressed the view that "for any government to permit [the Bolsheviks] to increase their power through commercial intercourse with its nationals would be to . . . invite the condemnation of all peoples desirous of restoring peace and social order." But early in 1920 the Allies lifted their blockade, and pressures began to grow for the State Department to relax its restrictions. After consultation with Wilson, the department announced in July that "restrictions which have heretofore stood in the way of trade and communication with Soviet Russia" had been removed.

The department went out of its way to insist that this action in no way constituted diplomatic recognition, and that businessmen seeking to deal with Soviet Russia would have to do so "on their own responsibility and at their own risk." Moreover, significant impediments to trade remained in the form of passport and visa restrictions, prohibitions on long-term credit, and a ban on the acceptance of Soviet gold in payment for purchases.[14] As

---

[14] Lansing to Ammission, August 2, 1919, *FR: 1919: Russia*, p.156; State Department press release, July 7, 1920, *FR: 1920*, III, 717. See also Joan Hoff Wilson, *Ideology and Economics: U. S. Relations with the Soviet Union, 1918–1933* (Columbia, Missouri: 1974), pp. 35–48; and Floyd J. Fithian, "Soviet-American Economic Relations, 1918–1933: American Business in Russia during the Period of Nonrecognition," (Ph. D. Dissertation, University of Nebraska, 1964), pp. 51–59.

one recent student of the period has noted, these restrictions apparently reflected "the Government's ambivalent desire to allow trade in theory but to make it somewhat difficult in practice in order to bring economic pressure to bear on the Soviet regime for ideological purposes."[15]

Lenin and his associates had high hopes that the new Republican administration of Warren G. Harding, presumably more "businesslike" than its predecessor, would further loosen restrictions on trade and authorize recognition. To this end, the All-Russian Central Executive Committee sent a note to the new president and Congress in March 1921, pointing out the special attitude the Russian government had always maintained toward the United States, and expressing the hope that the new administration "will clearly understand the immense advantage which will accrue to both Republics through the restoration of commercial relations."[16] There were in the Republican party several prominent critics of Wilson's Russian policy, among them Raymond Robins and Senator William E. Borah. There is even evidence that President Harding himself shared their views.[17] But Harding left foreign policy up to his secretary of state, Charles Evans Hughes, and Hughes quickly made it clear that there would be no change in Russian policy.

There could be no resumption of trade with Russia, Hughes announced, "until the economic bases of production are securely established." That would happen only when the Soviet government provided guarantees regarding "the safety of life, the recognition by firm guarantees of private property, the sanctity of contract, and the rights of free labor." In short, establishment of a normal economic relationship with Soviet Russia would require nothing less than fundamental change in the internal organization of the Soviet state. Lenin's expectation that economic opportunities would cause a truly "businesslike" administration to forget ideological differences proved to be ill-founded. "America . . . is a puzzle, its relations with Russia a

---

[15] Wilson, *Ideology and Economics*, p. 44.

[16] Note of March 20, 1921, Degras, ed., *Soviet Documents*, I, 244–245.

[17] On this point, see Bennett, *Recognition of Russia*, pp. 61–64; Fithian, "Soviet-American Economic Relations," pp. 60–61; and Robert K. Murray, *The Harding Era: Warren G. Harding and His Administration* (Minneapolis: 1969), pp. 348–353.

paradox," Foreign Minister Chicherin noted, early in 1922. "It would seem that everything should urge it towards meeting our desire for a *rapprochement* and for entering into close economic relations. . . . Up to the present the new American administration has not fulfilled these hopes."[18]

Hughes' policy was not as "inscrutable" as Chicherin made it appear. Like Wilson's, it was based on the assumption, increasingly pervasive in early twentieth-century American diplomacy, that the internal ideological orientation of a state would determine its behavior in the international arena.[19] This conviction had played a major role in shaping attitudes toward tsarist Russia and imperial Germany prior to World War I; now, in the postwar era, it continued to influence decisively Washington's policies toward the new Soviet republic.

III

Nevertheless, there was a certain ambivalence in United States policy toward Soviet Russia in the 1920s. Although, on the one hand, official Washington hoped to bring about changes in Russia by refusing to have anything to do with its government, it was, on the other hand, eager to promote overseas trade and investment opportunities for American businessmen.[20] These businessmen found it difficult to ignore the very considerable attractions of the Russian market which Lenin and his successors held out; moreover, in this period of relative *laissez-faire*, the government did not feel it proper to compel such businessmen to adjust their activities to official political positions. As a result, extensive contacts grew up in the 1920s between individual American firms and the Soviet government. And when, during the famine of 1921–1922, the issue of humanitarian aid arose, even the government stepped in, on a thinly disguised basis, to provide relief. The overall effect of United States policy during the nonrecognition period, there-

---

[18] Hughes to Litvinov, March 25, 1921, *FR: 1921*, II, 768; Chicherin report to Central Executive Committee, January 27, 1922, Degras, ed., *Soviet Documents*, I, 291–292.

[19] See, on this point, Chapter Two, above; also Lasch, *The American Liberals and the Russian Revolution*, pp. 218–220.

[20] Wilson, *Ideology and Economics*, pp. 29–30; Fithian, "Soviet-American Economic Relations" pp. 65, 145, 351.

fore, came close to being the very opposite from what Washington had intended: the United States inadvertently played a considerable role in laying the economic foundations of Soviet power.

The first and quite possibly the most important assistance the United States provided to the new Soviet state came in response to the devastating famine which hit major food-producing areas of that country in the summer of 1921. This crisis, partly the result of weather, partly of dislocations stemming from war, civil conflict, and forced requisitions of grain by the government, became known to the world in July when the famous author Maxim Gorky appealed for assistance. Some days later the Soviet government acknowledged the severity of the situation and officially requested aid.[21]

Much to the Russians' surprise, the quickest and most substantial response came from the United States. Herbert Hoover, secretary of commerce in the Harding cabinet, offered in his capacity as chairman of the quasi-private American Relief Administration to provide food, clothing, and medical supplies for up to a million Russian children. Hoover's motives in making this offer were the subject of much speculation, both in the United States and Russia. The ARA chief had been an outspoken opponent of the Bolshevik regime and had strongly supported Hughes' nonrecognition policy. Moreover, he had gained some notoriety during the Paris Peace Conference for advocating the use of food as a political weapon, both in withholding aid from the short-lived Bela Kun government in Hungary and in proposing the Hoover-Nansen plan for assistance to Russia, a scheme quite frankly intended to undermine Bolshevism. Finally, Hoover's organization had provided aid to the Whites during the Russian civil war. "Everything that is known of Mr. Hoover," an American liberal journal complained, "conveys ample assurance that he would use his position in Russia for political purposes; indeed that he could hardly help doing so if he tried." The Bolsheviks were even more suspicious, seeing Hoover's plan alternatively as a new form of interference in their internal affairs ("bread intervention") and as a reflection of an

---

[21] Benjamin M. Weissman, *Herbert Hoover and Famine Relief to Soviet Russia: 1921–1923* (Stanford: 1974), pp. 1–15.

economic crisis brought on by agricultural overproduction in the United States.[22]

Need overcame distrust, however, and in August 1921, Soviet representatives signed a "treaty" with ARA officials providing for the distribution of relief supplies "without regard to race, religion or social or political status." Over the next two years, the ARA furnished some 550,000 tons of food, clothing, and medicine to Russia, at a cost, primarily borne by American governmental and charitable sources, of around $50 million. (The Soviet government contributed an additional $11 million to the program in the form of gold shipments, which were allowed into the United States under a special relaxation of the gold ban.) At the height of its effort, the program was sustaining not 1 million people, as had originally been promised, but 10 million. ARA officials were given considerable latitude in determining how such aid should be distributed, and were allowed to work closely with local officials with minimal interference from Moscow. Nor were the Russians ungrateful: upon conclusion of its work the ARA received the following fulsome tribute from the Soviet government:

[T]he Council of People's Commissars, in the name of the millions who have been rescued, and of all the working-people of Soviet Russia and the Union Republics, considers it its duty, before the representatives of the entire world, to express its deepest gratitude to this organization, to its leader, Herbert Hoover, . . . and to declare that the people of the Union of Soviet Socialist Republics will never forget the help rendered to them through the ARA, perceiving in it a guarantee of the future friendship of the two nations.[23]

Subsequent Soviet accounts have been less generous. One recent discussion describes the ARA as an instrument for dumping surplus commodities, and accuses its representatives in

---

[22] Ibid., pp. 17–37. See also Mayer, *Politics and Diplomacy of Peacemaking*, pp. 24–27, 474–487; and George W. Hopkins, "The Politics of Food: United States and Soviet Hungary, March-August, 1919," *Mid-America*, LV(October, 1973), 245–270.

[23] Weissman, *Hoover and Famine Relief*, pp. 46–73, 177–178, 198–199. See also Benjamin M. Weissman, "Herbert Hoover's 'Treaty' with Soviet Russia: August 20, 1921," *Slavic Review*, XXVIII(1969), 276–288; and the official history of A. R. A. activities in Russia, H. H. Fisher, *The Famine in Soviet Russia, 1919–1923* (New York: 1927), especially pp. 553–557.

Russia of having preoccupied themselves with "espionage and the support of counter-revolutionary elements." American historians too have been skeptical of Hoover's disinterestedness; his program was, one scholar has commented, "simultaneously a self-aggrandizing, humanitarian, anti-Communist, anti-depression effort." Certainly the ARA chief would have welcomed the demise of Bolshevism, and may well have expected such an obvious demonstration of the regime's inability to feed its people to have that effect. But no evidence has been produced linking ARA personnel with anti-Bolshevik activities, and, as Hoover himself later admitted, the relief program wound up strengthening the Soviet government more than it weakened it. Doubtless the program benefited an American economy in which agricultural surpluses were an increasing problem; it should be recognized, however, that these surpluses were distributed in Russia at the expense of the American taxpayer. And while it is true that the operation enhanced Hoover's already considerable personal and political reputation, at the same time it is difficult to think of anyone else with the peculiar combination of organizational skills and anti-Communist credentials which the job required.[24] In the end the most satisfactory explanation, both for Hoover's actions and the support they received from the American people, may well lie in the characteristically American belief that humanitarian interests do, at times, take precedence over, and can be kept separate from, considerations of politics or ideology.

The timely aid the Bolshevik government received through the famine relief program was only one of several ways in which it benefited from economic contacts with the West, particularly the United States. Lenin's New Economic Policy, instituted early in 1921, marked the beginning of a concerted effort to harness the resources and skills of capitalism in support of the new Socialist order. Three particular areas of emphasis were concessions, trade, and technical assistance.

Following their embarrassing failures with Vanderlip and Sinclair, the Russians abandoned the use of concessions as in-

---

[24] P. M. Malakin, "Iz istorii ekonomicheskikh sviazei s SShA," *SShA: Ekonomika, Politika, Ideologiia,* 1970, #3, p. 18; Wilson, *Ideology and Economics,* p. 24; Weissmann, *Hoover and Famine Relief,* pp. 184–188.

struments of diplomacy and concentrated on employing them to attract foreign capital for reconstruction and development. Under the typical concessions contract, of which more than 300 were signed in the 1920s, the Soviet government would make available opportunities, usually in the area of mining or manufacturing, in return for which foreign businessmen would supply capital, technical expertise, and, of course, royalties. Several important concessions went to Americans. W. Averell Harriman, later ambassador to the Soviet Union, operated a massive manganese mining concession in the Caucasus between 1925 and 1928. Two brothers, Armand and Julius Hammer, held concessions for asbestos mining and pencil manufacturing. Even an American labor union, Sidney Hillman's Amalgamated Clothing Workers, formed a corporation which channeled capital into the development of the Soviet textile industry. Generally, though, American capitalists did not respond in large numbers to the opportunity to operate concessions in the Soviet Union. Bureaucratic and labor problems caused difficulties, and, except for Hammer's pencil factory, returns on investment seemed small. Many Americans still worried about the dangers of nationalization and preferred less risky forms of economic exchange. The Russians themselves eventually came to see the disadvantages of concessions and, under the First Five-Year Plan, initiated in 1928, shifted to a policy of relying on domestic capital to support industrialization.[25]

Domestic sources could not supply the technical skills needed for large-scale projects, however, and for this the Russians came to rely heavily on German and American engineers. Technical aid contracts, under which foreign firms or individuals provided engineering and managerial skills for a fixed fee, were negotiated with increasing frequency in the late 1920s. It has been estimated that as many as 1000 American engineers held individual technical aid contracts during the First Five-Year Plan, and many more were in Russia under contracts signed with American corporations. Especially noteworthy were the activities of the Albert Kahn Company, an industrial architec-

---

[25] Fithian, "Soviet-American Economic Relations," pp. 87–111, 183; Wilson, *Ideology and Economics,* pp. 71–73, 155–160; John P. McKay, "Foreign Enterprise in Russian and Soviet Industry: A Long Term Perspective," *Business History Review,* XLVIII(Autumn, 1974), 350–352.

ture firm which designed some 600 plants in Russia; the General Electric Company, which built the massive Dneiprostroy dam and provided other forms of technical assistance to the Soviet electrical industry; and the high priest of *laissez-faire,* mass-production capitalism himself, Henry Ford, whose company virtually single-handedly created the Soviet automobile and truck industry.[26]

Trade also flourished during the nonrecognition period, despite problems raised by the one-sided nature of the exchange (American products sold far better in the Soviet Union than Russian products did in the United States), the difficulty in securing credit brought about by Washington's refusal to allow the sale of Soviet securities in the United States, and the government's ban on Soviet gold shipments. Ways were found to circumvent these impediments, however, and by 1930, American exports to the Soviet Union exceeded those of any other country, constituting 25% of the total. Exports to Russia as a percentage of total American exports never exceeded 3.6% during this period (as opposed to 8.9% during the admittedly abnormal year which preceded American entry into World War I). But in certain key areas, trade with Russia was important. Cotton exports to Russia jumped from $1 million to $37 million, or from 0.1% to 3% of total cotton exports, in the single year from 1923 to 1924. In 1925, the Ford Motor Company sent 38% of its tractors manufactured for export to the Soviet Union, or about 10% of its total production that year. In 1930 and 1931, the Soviet Union was the largest single foreign purchaser for American agricultural and industrial equipment. The Soviet Union may not have been "the greatest undeveloped market in the world," as Senator William Borah extravagantly claimed in 1930, but it was important enough for both Americans and Russians, whatever their ideological differences, to make considerable efforts to promote it.[27]

---

[26] Fithian, "Soviet-American Economic Relations," pp. 219–348; McKay, "Foreign Enterprise," pp. 352–353.

[27] Robert Paul Browder, *The Origins of Soviet-American Diplomacy* (Princeton: 1953), pp. 24–48, 224–225; *Historical Statistics of the United States, Colonial Times to 1957* (Washington: 1960), pp. 537, 546; Fithian, "Soviet-American Economic Relations," pp. 179, 193; Philip S. Gillette, "Conditions of American-Soviet Commerce: The Beginning of Direct Cotton Trade, 1923–1924," *Soviet Union,* I, (1974), 74–93.

Foreign technology has always been important to Russian development; there seems little doubt that economic contacts with the United States, whether in the form of famine relief, concessions, technical aid contracts, or commerce, played an important role in stabilizing conditions in Russia during the first years of Soviet rule. The 1921–1922 famine in particular posed a serious crisis for the Bolsheviks; given conditions in the world at that time, it is difficult to see where outside aid in any volume could have come from if not from the United States. Similarly, private American technical assistance was very likely of critical importance to the success of the First Five-Year Plan.[28] All of this is not to say, of course, that the young Soviet republic could not have survived without American aid. Other sources of commerce, technology, and capital were available, notably in Great Britain and Germany, and were used. It is to say, however, that the United States possessed these commodities in sufficient variety, quality, and abundance to make the development of economic ties with America a matter of urgent priority for the Soviet government.

What is most striking about the aid the United States rendered to the Soviet Union in the 1920s is the inadvertent, almost accidental, manner in which it was provided. No one in Washington made the decision to aid Soviet economic development; indeed, to the extent that there existed any explicit official policy on this matter, it was inclined in the opposite direction. But as in the 1914–1917 period, the government found it difficult to align the nation's economic policies with its official ideological attitude. Partly, this situation arose from the fact that economic policy was still set in large part by the decisions of individual businessmen, not all of whom sought or abided by government advice. In part, too, the contradiction stemmed from an opportunistic ambivalence on the part of government officials, most of whom would not have disagreed with *Business Week*'s observation in 1930 that "the common-sense proceeding seems to be to sell the misguided fanatics all they are willing to

[28] Fithian, "Soviet-American Economic Relations," pp. 355–356; McKay, "Foreign Enterprise," pp. 352–354; Anthony C. Sutton, *Western Technology and Soviet Economic Development, 1917 to 1930* (Stanford: 1968), pp. 346–348.

pay for—business being what it is just now."[29] Whatever the case, the way in which Americans compartmentalized political and economic relations during the years of nonrecognition seemed to provide striking confirmation for the views of Lenin (who never engaged in such compartmentalization) that capitalists would industrialize Soviet Russia because they could not resist the short-term advantages, whatever the long-term dangers.

IV

Despite the increasingly important economic relationship between the United States and the Soviet Union, ideological antipathy remained strong. The Soviet Union constituted a unique phenomenon on the international scene in that it sought to carry on normal diplomatic relations with the capitalist world while simultaneously, and quite openly, plotting its destruction.[30] Its chief instrument for this purpose was the Third International, or Comintern, established in March 1919, in order to coordinate and direct revolutionary movements throughout the world. At no point in their history were the Soviets more preoccupied with world revolutionary ambitions; despite their almost total lack of success, their activities in this sphere provided the single most important impediment to the normalization of relations with the United States.

American officials had, from the first, been sensitive to the dangers of an international revolutionary movement, not because, as would be the case three decades later, they feared the military power of the Soviet state, but rather because they saw Bolshevism as a disease which would spread wherever chaos and disorder existed. "The spirit of Bolshevism is lurking everywhere," Wilson had noted, in the fall of 1918. "There is grave unrest all over the world. There are symptoms of it in this country—symptoms that are apparent although not yet dangerous." Bolshevism's appeal, Secretary of State Lansing noted, was "to the unintelligent and brutish elements of mankind to take from the intellectual and successful their rights and posses-

[29] Quoted in Fithian, "Soviet-American Economic Relations," p. 196.
[30] Ulam, *Expansion and Coexistence*, pp. 130–131.

sions and to reduce them to a state of slavery. . . . Bolshevism is the most hideous and monstrous thing that the human mind has ever conceived." Concerned about the spread of Bolshevism in the wake of war, the State Department ordered its representatives "to follow closely all efforts at Bolshevik propaganda both here and abroad."[31]

It is significant that the formation of the Comintern coincided with Lenin's efforts to normalize relations with the West through his reply to the Prinkipo invitation and his proposals to Bullitt; the apparent duplicity involved in these initiatives must be cited as one of several reasons why they were not accepted. Nor did the outbreak of the "Red scare" at home make United States officials any less sensitive to the Bolshevik "menace": by the fall of 1919 a note of hysteria had begun to creep into the rhetoric of Wilson himself:

> Do you honestly think, my fellow citizens, that none of that poison has got in the veins of this free people? . . . With the tongue of the wireless and the tongue of the telegraph all the suggestions of disorder are spread through the world. . . . And men look you calmly in the face in America and say they are for that sort of revolution.

Apocalyptic pronouncements of this type became less frequent as it became clear that Bolshevism was not going to take root in Europe and as the domestic "Red scare" waned. But the Comintern's activities did provide a convenient justification for nonrecognition. As Secretary of State Colby noted in his August 1920 policy statement: "We cannot recognize, hold official relations with, or give friendly reception to the agents of a government which is determined and bound to conspire against our institutions."[32] This argument, more than any other, became the basis upon which American policy toward the Soviet Union would be based for the next thirteen years.

"We recognize the right of revolution and we do not attempt to determine the internal concerns of other States," Secretary of

---

[31] Thompson, *Russia, Bolshevism, and the Versailles Peace*, pp. 14–15; Lansing to Page, November 6, 1918, *FR: 1918: Russia*, I, 726. See also ibid., p. 729.

[32] Wilson Des Moines speech, September 6, 1919, quoted in *FR: 1919: Russia*, p. 120; Colby to Avezzana, August 10, 1920, *FR: 1920*, III, 468. See also Browder, *Origins of Soviet-American Diplomacy*, pp. 12–13; and Robert K. Murray, *Red Scare: A Study in National Hysteria, 1919–1920* (Minneapolis: 1955), *passim.*

State Hughes observed in 1923. But recognition also depended, Hughes added, upon the willingness of the state recognized to accept the "obligations inherent in international intercourse." The Soviet regime had violated these obligations by abridging personal liberties, repudiating debts, and confiscating property. But "what is most serious is that . . . those in control at Moscow have not given up their original purpose of destroying existing governments wherever they can do so throughout the world." To illustrate this point, Hughes took to quoting the incendiary proclamations of Lenin, Trotsky, and Zinoviev, in one case before the assembled members of the Women's Committee for the Recognition of Russia. And when, in President Coolidge's first annual message to Congress in December 1923, a relatively innocuous reference to Russia elicited from Chicherin a renewed bid for recognition, Hughes torpedoed the initiative with the curt observation that "there would seem to be at this time no reason for negotiations." To add insult to injury, he had the State Department release, on the following day, intercepted instructions from the Comintern to the Communist Party of the United States, looking forward to the day, "in the not too distant future," when the party would "raise the red flag over the White House."[33]

American officials did not take Comintern activity lightly. A 1923 analysis from the United States legation in Riga, Latvia (which served, during this period, as a primary information-gathering center on Soviet affairs), reported Comintern propaganda in such diverse areas as Germany, Eastern Europe, Great Britain, Spain, Turkey, Persia, Afghanistan, India, China, and Japan. Early in 1924 Secretary of State Hughes sent the Senate Foreign Relations Committee an extensive file on Comintern activities in the United States. Secretary of State Kellogg gave extensive publicity to reports in 1927 that the Comintern had expanded its activities into Latin America; this prompted Litvinov to complain that soon "the enlightened statesmen of the great Powers [would] begin [ascribing] to the machinations of the Bolsheviks the earthquake in Japan and the floods in

---

[33] Hughes to Samuel Gompers, July 19, 1923, *FR: 1923*, II, 760–764; State Department press releases, March 21, December 18 and 19, 1923, ibid., pp. 755–758, 788–790.

America." On the occasion of the Sixth Comintern Congress in Moscow in 1928, the legation staff in Riga spent months compiling a detailed account of the proceedings and a list of participants which, when forwarded to Washington, filled hundreds of pages. "It would be truly ostrichlike," the American *chargé* there warned, "not to perceive that this 'General Staff of the World Revolution' is entirely in earnest in its determination to overthrow every non-Communist society and Government, and to erect a World Soviet Socialist Republic."[34]

"The Government of the United States feels no concern lest this systematic interference in our affairs . . . bring about the overthrow of our Government and institutions," Secretary Kellogg noted in 1928; "[it], however, does not propose to acquiesce in such interference by entering into relations with the Soviet Union." Or, as Robert F. Kelley, the influential chief of the State Department's Division of East European Affairs, put it in an internal memorandum in April 1929:

The essential difficulty lying in the way of the recognition of the Soviet government is not certain acts of the Bolshevik regime, such as repudiation of debts, the confiscation of property, and the carrying on of propaganda in the United States; but the Bolshevik world revolutionary purpose, of which these acts are manifestations. It is this fundamental purpose of the Bolshevik leaders which precludes the observance by them of the obligations ordinarily accepted as governing relations between nations. . . . This . . . is the idea underlying all our statements of policy towards the Bolshevik regime.[35]

Soviet world revolutionary activity thus became the chief justification used by the State Department, and by the government generally, in support of its nonrecognition policy.

In fact, however, the Comintern was not a conspicuously suc-

---

[34] F. W. B. Coleman to Hughes, November 8, 1923, *FR: 1923*, II, 771; Filene, *Americans and the Soviet Experiment*, pp. 91–92; Stephen John Kneeshaw, "The Kellogg-Briand Pact and American Recognition of the Soviet Union," *Mid-America*, LVI(January, 1974), 20–23; Litvinov statement of January 17, 1924, Degras, ed., *Soviet Documents*, II, 152; Sussdorff to Kellogg, October 19 and 25, 1928, and Coleman to Stimson, April 17, 1929, in DSR, 861.00 - Congress, Communist International VI/13, 21, 36 (M-316: 67).

[35] Kellogg to Butler, February 23, 1928, *FR: 1928*, III, 823–824; Kelley memorandum of April 12, 1929, DSR, 861.01/1415 (M-316: 76). See also Kelley to Robert Olds, February 10, 1928, quoted in Wilson, *Ideology and Economics*, pp. 99–100.

cessful organization. Although Communist parties under Soviet control were established throughout much of the world during the interwar period, the only country in which one actually came to power was Outer Mongolia. Efforts to spark revolutions in more important areas either failed completely, as in the case of Germany, or saw the revolution take an anti-Communist direction, as happened in China. Some of the reasons for this failure can be seen by examining the Comintern's relations with one of its more exotic creations, the Communist movement in the United States.

American communism in its formative years was riddled with factionalism; not until 1923 was some semblance of unity achieved. Whatever their differences, however, all American Communists mechanically sought guidance from the Comintern. "If the Comintern finds itself criss-cross with my opinions," William Z. Foster, one of the more durable party leaders commented, "there is only one thing to do and that is to change my opinions to fit the policy of the Comintern."[36] But because the Comintern had, since its formation, been in turn under the rigid control of the Communist Party of the Soviet Union, this kind of tight discipline made the fortunes of communism in the United States wholly dependent upon the ability of Soviet leaders to assess revolutionary prospects in a country few of them knew anything about.

The effects were not only destructive; they were at times ludicrous. On Comintern orders, American Communists supported Senator Robert LaFollette's third-party presidential bid in 1924, only to have these instructions abruptly reversed in mid-campaign. A year later the Comintern decided that LaFollette had been right after all, but that American Communists, as loyal Comintern members, had been right to withdraw their support from him. The Comintern insisted that the American party organize itself rigidly on the Russian model, even to the point of creating party cells in factories; the fact that American workers considered the factory both an inappropriate and wholly impractical location for political activity was not allowed to stand in the way. In 1928 the Comintern ordered the Ameri-

---

[36] Quoted in Theodore Draper, *American Communism and Soviet Russia: The Formative Period* (New York: 1960), p. 149.

can party to support formation of a separate black state in the South; this ambitious scheme represented nothing less than an effort on the part of Stalin himself to transfer his nationalities policy from the Caucasus and Central Asia to the far less hospitable territory of Alabama and Mississippi. Party officials patiently accommodated themselves to each successive manifestation of the Soviet leadership's collective wisdom, although not without occasional resistance on the part of the rank and file. American workers, one party organizer complained, greeted "the latest and most improved model" of the party line with a bewilderment comparable to that of "the Russian *muzhik* upon his first contact with the American tractor." "Why was the American Communist Party like the Brooklyn Bridge?" one wag asked, in what became a classic comment on the party's relationship to Moscow: "Because both were suspended on cables."[37]

"It would be wrong to ignore the specific peculiarities of American capitalism," Stalin told a delegation of American Communists in 1929:

But it would be still more wrong to base the activities of the Communist Party on these specific features, since the foundation of the activities of every Communist Party, including the American Communist Party, on which it must base itself, must be the general features of capitalism, which are the same for all countries, and not its specific features in any given country.[38]

This characteristically ponderous statement reveals much, not just about the Comintern's relationship to the American Communist party, but about its general failure in the interwar period. The Soviet autocrat's insistence on viewing capitalism as a monolith was in fact a backhanded justification for his own monolithic control of the international Communist movement. The resulting tactical inflexibility proved to be a major impediment to that movement's success. Communism would gain power, in the end, only where Stalin could impose it by force, or

---

[37] Ibid., pp. 96–118, 137, 192–193, 345–356, 390. See also Lowell K. Dyson, "The Red Peasant International in America," *Journal of American History*, LVIII(March, 1972), 958–973.

[38] Quoted in Draper, *American Communism and Soviet Russia*, p. 409.

where it could free itself from the debilitating effects of Stalin's control.

Ineffective as they were, the Comintern's efforts to provoke world revolution persistently undercut efforts of the Soviet Foreign Ministry to normalize diplomatic relations with the capitalist world. Attempts to start a revolution in Germany in 1923 partially undid the reconciliation between the two powers which had been arranged at Rapallo a year earlier. Comintern activity was a persistent irritant in relations with Great Britain, even to the point of causing a break in diplomatic relations in 1927. In China, the Russians followed an intricate policy of plotting against both the official government in Peking and Chiang Kai-shek's insurgent movement, while simultaneously attempting to carry on conventional relations with both: the result was one of the most disastrous failures in the history of Soviet foreign policy. And in the United States, the persistence of Comintern activity at home and abroad, while it posed no significant threat to the national security, provided opponents of recognition with their most persuasive arguments. As Alexander Gumberg, a close associate of Raymond Robins and one of the most tireless workers for recognition, complained, "These fellows still seem to be sitting up nights trying to think up some scheme which will get them in dutch with the rest of the world."[39]

V

In the summer of 1929, an official in the State Department's Division of East European Affairs, provoked by a prorecognition editorial in the *New Republic*, sat down to review the reasons why United States policy toward the Soviet Union should not be changed. The presence of official representatives in Moscow would not provide Washington with any significant amount of information it did not already have, he noted, given the efficiency of the Riga legation staff and the restrictions the Russians

---

[39] Quoted in Filene, *Americans and the Soviet Experiment,* p. 90. See also Ulam, *Expansion and Coexistence,* pp. 111–182; and Theodore H. Von Laue, "Soviet Diplomacy: G. V. Chicherin, People's Commissar for Foreign Affairs, 1918–1930," in Gordon A. Craig and Felix Gilbert, eds., *The Diplomats, 1919–1939* (Princeton: 1953), I, 234–281.

imposed on foreign diplomats' movements. Nor would recognition give the United States additional influence over the actions of the Soviet government—Soviet foreign policy was primarily the result of internal factors and would change only in response to them. It would not significantly improve economic contacts: indeed, since there was some evidence that the Soviet government had been placing massive orders in the United States to encourage prorecognition sentiment, the volume of trade might actually decline if recognition were granted. Finally, "it may be said that to recognize the Soviet Government now would necessarily signify that our policy in the past had been erroneous."[40]

At the time it was made, not many Americans would have quarreled with this analysis. There had always been advocates of recognition, but few of them had been able to point to any concrete benefits to be derived from extending it. Political figures like Senators William Borah and Burton K. Wheeler criticized nonrecognition as a form of intervention in the internal affairs of another state, but found it difficult to explain away the Comintern's all-too-obvious efforts along the same line. Businessmen who favored recognition on the grounds that it would increase trade found trade increasing anyway; the majority of the business community was entirely comfortable with the Republican compromise of simultaneously condemning the Bolshevik regime while profiting from economic contacts with it. Radicals and intellectuals found themselves torn between admiration for the idealistic goals of the Soviet "experiment" and repugnance for its autocratic, materialistic, at times inhumane methods. Though conspicuous in their reporting and writing on Russia, their impact on the debate over recognition was minimal.[41]

Antirecognition forces had the weight of informed opinion on their side during the 1920s; what is probably more important, they had effective organizational support. The Soviet Union's official atheism alienated all religious groups, but it so happened that the denomination which suffered the most direct outrage

---

[40] Memorandum by E. L. Packer, August 30, 1929, DSR, 861.01/1510½(M-316:76).
[41] Robert James Maddox, *William E. Borah and American Foreign Policy* (Baton Rouge: 1969), pp. 49, 203–208; Filene, *Americans and the Soviet Experiment*, pp. 91–92, 151–154.

was also the best organized. In March 1923, the vicar-general of the Roman Catholic Church in Russia was executed for counter-revolutionary activities. From this time on, the Catholic Church in the United States became one of the most vociferous and effective opponents of recognition. The American Federation of Labor also strongly opposed recognition; anti-Soviet activity had become such an important badge of respectability for the nation's largest labor union that Secretary of State Henry L. Stimson could describe it in 1931 as "our chief barrier against communism." Patriotic organizations such as the American Legion and the Daughters of the American Revolution found non-recognition a congenial issue; so, too, did major business groups like the National Association of Manufacturers, the National Civic Federation, and the United States Chamber of Commerce.[42]

But, in the end, the most effective organized opposition to recognition may well have existed among a relatively small number of key officials in the State and Commerce departments. The State Department's Division of East European Affairs was largely staffed with diplomats who had served in Russia during the traumatic years of intervention and civil war. As in the case of other Russian "experts," both before and after, proximity impaired objectivity, with effects which were to persist for years afterward in the form of hostility toward the Russian government. In the Commerce Department, resistance to recognition was very much the result of Herbert Hoover's personal impact as secretary of commerce. Despite his willingness to trade with and even feed the Bolsheviks, Hoover nursed a deep ideological aversion to the Soviet government which precluded normal diplomatic relations, and succeeded in transmitting these views to those who worked under him. As a consequence, antirecognition sentiment became institutionalized in these two departments; in the absence of strong incentives in favor of recognition, these bureaucratic constraints played a major role in perpetuating existing policies.[43]

---

[42] Ibid., pp. 82–84, 89, 157–160; Wilson, *Ideology and Economics*, pp. 64–67, 111; Stimson memorandum of conversation with Italian foreign minister Dino Grandi, July 9, 1931, *FR: 1931*, I, 541.

[43] Wilson, *Ideology and Economics*, pp. 20–21, 85–86, 91–92, 130–132.

After Hoover became president, however, circumstances combined to provide new arguments, both for and against recognition. One such circumstance was the onset of the Great Depression. Heavy Russian orders for industrial and agricultural equipment continued as other markets declined, leading some businessmen to see in Stalin's Five-Year Plan a means of bringing about economic recovery in the United States. Exports to Russia as a percentage of total exports remained small—2.9% in 1930, 3.6% in 1931—but recognition, it was thought, might drive the figures higher by making it easier for the Russians to get credit in the United States. It is important to note, however, that the depression cut both ways. It also forced the Russians to try to expand their own export markets by cutting prices; this led to such serious competition for American producers of lumber, matches, coal, manganese, and wheat that the Treasury banned imports of several of these commodities, charging the Russians with dumping and the use of forced labor. Recognition might therefore bring economic opportunities, but it could also bring dangers unless some way was found to restrict cheap Soviet imports. As a result, although recognition was much debated among businessmen, no clear consensus on the matter emerged.[44]

The Russians were well aware of the political leverage trade with the United States gave them during the depression and sought to use it to bring about recognition. As Boris E. Skvirskii, head of the Soviet Information Bureau in Washington, noted in 1930, "Events have shown that in times of crisis Americans feel the importance of Soviet markets and that the threat of losing them redounds to our benefit. . . . Knowing our decisive position, we should be prepared to use it." The Soviet government accepted Skvirskii's advice and, in the fall of 1931, cut back sharply on American orders. Nikolai N. Krestinskii, deputy commissar for foreign affairs, explained the strategy in a report to the Politburo:

The maximum contraction and eventual full cessation of our purchases will be our most important and convincing instrument for put-

---

[44] Fithian, "Soviet-American Economic Relations," pp. 189–211; Wilson, *Ideology and Economics*, pp. 103–120; Browder, *Origins of Soviet-American Diplomacy*, pp. 28–48; Filene, *Americans and the Soviet Experiment*, pp. 211–239.

ting pressure on America. The loss of Soviet markets, the importance of which has grown tremendously during the period of crisis, will more quickly impel American business and political circles to reconsider their traditional position of not recognizing the USSR.

The trade cutback did cause concern—exports to Russia came to only $12.6 million in 1932, down from $103.7 million the previous year—and some intensification of pressure among businessmen for recognition. But opposition from other business leaders worried about Soviet imports, together with the lack of any firm assurance that recognition really would increase Soviet orders, prevented Skvirskii's strategy from succeeding. The American "ruling circles" remained divided, leaving the government free to do what it wanted.[45]

A clearer and more decisive argument in favor of recognition grew out of the fact that the United States was now the only major country which had not established diplomatic relations with the Soviet Union. With Moscow becoming more and more active in international diplomacy, the absence of official ties had begun to cause embarrassments. One came in 1928, when Russian adherence to the Kellogg-Briand Pact on the renunciation of war raised the alarming possibility that the United States, by signing the same document, might have inadvertently recognized the USSR. Another occurred during a brief Sino-Soviet conflict in Manchuria the following year when Secretary of State Stimson undertook to "remind" both sides of their obligations under the pact, only to receive in return a sharp "reminder" from Litvinov that the United States, not having seen fit yet to recognize the existence of the Soviet Union, was hardly in a position to be giving it advice and "instructions."[46]

The absence of official relations between Washington and Moscow became more than just an embarrassment in 1931,

[45] Skvirskii to Soviet foreign ministry, August 13, 1930, *Dokumenty vneshnei politiki, SSSR,* XIII, 458; Krestinskii to Politburo, September 18, 1931, ibid., XIV, 527. See also Browder, *Origins of Soviet-American Diplomacy,* pp. 43–47; and Filene, *Americans and the Soviet Experiment,* pp. 235–237.

[46] Litvinov to Stimson, December 3, 1929, Degras, ed., *Soviet Documents,* II, 408. See also Kneeshaw, "The Kellogg-Briand Pact," pp. 23–31; Pauline Tompkins, *American-Russian Relations in the Far East,* (New York: 1949), pp. 220–246; and Robert H. Ferrell, *American Diplomacy in the Great Depression: Hoover-Stimson Foreign Policy, 1929–1933* (New Haven: 1957), pp. 45–67.

when Japan suddenly ejected China from Manchuria. Both the
United States and the Soviet Union sought to deter Japan from
further aggression, but without diplomatic relations, no concerted action was possible. Boris Skvirskii, the Russians' unofficial agent in Washington, launched a quiet campaign early in
1932 to promote American recognition of the Soviet Union as a
means of impressing Tokyo. Stimson was not unreceptive. He
had already publicly abandoned Wilson's practice of recognizing only constitutionally legitimate regimes and, unlike Kellogg,
generally deprecated the dangers of international communism.
Gravely concerned by the failure of the League of Nations to act,
he ordered subordinates in the State Department to study what
impact recognition would have on the Far Eastern situation and
even met secretly at the Geneva Disarmament Conference with
Karl Radek, one of Litvinov's lieutenants, to discuss the matter.
In the end, however, nothing was done. State Department officials concluded that Tokyo would interpret recognition as a hostile act; given Hoover's strong aversion to recognition and to any
kind of provocative action in the Far East, this argument carried
great weight. As Assistant Secretary of State James Grafton Ro-
gers told Skvirskii in June, the Japanese military had already
gone so far that recognition would not deter them from attack-
ing the Soviet Union if they were so inclined: "from them one
can expect anything."[47]

The very fact that recognition had been considered was encouraging to the Russians, however, and they anticipated action
as soon as the new and more "practical" Roosevelt administration took office. Skvirskii reported that the new president's advisers were leaning toward recognition, largely on the grounds
that it would strengthen the American position in dealing with
Japan. Nor did the Russians hesitate to take advantage of these
rumors. "In America there is an increasing number of people
who recognize the mistake of not have relations with us," Deputy Commissar for Foreign Affairs Karakhan told the Japanese

---

[47] Skvirskii to Litvinov, January 29, 1932, and to Narkomindel, February 2 and
June 4, 1932, *Dokumenty vneshnei politiki, SSSR*, XV, 69–70, 80, 351–352. See also
Stimson to Borah, September 8, 1932, *Foreign Relations: The Soviet Union,
1933–1939* (Washington: 1952), pp. 1–2; Bennett, *Recognition of Russia*, pp. 74–80;
and Tompkins, *American-Russian Relations*, pp. 247–263.

ambassador to Moscow in February 1933. "Thus, if America wants to correct its mistake, then we will not prevent it, if it wants to restore relations with us, we, of course, wish to restore normal relations with America."[48]

---

[48] Notes, meeting between Karakhan and Ota, February 27, 1933, *Dokumenty vneshnei politiki SSSR*, XVI, 129. See also Skvirskii to Narkomindel, July 8, December 2, 1932, January 28, February 21, April 1, 1933, ibid., XV, 403, 661–662, XVI, 60, 108, 210.

CHAPTER V

Recognition and Disillusionment: 1933–1941

I N RETROSPECT, IT IS CLEAR THAT THE UNITED STATES
AND THE SOVIET UNION HAD A COMMON INTEREST during the 1930s in resisting the growing power of Germany and
Japan. With the establishment of formal diplomatic relations in
1933, opportunities would appear to have existed for joint action
in pursuit of this aim. That such action did not occur must be
attributed to the influence, within both countries, of internal
constraints on foreign policy. In the United States, powerful
non-interventionist tendencies discouraged the Roosevelt administration from making commitments of any kind to oppose
aggression. The Soviet Union openly encouraged such commitments, but continued Comintern activity, together with a
series of gruesome purges, conveyed to the outside world the
impression that the USSR was an abnormal state, not to be dealt
with through the instruments of conventional diplomacy. The
result was an absence of collaboration between Washington and
Moscow until common enemies forced Russians and Americans
into a reluctant alliance in the interests of self-preservation.

I

The question of whether or not to recognize the Soviet Union
had attracted considerable public attention during the year preceding Roosevelt's inauguration but not in such a way as to
restrict the new president's freedom of action. To the extent that
its opinions can be reconstructed, given the rudimentary polling
techniques of the day, the general public appears to have fa-

vored recognition by a considerable margin. Organized opposition existed among business, labor, and religious communities, but prorecognition sentiment within those same groups tended to neutralize it. As a consequence, Roosevelt was free to follow his own inclinations, knowing he would meet neither unanimous support nor overwhelming opposition to whatever course he chose.[1]

Several considerations caused Roosevelt to favor establishing diplomatic ties. One was the simple fact that nonrecognition had not achieved its objectives: it had changed neither the internal configuration nor the external behavior of the Soviet state. Given Roosevelt's impatience with ineffective policies, given the low priority he attached to such things as ideological consistency, it was as easy for him to give up nonrecognition as it was to abandon Prohibition, another outdated policy which quickly fell victim to the new administration's affinity for the practical.

An equally important consideration, in Roosevelt's mind, was the fact that the world confronted several major problems which could be solved only with the Russians' active cooperation. One of these was the global economic crisis. Efforts to stabilize world wheat prices in the summer of 1933 brought about the first open contacts between American and Soviet officials since the Russian Revolution. Soon thereafter, negotiations began on the extension of Reconstruction Finance Corporation credits to support Soviet purchases of American cotton. Roosevelt did not expect recognition to bring dramatic improvements in either the international or domestic economic situations, but he did regard the USSR as too important an element in the world economy to justify a continued policy of aloofness.[2]

Nor could the Russians easily be excluded from efforts to maintain peace at a time when the World War I settlement seemed to be coming apart. Japan had already successfully challenged the League of Nations in Manchuria; the organization

[1] Thomas R. Maddux, "Years of Estrangement: American Relations with the Soviet Union, 1933–1941," (unpublished manuscript), pp. 6–34; Browder, *Origins of Soviet-American Diplomacy*, pp. 85–86.

[2] Ibid., pp. 90–95. See also Robert E. Bowers, "American Diplomacy, the 1933 Wheat Conference, and Recognition of the Soviet Union," *Agricultural History*, XL(January, 1966), 39–52.

would soon be under attack in Europe as well. Isolationism kept Roosevelt from contemplating direct action against the aggressors, but he had no intention of remaining completely neutral. Instead he sought ways, however subtle, to increase the strain and uncertainty under which Germany and Japan would have to operate, without at the same time committing the United States to specific measures of any kind. A diplomatic opening to Moscow fitted in well with this strategy.[3]

On May 16, 1933, Roosevelt included Soviet President Mikhail Kalinin among recipients of a public message, sent to fifty-two heads of state, appealing for the success of the Geneva Disarmament Conference and proposing a global nonaggression pact. The president denied that Kalinin's inclusion had any special meaning, but the significance of this first formal communication to the Soviet government could hardly be overlooked. Five months later, on October 10, Roosevelt sent a second letter to Kalinin proposing discussions with a view toward ending "the present abnormal relations between the hundred and twenty-five million people of the United States and the hundred and sixty million people of Russia." The Russians accepted with alacrity, and announced that Soviet Foreign Minister Maxim Litvinov would come to the United States himself to conduct the negotiations.[4]

Press and public reactions were generally favorable, but there were centers of resistance which worried the president. Working skillfully through personal contacts, he sought to blunt opposition among religious and labor groups by assuring them that recognition would not be granted without a price: "Leave it to me, Father," he told one Catholic critic, "I am a good horse trader." Roosevelt took the same position with the State Department, which he suspected of harboring reservations about recognition, and insisted on handling the negotiations personally. This does not mean that Roosevelt ignored his diplomats' advice: he accepted the department's recommendation that preconditions for recognition include acknowledgment of the Provisional Government's debts, a pledge of noninterference in

[3] Farnsworth, *Bullitt*, p. 91.
[4] Edgar B. Nixon, ed., *Franklin D. Roosevelt and Foreign Affairs: 1933–1937* (Cambridge, Massachusetts: 1967), I, 126–129; *FR: Soviet Union*, pp. 17–19.

American domestic affairs, and a promise to respect the religious freedom of Americans inside the Soviet Union. But the president rejected State's suggestion that secret preliminary discussions be held to establish areas of agreement and disagreement. Nor did he pay any attention to the concern of some elements within the department over Comintern activity in Cuba.[5]

Litvinov arrived in Washington in early November, expecting immediate recognition. He was surprised, and somewhat offended, to find that commitments were expected in advance on debts, religious rights, and communist activity inside the United States. The Soviet foreign minister regarded these conditions largely as gestures intended to placate American critics of recognition: "My general impression," he reported to Moscow, "is that Roosevelt doubtlessly is striving for the establishment of the best relations, but that he is really frightened of the opponents of recognition." The agreement on religious rights for Americans in the Soviet Union was not difficult to achieve, but Litvinov balked at promising an end to communist activities in the United States, on the grounds that the Soviet government had no authority over the Comintern. He also resisted an ingenious suggestion from Roosevelt that Comintern headquarters be transferred from Moscow to that other center of international activity, Geneva. In the end, Litvinov signed a statement, drafted by the State Department, promising that the Soviet Union would not

permit the formation or residence on its territory of any organization or group . . . which has as an aim the overthrow or the preparation for the overthrow of, or the bringing about by force of a change in, the political or social order of the whole or any part of the United States, its territories or possessions.

By design, however, the pledge said nothing about the Comintern, in the belief that if it were mentioned specifically the Russians could evade the agreement by simply changing the

[5] Maddux, "Years of Estrangement," pp. 44–52; Browder, *Origins of Soviet-American Diplomacy*, pp. 106–107, 112–115, 125; Robert E. Bowers, "Hull, Russian Subversion in Cuba, and Recognition of the U.S.S.R.," *Journal of American History*, LIII(December, 1966), 542–554.

organization's name. Litvinov, in turn, made it clear that he did not regard the Comintern as covered by the agreement in the first place.[6]

Roosevelt and Litvinov reached no final agreement on the touchy question of debts, but they did arrive at an understanding whereby the Russians would pay no less than $75 million (as against a total debt of $188 million), in the form of extra interest on a loan extended to finance Soviet purchases in the United States. Roosevelt and the State Department viewed this arrangement as a "credit" which would allow Washington to control purchases made, but through careless drafting the word "loan" crept into the document the president and Litvinov signed. The Americans also failed to specify that the Russians would be expected to pay interest on the Kerensky government debt, another misunderstanding which would cause problems later on. On this less than precise basis, the agreement establishing formal diplomatic relations was signed on November 17, 1933.[7]

Despite the acrimonious nature of the negotiations, Litvinov did have reason to expect positive diplomatic benefits from them. He reported to Moscow that Roosevelt had referred specifically to Germany and Japan as sources of military danger in the world, and had raised the possibility that the United States and the Soviet Union, acting together, might be able to "stave them off." The president made it clear that the United States could not go to war, but he expressed the hope that both Germany and Japan would exhaust themselves, and that no war would be necessary. In the meantime, the United States was prepared to give the Soviet Union "100% moral and diplomatic support." Roosevelt then suggested the possibility of a triangular nonaggression pact between the United States, the Soviet Union, and Japan, and gave Litvinov the impression that, if Japan refused to

---

[6] Litvinov to Soviet foreign ministry, November 8, 1933, *Dokumenty vneshnei politiki SSSR*, XVI, 609–610; Litvinov to Roosevelt, November 16, 1933, *FR: Soviet Union*, p. 29. See also Donald G. Bishop, *The Roosevelt-Litvinov Agreements: The American View* (Syracuse: 1965), pp. 27–31.

[7] For negotiation of the Roosevelt-Litvinov agreements, see Browder, *Origins of Soviet-American Diplomacy*, pp. 127–141, 181–183; and Bishop, *The Roosevelt-Litvinov Agreements*, pp. 148–152.

sign, the United States would conclude such a pact with the Soviet Union alone.[8]

For the moment, it appeared as if the basis for cordial relations had been laid. Litvinov departed Washington in a cloud of friendly rhetoric, and Roosevelt impressed the Russians by naming as the first American ambassador to the Soviet Union William C. Bullitt, Wilson's secret emissary to Lenin and Trotsky in 1919 and a long-standing advocate of Soviet recognition. Bullitt's reception in Moscow the following month did nothing to disappoint him. President Kalinin solemnly assured the new envoy of the Russians' realization that President Roosevelt "really cared about the welfare of the laboring men and the farmers and was not engaged in protecting the vested rights of property." Stalin did Bullitt the unprecedented courtesy of attending a lavish feast in his honor, accompanied by innumerable toasts, which ended with the Soviet dictator planting a wet kiss on the cheek of the astonished diplomat. Stalin also agreed to the construction of an American embassy modeled on Jefferson's Monticello, to be built on a bluff overlooking the Russian capital. ("I like the idea of planting Thomas Jefferson in Moscow," Roosevelt later noted.) "It is obvious," Bullitt reported to the president, "that our representatives in the Soviet Union today can have a really immense influence."[9]

II

Disillusionment soon crept into the new Soviet-American relationship, however, as it became clear that both sides had misunderstood what the other had expected from the Roosevelt-Litvinov agreements. This occurred first with respect to the question of Japan. Since no records were kept on the American side, it is impossible to confirm Litvinov's account of what Roosevelt had said to him on this subject. While the president may well have talked about a Far Eastern nonaggression pact, it seems doubtful that he regarded these discussions as anything

---

[8] Litvinov to Soviet foreign ministry, November 8, 17, 1933, *Dokumenty vneshnei politiki SSSR,* XVI, 609, 658–659.

[9] Bullitt to Roosevelt, January 1, 1934, in Orville H. Bullitt, ed., *For the President: Personal and Secret: Correspondence between Franklin D. Roosevelt and William C. Bullitt* (Boston: 1972), pp. 63–70; Roosevelt to Cordell Hull, February 16, 1934, Nixon, ed., *F. D. R. and Foreign Affairs,* I, 647.

other than "brainstorming." The Russians, however, took them seriously. Moscow press commentaries contained considerable speculation about joint Soviet-American cooperation against Japan, and Bullitt found his first days in the Russian capital filled with rumors of war in the Far East, together with hints of what the United States could do to help. Stalin himself suggested the immediate shipment of 250,000 tons of steel rails to reequip the Trans-Siberian Railroad, while V. M. Molotov, chairman of the Council of People's Commissars, publicly observed that "the most reactionary Japanese militarists fear that such countries as the U.S.S.R., the United States, and China, may work together against the instigators of a new Far-Eastern war."[10]

In fact, public and Congressional opposition to foreign commitments made any form of active United States cooperation with the Soviet Union against Japan virtually impossible. The Roosevelt administration viewed the Far Eastern situation with extreme caution, and although the president himself clearly hoped that the normalization of Soviet-American relations might inhibit the Japanese, he was at no point in a position to take more positive action. The Russians' failure to see this fact must be attributed in part to wishful thinking, in part to their chronic lack of sophistication in analyzing American politics, and in part to a tendency, shared by many others, to confuse Rooseveltian banter with national policy.

Ideological blinders compounded the confusion. Long-anticipated "contradictions of capitalism" had, Russian officials believed, forced the non-fascist West into seeking cooperation with the Soviet Union. The United States, *Izvestiia* noted at the time of recognition, had been "compelled" to deal with the USSR in order to ward off the twin dangers of global depression and fascist aggression.[11] But in the view of the Roosevelt administration, it was the Soviet Union which was acting under compulsion and should be willing to pay whatever price was necessary to achieve such limited cooperation as American opinion might allow. As Bullitt put it in a letter to the president, "It is obvious that the Soviet Government values so highly the moral

---

[10] Bullitt to Roosevelt, January 1, 1934, in Bullitt, ed., *For the President*, pp. 67–68; Molotov speech of December 28, 1933, Degras, ed., *Soviet Documents*, III, 46–47. See also Browder, *Origins of Soviet-American Diplomacy*, pp. 153–156.
[11] *Izvestiia*, November 20, 1933, quoted in *FR: Soviet Union*, p. 44.

support it may receive from the United States in the matter of preventing war with Japan that there is almost nothing we may not ask for and obtain at the present time."[12]

Once Bullitt made it clear that "moral support" was all the Russians could expect in the Far East, the atmosphere in Moscow chilled noticeably. When negotiations on debts and credits began in March 1934, the Russians were firm and unyielding. Roosevelt's agreement with Litvinov had left important issues unresolved—notably whether a loan or a credit was to be extended to finance Soviet purchases inside the United States, how much of the Kerensky government's debt the Soviets would pay, and whether this debt would be paid with interest. The Russians clearly were interested in securing American economic assistance, but not to the point of yielding the right to control Soviet purchases in the United States or of accepting the American position on the Kerensky debt, something that would have to be done, under the Johnson Act of 1934, if a loan were to be extended. Stalin might have compromised in return for an open American stand against Japan, but public opinion made this course unfeasible for the Roosevelt administration, while a gradual improvement in Soviet-Japanese relations made it seem, after a time, less vital to the Russians.[13]

Bullitt at first attributed the breakdown in negotiations to "misunderstandings," but by the spring of 1934 he was reporting that "the honeymoon atmosphere has evaporated completely." The Russians were convinced that the Japanese were not going to attack; moreover they expected pressure from export-hungry businessmen to make Washington compromise on the debt negotiations. "I do not take the matter so tragically," Litvinov told an infuriated Bullitt: "No nation today pays its debts." The Soviet foreign minister and the American ambassador were soon reduced to hurling insults at one another, and the Russians withdrew their offer of land for a new Monticello in Moscow. Bullitt's efforts to improve the situation by organizing polo matches and baseball games with Soviet officials had little effect. "The nub of the matter is this," he reported to the State

---

[12] Bullitt to Roosevelt, January 1, 1934, in Bullitt ed., *For the President*, pp. 72–73.
[13] Maddux, "Years of Estrangement," pp. 77–85; Bishop, *The Roosevelt-Litvinov Negotiations*, pp. 152–178.

Department: "If the Soviet Government should again become convinced that an attack by Japan was likely or imminent we should probably find Litvinov willing to reach an agreement on the basis of our proposals. So long as the Soviet Union feels completely secure I believe that no agreement acceptable to us will be acceptable to the authorities in Moscow."[14]

The final disillusionment, for Bullitt, came over the question of the Comintern's relationship with the Communist Party of the United States. Litvinov had indicated orally that he did not regard his agreement with Roosevelt as applying to Comintern activities, and it seems doubtful that administration officials really expected a cessation of communist activities in the United States. Roosevelt was under considerable domestic pressure to secure strict compliance with the agreement, however, and when plans for a seventh Comintern Congress became known in Moscow in the summer of 1935, Bullitt, with the State Department's approval, made it clear that Washington would regard participation by American communists as a violation of the Roosevelt-Litvinov pledge. Litvinov's only response was to feign ignorance of the forthcoming meeting.

The Comintern Congress did meet, American communists did participate, and Soviet newspapers published their attacks on the United States. Bullitt viewed these developments as "a flagrant violation of Litvinov's pledge to the President" and recommended, in retaliation, restrictions on Soviet visas and consular privileges. Roosevelt rejected these reprisals but did authorize a stiff note, released simultaneously to the press, threatening "most serious consequences" if the USSR failed to prevent further acts in violation of Litvinov's promise. The Russians responded predictably by disavowing responsibility for the Comintern and charging interference in Soviet internal affairs by anti-Bolshevik Russian émigrés in the United States. Soviet Ambassador Alexander Troyanovsky concluded the exchange somewhat less predictably with the Biblical interrogatory: "Why beholdest thou the mote which is in thy brother's

---

[14] Bullitt to Hull, March 28, May 21, June 16, 1934, *FR: Soviet Union*, pp. 74, 100, 109–111; Bullitt to Roosevelt, April 13 and August 5, 1934, in Bullitt, ed., *For the President*, pp. 83, 93.

eye, but perceivest not the beam that is in thine own eye?"[15]

"It is perfectly clear, Bullitt wrote in July 1935, "that to speak of 'normal relations' between the Soviet Union and any other country is to speak of something which does not and cannot exist." Litvinov, for once, agreed. He admitted to the American ambassador some months later that "there was no such thing as friendship or 'really friendly' relations between nations." The truth was that the United States wanted "to remain aloof from all active interest in international affairs." For this reason, he implied, friendly relations with the United States were not of great importance to the Soviet Union.[16]

Both sides had expected too much from recognition. The Russians anticipated that establishing formal relations with the United States would help counterbalance the growing power of Germany and Japan. Convinced that the United States had been "compelled," for similar reasons, to deal with the Russians, Kremlin officials failed to understand why American diplomats attached greater importance to strict implementation of the Roosevelt-Litvinov agreements than to common action against the aggressors. Only gradually did they come to realize that the Roosevelt administration's preoccupation with unpaid debts and Comintern activities had been sincere; that, because of the depth of American isolationism, whatever prospects of cooperation against aggression Roosevelt had held out lay more in the realm of rhetoric than reality.[17]

For the Americans, recognition had been expected to achieve what nonrecognition had not: a fundamental change in the external behavior of the Soviet Union which would make it an acceptable member of the international community. The new policy turned out to be no more successful than its predecessor, for the simple reason that neither the existence nor absence of relations with the United States provided sufficient incentive to Stalin to change the internal structure of his regime, upon which

---

[15] *FR: Soviet Union*, pp. 221–223, 244–245. See also Bishop, *The Roosevelt-Litvinov Agreements*, pp. 31, 44–53.

[16] Bullitt to R. Walton Moore, July 15, 1935, and to Hull, November 9, 1935, *FR: Soviet Union*, pp. 134, 265.

[17] On this point, see Keith David Eagles, "Ambassador Joseph E. Davies and American-Soviet Relations, 1937–1941," (Ph. D. Dissertation, University of Minnesota, 1966), pp. 49–50.

foreign policy ultimately depended. The Americans' preconditions for recognition meant little, partly because they were so
vaguely worded as to be susceptible of varying interpretations,
partly because, once recognition had been granted, there was no
sure way to compel compliance.[18] Both sides, in sum, exaggerated the effects establishing formal diplomatic relations would
have on the other; the failure of the Roosevelt-Litvinov agreements must be seen, in the end, as a triumph of internal over
external considerations in foreign policy.

III

The disillusionment which followed the breakdown of negotiations on the debt question coincided with the beginning of the
massive purges which were to mark the consolidation of Stalin's
dictatorship. It was a period when surface appearances coincided only sporadically with what was in fact taking place: it is
symptomatic that the new Soviet constitution of 1936, guaran-
teeing free elections and the rights of Soviet citizens, went into
effect four months after the first great purge trial and one month
before the second. This disparity between appearance and reality made it unusually difficult for American observers to come to
grips with the phenomenon of Stalinism.

There was by this time a core of professionally trained Russian
experts on the staff of the American Embassy in Moscow,
among them George F. Kennan and Charles E. Bohlen, both of
whom would later play a significant role in shaping United
States policy toward the Soviet Union. Another influential
career diplomat, Loy W. Henderson, though not specifically a
Russian specialist, served in Moscow from 1934 to 1938. These
officials had, in turn, been much influenced by the long-time
chief of the State Department's Division of East European Affairs, Robert F. Kelley. The purport of their voluminous reports
back to Washington during this period was that there existed
little reliable basis for cooperation with the Soviet Union, even
against potential adversaries. As Kennan later put it, "Never
—neither then nor at any later date—did I consider the Soviet

---

[18] Bishop, *The Roosevelt-Litvinov Agreements*, p. 15.

Union a fit ally or associate, actual or potential, for this country."[19]

The Soviet specialists based this view in part on ideological considerations. "I am convinced," Henderson wrote in 1936, "that the establishment of a Union of World Soviet Socialist Republics is still the ultimate objective of Soviet foreign policy." Henderson conceded that the prospect of world revolution was not as bright, in the eyes of Russian leaders, as it once had been. He even raised the possibility that "Soviet leaders might eventually become so engrossed in the accomplishment of their more immediate objectives that they will lose sight of it altogether." But, for the moment, the Soviet Union was clearly seeking to control revolutionary movements throughout the world, both to promote its own foreign policy interests and also out of "fear that if it loses all guidance over those forces they are likely to develop into implacable foes of the Soviet Union and the Soviet system." Such considerations could not be ignored in assessing bases for cooperation between Washington and Moscow.[20]

Henderson and his colleagues did not go so far as to share the view Bullitt had come to by this time—that relations with the Soviet Union were merely "a subordinate part of the problem presented by communism as a militant faith designed to produce world revolution and the 'liquidation,' (that is to say, murder) of all non-believers."[21] The Soviet specialists always tended to see ideology more as the instrument rather than the determinant of Stalin's policy. Still, international communism was a matter of sufficient concern to cause embassy experts to discount Moscow's sincerity in seeking a united front against the aggressors. Henderson, for example, interpreted Russian aid to the Spanish Republicans as a demonstration of sympathy for the world revolutionary movement, while Kennan regarded

---

[19] George F. Kennan, *Memoirs: 1925–1950* (Boston: 1967), p. 57. See also Thomas R. Maddux, "American Diplomats and the Soviet Experiment: The View from the Moscow Embassy, 1934–1939," *South Atlantic Quarterly*, LXXIV(Autumn, 1975), 470–471; Franz Knipping, *Die Amerikanische Russlandpolitik in der Zeit des Hitler-Stalin-Pakts, 1939–1941* (Tübingen: 1974), pp. 25–26.

[20] Henderson to Hull, November 16, 1936, *FR:Soviet Union*, pp. 310–311, 313. See also Maddux, "Years of Estrangement," pp. 106–111; and Eagles, "Davies," pp. 206–207.

[21] Bullitt to Hull, April 20, 1936, *FR: Soviet Union*, p. 292.

Chinese Communist efforts to form an anti-Japanese coalition with Chiang Kai-shek as an attempt by Moscow, using Trojan horse tactics, to take over China.[22] In neither case were these assessments necessarily in error as far as Moscow's ultimate objectives were concerned. But they did downplay more than appears warranted in retrospect the Kremlin's interest in resisting Germany and Japan.

Another problem which served to inhibit Soviet-American cooperation, in the view of the Russian specialists, was the Stalin regime's increasing suspicion of foreigners. Xenophobia was, of course, nothing new in Russia—Bullitt in 1936 submitted a long report on the subject taken entirely from the dispatches of Neill Brown, the American minister in St. Petersburg in the early 1850s. But the scope and intensity of Stalin's antiforeign campaign soon surpassed anything achieved by Nicholas I. It took the form of restrictions on travel, intimidation of Soviet citizens to discourage contacts with outsiders, discriminatory currency exchange rates, repeated attempts to penetrate embassy security, and even, in 1937, an accusation that an American cotton expert had tried to import the boll weevil into Soviet Turkestan. "One is inclined to wonder," Henderson observed, "whether, in view of the manner in which the Soviet Government is inculcating hatred for, and suspicion of, all foreigners, . . . that Government seriously desires genuinely friendly relations between the Soviet Union and any other country."[23]

The brutal purges of the 1936–1938 period only confirmed this view. Although skeptical of official charges that there had been a conspiracy directed against Stalin's regime, the embassy staff despaired of proving their falsity. "The Russian mind," Kennan noted, "sometimes carries both truth and falsehood to such infinite extremes that they eventually meet in space, like parallel lines, and it is no longer possible to distinguish between them." They were unanimous, however, in their belief that these internal upheavals had so weakened the Soviet government and military that it would be difficult, in the immediate future, for

---

[22] Henderson to Hull, October 17, 1936, *FR: 1936*, II, 540; Dorothy Borg, *The United States and the Far Eastern Crisis of 1933–1938* (Cambridge, Massachusetts: 1964), pp. 232–234.

[23] Henderson to Hull, August 20, 1937, *FR: Soviet Union*, p. 390. See also Bullitt to Hull, March 4, 1936, ibid., pp. 289–291.

Moscow to play a major role in world affairs. And despite their training, which encouraged a dispassionate and reasoned approach to events, the embassy staff could not help reacting with horror and repugnance at the events they were witnessing. "I felt that the top of my head was coming off," Bohlen recalled, after sitting through the sentencing of eighteen leading Bolsheviks "to be shot." "So prolonged and incessant were the hammer-blow impressions," Kennan later wrote, "each more outrageous and heartrending than the other—that the effect was never to leave me. Its imprint on my political judgment was one that would place me at odds with official thinking in Washington for at least a decade thereafter."[24]

There was another interpretation of events in the Soviet Union, however, and this was provided by Bullitt's successor, Joseph E. Davies, a wealthy lawyer with no diplomatic experience whom Roosevelt named ambassador to the Soviet Union in November 1936. Davies went to Russia at a time when relations were so bad that they could hardly do anything but improve. Instructed by the President to evaluate elements of strength in the Soviet system, Davies saw what he wanted to see, and his impressions, often very different from those of his staff, formed the basis of his reports back to Washington. Certain that the combination of capitalism and nationalism constituted the strongest possible base of national power, Davies persuaded himself that both were developing inside the Soviet Union. Revolutionary internationalism, he argued, was a thing of the past:

To maintain its existence, this Government has to apply capitalistic principles. Otherwise it will fail and be overthrown. . . . I expect to see this Government, while professing devotion to Communism, move constantly more to the Right, in practice, just as it has for the past eight years.

Fabian socialism, Davies thought, might be the end product of Stalin's gradual evolution away from communism.[25]

Like his staff, Davies found the purges "horrifying." Stalin's tyranny continued indefinitely, he argued, would provoke the

---

[24] Kennan memorandum, February 13, 1937, *FR: Soviet Union*, p. 369; Charles E. Bohlen, *Witness to History, 1929–1969* (New York: 1973), p. 51; Kennan, *Memoirs; 1925–1950*, p. 70.

[25] Davies to Hull, June 6, 1938, *FR: Soviet Union*, p. 557. See also Eagles, "Davies," pp. 208–212.

Russian people into destroying their own government. But, unlike his subordinates, Davies saw legitimate reasons for the terror. Foreign plots against the government had been real, in his view; the trials and the terror which surrounded them had been an unpleasant necessity. ("Great revolutions cannot be projected by spraying perfume," he quoted Soviet officials as arguing.) Stalin and his associates were wrapping themselves "in the mantle of angels to serve the devil. They are undoubtedly a strong, able group of ruthless idealists. But tyranny is tyranny." Despite this ambivalence, Davies did not see the purges as significantly weakening the Soviet Union, because of its almost unlimited supplies of manpower and massive industrial base. Nor did these events preclude cooperation against the aggressors: the purges had, after all, been directed against German and Japanese influences. An isolated Soviet Union might threaten world economic and political security, but "friendly relations in the future may be of great general value."[26]

Both Davies and his staff agreed that, despite all difficulties, diplomatic relations with the Soviet Union should be maintained. Whatever happened to Stalin's regime, the USSR was too important to ignore; bad relations were better than no relations at all. But the ambassador and the career diplomats disagreed sharply over the question of whether two governments with such diametrically opposed political systems could find any basis for joint action in the pursuit of common interests. The question has bedeviled Soviet-American relations ever since. The negative answer of Kennan, Bohlen, and Henderson would, in time, gain its hearing, but for the moment it was Davies' affirmative reply which found a response where it counted—in the White House.

IV

Roosevelt had, of course, regretted the failure of his agreement with Litvinov, but he never let his disappointment carry

---

[26] Davies to Hull, April 1 and June 6, 1938, *FR: Soviet Union*, pp. 546, 549, 557–559. See also Eagles, "Davies," pp. 216–225, 250–251; Richard H. Ullmann, "The Davies Mission and United States-Soviet Relations, 1937–1941," *World Politics*, IX(January, 1957), 220–239; and James S. Herndon and Joseph O. Baylen, "Col. Philip R. Faymonville and the Red Army, 1934–43," *Slavic Review*, XXXIV(September, 1975), 493–499.

him to the point of accepting Bullitt's view that Soviet communism posed a greater danger to the world than German fascism. Whatever its methods, the president took the view that the ultimate intentions of communism were meritorious—the improvement of the human condition. And he had never given up his original hope of working with the Russians to increase the strain under which Germany and Japan operated.[27] Accordingly, Roosevelt found Davies' assessment of the Russian situation more credible than that of the State Department. (It seems doubtful that the president ever saw the reports of the Moscow embassy staff, but he was familiar with the position of top State Department officials, which paralleled theirs.) And, following his triumphant reelection in 1936, he took steps to try to rebuild the briefly cordial Soviet-American relationship.

Davies' appointment in November 1936 had been one of those steps. The president instructed his new ambassador not to raise the old issue of debts but to concentrate on learning as much as possible about the Soviet Union's economic and military potential, with a view toward determining which side Moscow would likely support in the event of a European war. Davies resolved, presumably with the president's approval, to approach his mission "free from prejudice and with an open mind." In what was probably not an unrelated move, Roosevelt authorized, or at least did not oppose, a reorganization of the State Department in the spring of 1937 which eliminated Robert Kelley's Division of East European Affairs, a major center of skepticism regarding the possibility of cooperation with the Russians.[28]

Later that year, concerned about the resumption of Sino-Japanese hostilities, Roosevelt began toying with ideas for organizing resistance to Japan. These included a refusal to invoke provisions of the Neutrality Act, on the grounds that an arms embargo would only hurt China, and the October 5 "quarantine speech," in which he called for joint action against the aggres-

---

[27] Knipping, *Die Amerikanische Russlandpolitik*, pp. 5–6; Sumner Welles, *Where Are We Heading?* (New York: 1946), pp. 37–38; William L. Langer and S. Everett Gleason, *The Challenge to Isolation: The World Crisis of 1937–1940 and American Foreign Policy* (New York: 1952), pp. 126–127.

[28] Joseph E. Davies, *Mission to Moscow* (New York: 1941), pp. xii–xiv, xvii, 6. See also Kennan, *Memoirs: 1925–1950,* pp. 83–85; and Bohlen, *Witness to History,* pp. 39–41.

sors. They also involved highly tentative discussions with the State Department on the feasibility of United States collaboration with the British, the French, and the Russians to preserve peace in the Far East. Precisely what Roosevelt had in mind is not clear, but State's reaction, despite the abolition of Kelley's division, was not favorable. Secretary Hull and his advisers distrusted Soviet intentions in China, suspected Moscow of seeking a Japanese-American war, and, in the light of the purges, doubted the effectiveness of the Red Army in any Far Eastern conflict. Roosevelt did not object when the department sought unsuccessfully to block Soviet participation at the Brussels Conference on the Far East in November, or when United States representatives at that conference rebuffed inquiries from Litvinov about prospects for common action against Japan.[29]

The bombing of the American gunboat *Panay* in December, however, pushed Roosevelt again toward the idea of an anti-Japanese coalition. The president secretly proposed to the British consideration of a naval blockade against Japan, and dispatched Captain Royal E. Ingersoll, director of the Navy's War Plans Division, to London to discuss the matter. He also instructed Ambassador Davies, in January 1938, to suggest to the Russians an exchange of military information regarding Pacific problems in general, and Japan in particular. Significantly, Roosevelt instructed Davies to keep this initiative secret from both the State Department and the Moscow embassy staff. Litvinov responded lukewarmly to Davies's proposal, complaining that without a definite pact there seemed to be little purpose to the plan, but in June, Stalin himself endorsed it. By this time, though, the Ingersoll mission had become public and Roosevelt, fearing further revelations, refused to pursue the initiative.[30]

The president had, however, given the Russians reason to hope that military cooperation might be possible in another

---

[29] Maddux, "Years of Estrangement," pp. 201–205; Eagles, "Davies," pp. 178–192.

[30] Davies to Hull, January 17, 1939, *FR: Soviet Union,* pp. 596–597. See also Maddux, "Years of Estrangement," pp. 205–208; Langer and Gleason, *The Challenge to Isolation,* p. 127; and John McVickar Haight, Jr., "Franklin D. Roosevelt and a Naval Quarantine of Japan," *Pacific Historical Review,* XL(May, 1971), 203–226.

area. In November 1936, the Soviet government began a campaign, which it was to pursue with remarkable patience and tenacity over the next three years, to have private American firms construct warships for the Soviet navy. Stalin was seeking, at this time, to build a substantial balanced fleet, but the USSR lacked the facilities for constructing large vessels, and, for political reasons, the use of German, Japanese, British or French firms was impractical. The proposal required Washington's approval, since it involved the release of confidential specifications, but the State Department and the White House quickly made it clear that they had no objections. Even Robert Kelley approved, on the grounds that if the Soviet Union evolved eventually "into a purely national Government, the strengthening of the naval forces of the Soviet Union would not run counter to the national interests of the United States."[31]

However, the Navy Department, and, in particular, Admiral William D. Leahy, Chief of Naval Operations, had deep reservations about the propriety both of building foreign warships in the United States and of aiding a communist country. Navy officials privately let it be known that American firms cooperating with the Russians might not, in the future, receive Navy contracts, and this threat was enough to halt all action on the proposal. The Russians made repeated efforts to revive it, even promising to station the vessels in question at Vladivostok, where they could be used against the Japanese, but without success. Roosevelt complained in May 1939 of the Navy's tendency to consider "as a military secret every possible item of naval equipment" and reiterated that he "wanted this deal . . . to go through." But by this time, domestic shipbuilding capacity was almost wholly committed to American naval rearmament, and this situation, together with the rapid deterioration in Soviet-American relations that followed the Nazi-Soviet Pact in August, prevented further action.[32]

---

[31] Kelley memorandum of March 24, 1937, *FR: Soviet Union*, p. 466.

[32] The Soviet effort to have warships built in the United States is fully documented in *FR: Soviet Union*, pp. 457–490, 670–707, 869–903. See also Robert Ward Herrick, *Soviet Naval Strategy: Fifty Years of Theory and Practice* (Annapolis: 1968), pp. 36–38; and Thomas R. Maddux, "United States-Soviet Naval Relations in the 1930's: The Soviet Union's Efforts to Purchase Naval Vessels," *Naval War College Review*, XXIX(Fall, 1976), 28–37.

Given presently available evidence, it is difficult to know how seriously the Russians regarded prospects for American participation in an anti-Japanese coalition. Certainly the petty harassment of American diplomats in the Soviet Union continued throughout this period, and the Russians were never willing to make significant compromises on debts. Stalin does appear to have attached great importance to his plan for the construction of warships by American firms—otherwise, it is difficult to account for the persistence with which he pursued that objective, in the face of continual discouragement. Nor does it seem likely that Soviet officials had abandoned the hopes they had held in 1933 for diplomatic cooperation in the Far East, though what form they expected it to take remains unclear.

In fact, however, the possibility of joint Soviet-American action of any kind was remote. Fears of "entanglements" were still strong enough to inhibit positive moves by the Roosevelt administration to resist the aggressors. And even if these sentiments had not been a problem, there still would have been significant constraints on the Soviet-American relationship. For one thing, although Roosevelt worried about the rise of Germany and Japan, he did not become clear in his own mind until after Munich as to whether accommodation or resistance was the best way to handle these countries.[33] Nor was he willing to devote the kind of sustained attention to foreign affairs which would have allowed him to override objections to Soviet-American cooperation within the State and Navy Departments. And even if all these impediments had been removed, there still would have been the problem of internal differences between the two countries—differences which had never been more obvious than they were in the late 1930s.

The reality of the situation was simply that Stalin, in his desperate effort to secure his regime at all costs against internal challenge, had made the Soviet Union in the eyes of the external world an unacceptable partner in the task of keeping peace. Englishmen, Frenchmen, Poles, and Czechs were no more wil-

---

[33] See, on this point, Langer and Gleason, *The Challenge to Isolation,* p. 23; and Francis L. Loewenheim, "An Illusion That Shaped History: New Light on the History and Historiography of American Peace Efforts Before Munich," in Daniel R. Beaver, ed., *Some Pathways in Twentieth Century History* (Detroit: 1969), pp. 219–220.

ling to join in Litvinov's anti-fascist crusade than were Americans, whose interests were far less directly engaged. The Munich agreement of September 1938 represented the triumph of a widely shared view that communism was at least as dangerous as fascism, if not more so. It was a view which was to persist until Hitler's violation of that agreement six months later made his ultimate intentions clear. But by that time the Soviet Union had decided that, in the absence of cooperation from the West, the best chance of preventing war lay in collaboration with Hitler, not resistance to him.

V

Despite its revolutionary implications for Russian foreign policy, the Nazi-Soviet Pact of August 1939 came as no surprise in Washington. Davies had expressed fears of a German-Russian rapprochement if the West made no effort to join with the USSR in resisting the aggressors, and rumors of such a reconciliation periodically reached the Moscow embassy staff. During the summer of 1939, leaks from a German diplomat in that city gave United States officials the opportunity to monitor the secret Ribbentrop-Molotov negotiations on almost a day-by-day basis.[34] Still, the pact, when it came, was a bitter disappointment to those who had hoped for some improvement in Soviet-American relations. For those who had thought such improvement unlikely, it was a striking confirmation of their belief that the Russians could not be trusted.

Stalin's actions during the next six months only reinforced that judgment. The Nazi-Soviet Pact made it possible for Hitler, on September 1, to invade Poland, an action which, in turn, provoked British and French declarations of war. On September 17, in accordance with secret provisions of that pact, the Red Army entered Poland from the East, seizing almost half the country. By the end of October, the Russians had demanded and obtained base rights in the Baltic states of Latvia, Lithuania,

---

[34] Bohlen, *Witness to History*, pp. 67–87. See also *FR: Soviet Union*, pp. 373, 555, 584, 750: *FR: 1939*, I, 312–337; and Davies, *Mission to Moscow*, pp. 450, 453–454.

and Estonia. Finland's refusal to grant similar rights and boundary concessions brought about a Soviet invasion of that country on November 30, but unexpected resistance delayed the Red Army's victory until the following March. By the summer of 1940, Stalin had extracted territorial concessions from the Rumanians as well and had incorporated the Baltic states into the Soviet Union. These boundary changes regained for the Russians most of the territory lost during the Revolution and Civil War, but the fact that they had been achieved by intimidation and force made Moscow's actions seem, in the eyes of Western observers, little different from those of the Germans or the Japanese.

Nonetheless, the Roosevelt administration chose quite deliberately to make a fundamental distinction between the behavior of the Soviet Union and that of Germany and Japan. Tentatively at first, but by the summer of 1940 with increasing purposefulness, official Washington moved toward a strategy of seeking to undermine the Hitler-Stalin alliance while at the same time working to prevent a similar relationship from developing between Moscow and Tokyo.[35]

There had been intimations from the first that the Nazi-Soviet association could not last. "It reverses the processes of men's minds in a way which I do not believe can be permanent," Assistant Secretary of State Adolf Berle noted in September 1939; "winning or losing, that combination must eventually break up." The problem, though, was to determine how long such a development might take. Reports from the Moscow embassy stressed Russian-German cooperation, giving little reason to hope for an early break. State Department officials worried that the Hitler-Stalin split might come only after the Germans had defeated the Western democracies, and that the eventual outcome would be the Soviet domination of Europe. To some, including Assistant Secretary of State Breckinridge Long and Joseph P. Kennedy, United States ambassador to Great Britain, such thoughts suggested the wisdom of encouraging the British and French to make peace with Hitler. "It would be a shame," Long noted, "[to] continue a war which would mean the victory

---

[35] Knipping, *Die Amerikanische Russlandpolitik*, pp. 34–35.

of Communism in Europe and confront us with our eventual enemy—Russia.''[36]

For Roosevelt, however, the ultimate enemy had always been Germany. Accordingly, he categorically refused to promote negotiations with Hitler to keep Stalin out of Europe, and set about doing what was possible, within the framework of existing neutrality legislation, to aid the Western democracies. At the same time, he avoided actions which might unnecessarily antagonize the Russians. Despite its use of military force against Poland, Roosevelt chose not to regard the Soviet Union as a belligerent and so avoided invoking the arms embargo which had, since September, been in effect against Germany and its opponents. Nor did the administration make an issue over Soviet demands on the Baltic states, which, for the moment, remained nominally independent. In the Far East, Roosevelt encouraged the Chinese to maintain good relations with Moscow, with a view, as he put it, "to keep[ing] Russia and Japan apart."[37]

But the Soviet invasion of Finland on November 30, 1939, greatly complicated Roosevelt's strategy. The attack came at a time when the war between Germany and the Allies had lapsed into inactivity and so received full media coverage in the United States. Finland quickly became an object of sympathy, because not only had the Russians launched an unprovoked attack against a small democracy which had close ethnic ties to the United States; they had also managed to invade the only European country which had maintained regular payments on its World War I debts. The Russians further compounded their problems by failing to defeat the Finns quickly, thereby earning for themselves the reputation not only of predators but of inefficient ones at that.

---

[36] Berle Diary, September 3, 1939, quoted in Langer and Gleason, *The Challenge to Isolation*, p. 203; Long Diary, October 11, 1939, Fred L. Israel, ed., *The War Diary of Breckinridge Long* (Lincoln: 1966), p. 27. See also Kennedy to Hull, September 11 and 25, 1939, *FR: 1939*, I, 423–424, 454.

[37] Maddux, "Years of Estrangement" pp. 233–237. See also Langer and Gleason, *The Challenge to Isolation*, pp. 245, 320–321; John Morton Blum, *From the Morgenthau Diaries: Years of Urgency, 1938–1941* (Boston: 1965), p. 124; Robert A. Divine, *Roosevelt and World War II* (Baltimore: 1969), p. 78.

Roosevelt made no attempt to conceal his disgust. "The whole of the United States is not only horrified but thoroughly angry," he wrote, on November 30. "People are asking why one should have anything to do with the present Soviet leaders because their idea of civilization and human happiness is so totally different from ours." Congress had repealed the arms embargo by this time, but after Soviet planes bombed Finnish cities, the president did invoke a "moral embargo," discouraging American firms from shipping aircraft and related equipment to the USSR. On December 22, he instructed the State Department to let the Russians know that their attitude showed "such a complete disregard for the ordinary politeness and amenities between civilized governments that the President honestly wonders whether the Soviet Government considers it worthwhile to continue diplomatic relations." And on February 10, 1940, he publicly characterized the USSR as a "dictatorship as absolute as any other dictatorship in the world."[38]

Nonetheless, the president held fast against pressure, which quickly became considerable, to break relations with the Soviet Union or to place the Russians in the same category with Nazi Germany. Despite a strong personal inclination to help the Finns, Roosevelt yielded to Hull's objections against sending surplus military equipment and agreed to refer consideration of a loan to Congress, which failed to act until it was too late. The administration's restraint in this matter may have been motivated as much by fear of isolationist criticism as by the hope of playing the Russians off against the Germans, but the latter consideration was present as well and was not inconsistent with the first.[39] Settlement of the Russo-Finnish War in March 1940, together with the German invasion of Denmark and Norway in April and the attack on France and the Low Countries in May, reinforced Roosevelt's belief that the Germans were more dangerous than the Russians. Following France's unexpectedly

---

[38] Roosevelt to Joseph Grew, November 30, 1939, in Elliott Roosevelt, ed., *F. D. R.: His Personal Letters, 1928–1945* (New York: 1950), II, 961; Roosevelt to Hull and Welles, December 22, 1939, *FR: Soviet Union*, p. 869; Samuel I. Rosenman, ed., *The Public Papers and Addresses of Franklin D. Roosevelt* (New York: 1938–1950), IX, 93.

[39] Maddux, "Years of Estrangement," pp. 253–260.

quick defeat in June, the State Department, with the president's approval, began a concerted effort to try to improve United States relations with the Soviet Union.

This initiative took the form of a long series of negotiations, beginning in late July 1940, between Under Secretary of State Sumner Welles and Constantine Oumansky, the Soviet ambassador to the United States. The atmosphere under which these talks were conducted was hardly promising. The Russians had just completed their absorption of the Baltic states into the Soviet Union, and the administration had responded by freezing assets of those countries in the United States and by continuing to recognize them as independent states. The moral embargo on aircraft equipment remained in effect, and with American rearmament getting under way, the Russians experienced increasing difficulties in obtaining export licenses for other strategic materials which they wanted to purchase. Soviet espionage had become a matter of increasing concern with the discovery in May 1940 that a code clerk in the London embassy had been passing secret communications to the Russians and, presumably, the Germans. Soviet Foreign Minister Molotov was not exaggerating the situation when he commented in a speech on August 1: "I will not dwell on our relations with the United States of America, if only for the reason that there is nothing good that can be said about them."[40]

But both Moscow and Washington had by this time developed enough common concerns to keep the negotiations going. The United States had committed itself to providing all aid to Britain short of war; uncertainty on Germany's part about Russian intentions would obviously ease Britain's task. Uncertainty might also be useful in the Far East, where Japan was attempting to settle its differences with the Soviet Union to facilitate expansion into Southeast Asia. For the Russians, Hitler's rapid victories upset expectations that the Germans would be tied down in Western Europe for some time to come, while growing German activity in the Balkans and Finland hinted at the direction in which Hitler might move next. The Tripartite Pact, signed late in September 1940, further surprised

---

[40] Molotov speech of August 1, 1940, Degras., ed., *Soviet Documents*, III, 468. See also Maddux, "Years of Estrangement," pp. 264–267, 277–280.

the Russians, raising the possibility of a Berlin-Rome-Tokyo axis directed against Moscow.[41] Stalin was by no means ready to break his ties with Hitler at this stage, but this series of events did make clear the advantages of projecting a bit of unpredictability himself. For this purpose, the Welles-Oumansky negotiations were useful.

These talks did not go smoothly. Oumansky's abrasive personality alone was enough to try the patience of any diplomat, and he remained unrepentant in his insistence that the United States recognize Soviet territorial conquests and sell the Russians whatever was necessary for their defense efforts. Still, the discussions did provide Washington with assurances that the Russians had no immediate plans to align themselves with Japanese; on its part, the Roosevelt administration agreed early in 1941 to end the moral embargo. Few concrete results grew out of these exchanges, but the psychological atmosphere had definitely improved. Even Molotov admitted that the United States had demonstrated "in a very small way" a desire to improve relations with the Soviet Union.[42]

The Welles-Oumansky negotiations were not popular with Soviet specialists in the Department of State or in the Moscow embassy. The tendency in these quarters had been to stress Russo-German solidarity and to warn strongly against making unilateral concessions which Moscow would only interpret as a sign of weakness. The Russians feared a German attack, Ambassador Laurence A. Steinhardt argued in a letter from Moscow in October 1940, but they would never risk such an attack merely to improve relations with the United States or Great Britain. Similarly, in the Far East, the true Soviet interest was to get the United States embroiled in a war with Japan from which only the Russians would benefit. "If I am correct in this interpretation," Steinhardt noted, " . . . the best policy to pursue is one of aloofness, indicating strength, rather than an approach which can have no prospect of success."[43]

But the Russians were not to enjoy the luxury of deciding whether to remain aligned with Germany. Hitler had been

---

[41] Ulam, *Expansion and Coexistence,* pp. 296–303.

[42] *FR: 1940,* III, 440.

[43] Steinhardt to Henderson, October 20, 1940, *FR: 1940,* III, 407. See also Maddux, "Years of Estrangement," pp. 287–288.

planning an invasion of the Soviet Union since the summer of
1940, and by January 1941 the American embassy in Berlin, with
the help of a disaffected official in the German foreign ministry,
had obtained hard evidence to this effect. Steinhardt opposed
telling the Russians, on the grounds that the information would
encourage them to settle their differences with Japan and try to
appease Hitler, but Welles, presumably with Roosevelt's approval, went ahead. On March 1, 1941, he gave Oumansky the
news. "Oumansky turned very white," Welles recalled, and
then briefly expressed thanks. Further exchanges with Welles
provided additional information, which the Russians were able
to confirm from the British and from their own intelligence
service.[44] As a result, by the spring of 1941, Stalin had clear
indications of what to expect.

Meanwhile, the Roosevelt administration was working to ensure that the United States could assist the Russians if it chose to
when the German invasion came. In January 1941, the president
had submitted the Lend-Lease Act to Congress. The bill's primary purpose was to facilitate aid to Great Britain, but Roosevelt
carefully insisted on having language inserted authorizing assistance to *any* country whose defense he deemed vital to that of
the United States. Congressional critics pointed out that such
wording would make it possible to aid even the Soviet Union,
however remote that prospect might seem, but Roosevelt, in
possession by now of secret information suggesting that the
prospect was not remote at all, refused to accept amendments
specifically excluding the USSR. The bill passed on this basis,
and Roosevelt signed it on March 11, slightly more than a week
after Welles had informed Oumansky of the impending German
attack.[45]

If the Russians were grateful for the information the Americans had provided them or for Roosevelt's cautious handling of
the Lend-Lease bill, they did painfully little to show it. Instead,

---

[44] *FR: 1941,* I, 712–714; Sumner Welles, *The Time for Decision* (New York: 1944), pp.
170–171; William L. Langer and S. Everett Gleason, *The Undeclared War: 1940–1941*
(New York: 1953), pp. 336–345; James E. McSherry, *Stalin, Hitler, and Europe*
(Cleveland: 1970), II, 202–203, 218–220.
[45] Raymond H. Dawson, *The Decision to Aid Russia, 1941: Foreign Policy and Domestic Politics* (Chapel Hill: 1959), pp. 22–41.

as Steinhardt had predicted, Stalin moved to appease Berlin and repair his relations with Tokyo. The Soviet dictator made no protest early in April when Hitler invaded Yugoslavia one day after the Russians had signed a treaty of friendship with that country. Later that month, the Soviet Union negotiated a treaty with Japan pledging both countries to remain neutral if the other became involved in war with a third power. "Now that the Soviet Union and Japan have arranged their affairs," Stalin told the departing Japanese foreign minister, "Japan will straighten out the East, and the Soviet Union and Germany will take care of Europe and later on between them they will take care of the Americans." In May, the Russians withdrew recognition from the Norwegian, Belgian, and Yugoslav governments-in-exile, all of them victims of German aggression. Soviet economic deliveries to Germany were actually increased in the weeks before the German attack, and on June 14, a week before the invasion, TASS branded as an "obvious absurdity" rumors of an impending Russo-German war.[46]

The Roosevelt administration's policy of seeking to undermine the Hitler-Stalin alliance by improving relations with Moscow had not been easy to maintain, given the contempt the Russians showed for world opinion during their period of alignment with Germany, given the intensely hostile American public reaction to their behavior. Nor can it be said that the policy was successful—Stalin, after all, clung to his pact with Hitler until after German troops had begun marching into the Soviet Union. But the fact that the effort was made did ease problems of Soviet-American cooperation after June 22, 1941. It also provides interesting evidence that American policymakers, are, from time to time, capable of balancing interests against principles with some degree of sophistication and realism.

---

[46] McSherry, *Stalin, Hitler, and Europe*, II, 209–221; Ulam, *Expansion and Coexistence*, pp. 307–311.

CHAPTER VI

The Grand Alliance: 1941–1945

A FUNDAMENTAL PRINCIPLE IN THE CONDUCT OF INTERNATIONAL RELATIONS, it has been argued, is that great nations should not unnecessarily increase the number of adversaries with which they have to deal.[1] Like most principles of strategy and diplomacy, this one appears self-evident when stated. Practical implementation, however, has been surprisingly infrequent. A rare demonstration of the principle correctly applied can be found in Roosevelt's policy of trying to maintain some semblance of friendly relations with the Soviet Union during the difficult period from September 1939 through June 1941. For an egregious example of a failure to apply the principle, one need only turn to Hitler's diplomacy between June and December of 1941, a period which saw him perform the remarkable feat, within six months, of declaring war on *both* the Soviet Union and the United States. The result was to make possible the association of the United States, Great Britain, and the Soviet Union in what Winston Churchill called a "Grand Alliance" against their common German foe.

I

There is great irony in the fact that Stalin, who habitually trusted no one, was virtually the last person in a position of high responsibility to become convinced of Hitler's intention to attack the Soviet Union. Soviet intelligence had picked up numerous indications that an invasion was imminent, and both the Americans and the British had warned the Russians as well. But intelligence is no better than the preconceptions national leaders

---

[1] See Frederick H. Hartmann, *The Relations of Nations*, Fourth Edition (New York: 1973), pp. x, 82–83.

bring to its evaluation. Wanting to believe that his policy of buying time for Russia had not failed, Stalin refused until the very night of the attack to allow defensive preparations, with the result that the Soviet Union suffered such severe early losses in men, equipment, and territory as to make problematic its continuation in the war.[2]

Few in Washington failed to recognize the earthshaking implications of the Russo-German conflict, but there was from the start disagreement as to what to do about it. Obviously, it could only benefit the Anglo-American cause to have Britain's chief enemy tied down in the East. But if, as seemed likely, the Russians collapsed as Hitler's previous victims had done, then the British would have enjoyed at best a temporary respite. Any aid sent to Russia would only detract from Britain's ability to repel the renewed German offensive which would soon be hurled against it. If, on the other hand, there could be assurance that the Russians would fight, then it would clearly be advantageous to send them all possible aid. But a victory achieved in collaboration with the Soviet Union would raise serious questions about the peace settlement, since congruence between Stalin's war aims and those of his Western allies could not be assumed. Roosevelt's military and diplomatic advisers, accordingly, recommended caution in responding to this new development.[3]

From London, however, there came another view, powerfully and eloquently expressed. "I have only one purpose, the destruction of Hitler, and my life is much simplified thereby," Winston Churchill proclaimed. "If Hitler invaded Hell, I would make at least a favorable reference to the Devil in the House of Commons." Churchill had already sounded out Roosevelt on the idea of publicly welcoming Stalin as an ally if the Germans attacked. The President had raised no objections; hence, on the evening of June 22, the British prime minister announced in a radio address that "any man or state who fights on against

---

[2] See, on the early course of the Russo-German war, Albert Seaton, *The Russo-German War, 1941–45* (London: 1971), pp. 70–152; Adam B. Ulam, *Stalin: The Man and His Era* (New York: 1973), pp. 536–539; Alexander Werth, *Russia at War, 1941–45* (New York: 1964), pp. 131–260; John Erickson, *The Road to Stalingrad* (New York: 1975), pp. 50–222.

[3] Langer and Gleason, *The Undeclared War*, pp. 537–541; Dawson, *The Decision to Aid Russia*, pp. 112–118.

Nazidom will have our aid. Any man or state who marches with Hitler is our foe. . . . It follows, therefore, that we shall give whatever help we can to Russia and the Russian people."[4]

Roosevelt wholeheartedly agreed. To a greater extent than has been appreciated, his approach to strategy and diplomacy during the early years of World War II rested on a coherent set of assumptions, chief among which was the conviction that the security of the Western Hemisphere required Britain's survival as an independent state. It followed from this premise that, to the extent that other nations could be enlisted in the anti-German cause, Britain's plight would be eased thereby. Germany's invasion of the Soviet Union, he recognized, might provide such an opportunity. If it proved to be more than a diversion, he wrote on June 26, "it will mean the liberation of Europe from Nazi domination—and at the same time I do not think we need worry about any possibility of Russian domination."[5]

This last observation reflected Roosevelt's long-standing belief that although the Soviet Union was a dictatorship, officially committed to a repellent ideology, it was by no means as dangerous to American interests as was Hitler's Germany. "Russia is defending its own soil," he argued. "At the present time Russia is in no sense the aggressor nation—Germany is." It was true, the president noted, that the Russians had, in the past, used propaganda to try to spread their influence beyond their borders. But the Germans used force as well, a major difference. "The survival of Russia is less dangerous to religion, to the church as such, and to humanity in general than would be the survival of the German form of dictatorship," he wrote to Pope Pius XII on September 3. "I can't take communism nor can you," he explained to former Ambassador Joseph Davies,"but to cross this bridge I would hold hands with the Devil."[6]

Roosevelt had the authority, under the Lend-Lease Act, to

---

[4] Winston S. Churchill, *The Grand Alliance* (Boston: 1950), pp. 369–372.

[5] Roosevelt to William D. Leahy, June 26, 1941, in Roosevelt, ed., *F. D. R., His Personal Letters*, II, 1177.

[6] Roosevelt to Myron C. Taylor, September 1, 1941, Franklin D. Roosevelt Papers, PSF: Italy, Franklin D. Roosevelt Library, Hyde Park, New York; Roosevelt to Pius XII, September 3, 1941, in Roosevelt, ed., *F. D. R., His Personal Letters*, II, 1205; Eagles, "Davies," p. 328.

make American aid available to the Soviet Union, but Congress
retained control of appropriations and could, if it disagreed with
the president's decision, cut off funds. This possibility could not
easily be dismissed, given public attitudes toward the Soviet
Union in the summer of 1941. Russian actions in Poland, Finland, and the Baltic states during the previous two years had
provoked bitterness which even the German attack could not be
expected to dispel overnight. Isolationists found in the Soviet
Union's association with Great Britain all the more reason why
the United States should have nothing to do with the war. Even
interventionists had difficulty in rationalizing cooperation with
a power so recently Germany's ally. Public opinion polls reflected ambivalence: while an overwhelming majority of the
public wanted the Russians to defeat the Germans, only a
minority expected them to, or thought that the United States
should assist them.[7]

The president thus had to move warily. He authorized an
interim program of aid to Russia, but carefully refrained from
financing it under Lend-Lease. Instead he worked behind the
scenes to float trial balloons, disarm opponents, and allow pro-
Soviet sentiment gradually to build. He encouraged former
Ambassador Davies to speak in favor of all-out aid to the USSR
and to publish a sanitized version of his largely pro-Russian
1937–1938 dispatches from Moscow. In hopes of defusing opposition from religious organizations, Roosevelt cajoled the Kremlin
into issuing a largely meaningless affirmation of the right of
religious freedom in the Soviet Union, and worked simultaneously through the Vatican to discourage criticism of Russia by
American Catholics. When critics in Congress attempted in October to exclude the USSR from future Lend-Lease aid, the president lobbied quietly but successfully to defeat their amendment
while refraining from public opposition.[8]

Roosevelt had, by this time, received a series of increasingly

---

[7] Dawson, *The Decision to Aid Russia*, pp. 99–101, 218–230; George C. Herring, Jr.,
Aid to Russia, 1941–1946: Strategy, Diplomacy, the Origins of the Cold War (New
York: 1973), pp. 6–7.

[8] Maddux, "Years of Estrangement," pp. 310–311; Dawson, *The Decision to Aid
Russia*, pp. 230–238, 274–282; Langer and Gleason, *The Undeclared War*, pp.
793–798, 816–818; Herring, *Aid to Russia*, pp. 18–24.

optimistic reports regarding the Russians' capacity to resist, notably from Harry Hopkins, who had gone to Moscow in late July, and from W. Averell Harriman, who visited the Soviet capital in September with Lord Beaverbrook, British minister of supply. American and British military leaders, who had at first resented the diversion of vital supplies to the USSR, had come now to see the strategic value of this course of action: "The maintenance of an active front in Russia," the American Joint Board noted in September, "offers by far the best opportunity for a successful land offensive against Germany." Public opinion polls detected decreasing opposition to helping the Russians, along with a growing conviction that a Soviet victory would be in American interests. Accordingly, President Roosevelt encountered little opposition when, on November 7, 1941, he made Lend-Lease available to the Kremlin, on the grounds that the defense of the Soviet Union was vital to the security of the United States.[9]

Events had, in the course of two years, transformed the Russians from aggressors to allies, a process greatly facilitated by Roosevelt's concentration on congruities of interests between the United States and the Soviet Union, not differences of principle. There remained only Washington's formal affiliation with what was already in fact a tripartite coalition against Germany. This came about in an unexpected way on December 7, 1941, when the Japanese, taking advantage of a major American failure of intelligence, attacked Pearl Harbor. Hitler's declaration of war followed within three days. Three weeks later, on January 1, 1942, representatives of the United States, Great Britain, and the Soviet Union signed in Washington a "Declaration of the United Nations," committing each signatory to fight until victory had been achieved.[10] Hitler's inadvertent creation, the Grand Alliance, was now complete.

II

Churchill claims to have worried that, in view of all that had transpired between 1939 and 1941, the Russians might be shy

---

[9] Joint Board estimate of September 11, 1941, quoted in Langer and Gleason, *The Undeclared War*, p. 792. See also Dawson, *The Decision to Aid Russia*, pp. 282–289.
[10] Rosenman, ed., *Roosevelt Public Papers*, XI, 3–5.

about requesting help from the West in their fight against Hitler. Such proved not to be the case. As early as July 1941, Stalin asked the British, who were in no position to comply, to invade northern France. Later that month, he told Harry Hopkins that he would welcome American troops, under American command, anywhere on the Russian front. In September, he argued that Churchill could "without risk" send "twenty-five or thirty" British divisions to Archangel or the Caucasus—this at a time when London was straining shipping capabilities to the limit just to put two additional divisions into the Middle East. "By her passive attitude Britain is helping the Nazis," Stalin complained to the Soviet ambassador in London: "Do the British realise this? I think they do. What is it then that they want? It seems they want us to be weakened."[11]

This was an unjust accusation, but it did reflect the frustrations the Russians felt over a fundamental strategic fact of life in World War II: neither Great Britain nor the United States had come under direct ground attack. Both enjoyed, as a result, a certain flexibility in deciding how and when to strike back at the enemy. For the Russians, there could be no such choice: reeling from invasion on a broad front, their only option, short of capitulation, was all-out resistance. Obtaining relief from this pressure, whether through the dispatch of American and British troops to the Soviet Union or the creation of a second front against the Germans in Europe, accordingly became Stalin's chief diplomatic priority.

Roosevelt was not, at first, averse to creating an early second front. His military advisers, trained in the tradition of striking the enemy in the most direct manner and concerned about the strategic implications of a Soviet defeat, pushed strongly for an attack across the English Channel as soon as possible. Roosevelt, too, favored such an operation, partly out of a desire to stave off growing pressures inside the United States for an all-out offensive against Japan, partly out of fear that delay in confronting the Germans might lead Stalin to seek a separate

---

[11] Churchill, *The Grand Alliance*, pp. 380, 384, 462–465; Hopkins to Roosevelt, July 31, 1941, *FR: 1941*, I, 814; Stalin to Maisky, August 30, 1941, quoted in "Diplomatic History of the Opening of the Second Front in Europe, 1941–1944," *International Affairs* (Moscow), April, 1970, #4, p. 74.

peace, partly as an inducement to the Soviet leader to postpone discussion of postwar territorial claims in Europe, which Roosevelt feared might disrupt the common war effort. (That Stalin would not have been thinking about postwar territorial claims had he not expected to win does not seem to have occurred to the president, whose ability to see the interconnection of military and diplomatic problems was sometimes limited.) Accordingly, in June 1942, Roosevelt publicly promised Soviet Foreign Minister Molotov that a second front would be established somewhere in Europe before the end of the year. [12]

In the end, however, Roosevelt had to break this promise. The slow pace of American mobilization and training ensured that any 1942 attack would be primarily a British operation, and Churchill, haunted by memories of World War I trench warfare, was not inclined to launch costly attacks to relieve an ally whose concern over Britain's plight between 1939 and 1941 had been minimal. And even if the British had been willing, it would not have been possible in 1942 to accumulate sufficient transports to launch an invasion of Europe with any prospect of success. As a result, Roosevelt and Churchill agreed on a substitute plan involving joint Anglo-American landings in Vichy-occupied North Africa in November 1942. This operation met Roosevelt's desire to get American troops into action against the Germans before the end of the year, but it did little to take pressure off the Red Army. Delays in clearing the Germans out of Africa in turn made it impossible to launch a cross-Channel attack in 1943—the invasion of Italy, and that state's forced withdrawal from the Axis coalition, was, for the Russians, small comfort. The true second front would not come until June 1944, a year and a half later than Roosevelt had promised. [13]

The Russians believed at the time, and have charged since, that the delay in constituting the second front was deliberate. Roosevelt and Churchill, the argument runs, resolved to let the Soviet Union bear the brunt of the fighting, leaving the British

[12] Press release of June 11, 1942, *FR: 1942*, III, 594. See also Robert Beitzell, *The Uneasy Alliance: America, Britain and Russia, 1941–1943* (New York: 1972), pp. 14–42; and Richard W. Steele, *The First Offensive: 1942* (Bloomington: 1973), pp. 1–142.

[13] Ibid., pp. 143–182; Beitzell, *The Uneasy Alliance*, pp. 42–107, 303–365.

and Americans to step in at the last moment to shape the peace settlement.[14] There can be no doubt that it was the Russians who, as Churchill put it, "tore the guts" out of the German army. Total German losses, including killed, wounded, and missing, came to over six million on the eastern front, as compared to just over one million in Western Europe and the Mediterranean. Throughout most of the war the Red Army was confronting, on the eastern front, more than 200 enemy divisions. Prior to the Normandy landings in June 1944, the British and Americans rarely faced more than 10 German divisions at any one time. A recent Soviet account has noted pointedly but accurately that for every American killed in the war against the Axis, fifty Russians died.[15]

It is frequently forgotten, though, that the British and the Americans had their own second front problem in the Far East, where the Soviet Union had refrained from declaring war on the Japanese. Roosevelt and Churchill appreciated the Russians' unwillingness to take on an additional enemy at a time when the German army was just outside Moscow. At no point did they ask Stalin to enter the Far Eastern war until after Germany's defeat. But requirements of the war against Japan did significantly restrict the United States' ability to amass the troops and equipment—particularly landing craft—necessary to launch an early cross-Channel attack in Europe.[16] The delayed second front was, thus, part of the price the Russians paid for neutrality in the Far East.

It is also not often taken into account what impact the recruitment of additional manpower would have had on American war production, much of which went to Great Britain and the Soviet Union in the form of Lend-Lease. Some $43.6 billion, or 14% of total American defense expenditures in World War II, was allocated for Lend-Lease; of this, approximately $11 billion,

---

[14] See, for example, "Diplomatic History of the Opening of the Second Front," p. 76; B. Ponomaryov, A. Gromyko, and V. Khvostov, eds., *History of Soviet Foreign Policy, 1917–1945* (Moscow: 1969), p. 428.

[15] N. N. IAkovlev, "SSSR-SShA: Motivy sotrudnichestva i konflikta (1941–1945)", *SShA: Ekonomika, Politika, Ideologiia,* 1970, #5, p. 21. See also Seaton, *The Russo–German War,* p. 586; and Beitzell, *The Uneasy Alliance,* p. 369.

[16] Kent Roberts Greenfield, *American Strategy in World War II: A Reconsideration* (Baltimore: 1963), pp. 30–41.

or 3.5% of total expenditures, went to the Soviet Union. As it was, the United States mobilized almost as high a percentage of its population as did the USSR (12% versus 13%); its factories produced 35% of all the combat munitions used against Germany and its allies and 85% of those used against the Japanese. The United States might have been able to collect enough men in Britain in 1943 to launch a second front, but only by taking pressure off Japan in the Far East (thereby increasing the Soviet Union's security problems in that part of the world) and cutting back on the industrial production which played such a vital role in shaping the outcome of the war.[17]

Anglo-American reluctance to incur casualties also worked to delay the second front. Churchill's preoccupation with this matter has been well documented; less well known is the extent to which Roosevelt shared this concern.[18] The Russians, denied the luxury of deciding how to use their manpower, naturally resented this situation. But the fact that the British and Americans refused to launch suicide attacks to take pressure off the Red Army does not necessarily imply a determination on their part to deny Stalin the legitimate fruits of victory. Had such been their intent, the best strategy would have been to invade Europe at once regardless of casualties, so as to keep the Russians out of as much of it as possible. Rather, Anglo-American strategy reflected the rational balancing of objectives and resources which any wise statesman will engage in, *if he has the choice.* Stalin, in part as a result of his own bungling diplomacy between 1939 and 1941, was simply unfortunate enough not to have had that choice.

III

Anglo-American military strategy was not without its price, though. The caution Roosevelt and Churchill demonstrated in planning military operations gave the Russians a credible basis

---

[17] Richard M. Leighton, "The American Arsenal Policy in World War II: A Retrospective View," in Daniel R. Beaver, ed., *Some Pathways in Twentieth Century History* (Detroit: 1969), pp. 221–252. See also Robert Huhn Jones, *The Roads to Russia: United States Lend-Lease to the Soviet Union* (Norman, Oklahoma: 1969), pp. 238–239.

[18] W. Averell Harriman and Elie Abel, *Special Envoy to Churchill and Stalin, 1941–1946* (New York: 1975), p. 74.

for claiming that, having borne a disproportionate share of the costs of fighting the war, they should in turn enjoy disproportionate influence in determining the postwar settlement.[19] There is, to be sure, nothing automatic about the proposition that investments in blood necessarily produce equivalent dividends in political influence; if anything, the World War I experience had demonstrated precisely the opposite. Stalin's great fear was that Roosevelt and Churchill might try to repeat Wilson's performance in that earlier conflict—let the major belligerents bleed each other white, then demand, at a decisive moment, the right to shape the peace settlement. But for a variety of reasons, London and Washington failed to take advantage of their strategic flexibility to secure for themselves a decisive role at the peace table. Much to his surprise, Stalin found himself being petitioned to grant concessions to the West, rather than the other way around.[20]

Stalin probably had no precise blueprint for the kind of settlement he wanted, but he did have a set of operating assumptions which had consistently governed his foreign policy. These included the convictions: (1) that the outside world would, for the foreseeable future, remain hostile to the Soviet Union; (2) that, despite this circumstance, the security of the USSR should not be risked to promote world revolution; (3) that such security could best be obtained (a) by taking advantage of conflicts between potential adversaries to keep them divided, and (b) by dominating spheres of influence along Russia's periphery, in order to place as much controlled territory between the Soviet Union and its enemies as possible.[21] These principles had governed Stalin's diplomacy during his abortive period of collaboration with Hitler; given the opportunity, he could be expected to apply them as well in his dealings with his Western allies.

The Soviet leader had sought as early as December 1941 to have the British confirm the territorial gains Russia had made from the Nazi-Soviet Pact—eastern Poland, the Baltic states, and parts of Finland and Rumania. "All we ask for," he told Anthony Eden, "is to restore our country to its former fron-

[19] Frederick C. Barghoorn, *The Soviet Image of the United States* (New York: 1950), p. 51.
[20] Ulam, *Stalin,* pp. 564–565.
[21] This analysis follows Ulam, *Expansion and Coexistence,* pp. 345–348, 360–361.

tiers." Stalin advanced these claims cautiously, however, and when the Americans objected, agreed not to press them, for fear of destroying chances for an early second front.[22] By 1943, however, Soviet military fortunes had decidedly improved, even without a cross-Channel attack. Gradually Stalin let it be known that he would insist, not just on a return to his 1939–1941 frontiers, but on the installation as well of governments "friendly" to the Soviet Union throughout Eastern Europe and the Balkans. The result promised to be an intrusion of Russian power into Europe unprecedented since the days of Alexander I.

Such a development would pose great problems for Britain and the United States, whose policies, both in World Wars I and II, had been based on the proposition that a balance of power on the European continent was crucial to their security. Complicating the issue was the fact that Roosevelt had chosen to justify American entry into the war, not solely in terms of the considerations of power politics which weighed most heavily in his own mind, but in idealistic terms as well. Thus the president, with Churchill, had pledged himself in the Atlantic Charter to oppose "territorial changes that do not accord with the freely expressed wishes of the peoples concerned," and to seek to have "sovereign rights and self government restored to those who have been forcibly deprived of them."[23] Whether on grounds of *realpolitik* or Wilsonian ideals, therefore, the massive expansion of Soviet power in Europe was not a prospect Anglo-American leaders could view with equanimity.

Options for avoiding this prospect, however, were decidedly limited. One would have been to negotiate a separate peace with Germany before the Soviet Union had moved into a position of dominance. Certainly Stalin feared this possibility—his suspicious mind could never completely free itself from the fear that his capitalist allies might make common cause with his capitalist foes.[24] In fact, though, such an arrangement was never seriously considered. Roosevelt and Churchill stuck strictly to

---

[22] *The Reckoning: The Memoirs of Anthony Eden, Earl of Avon* (Boston: 1965), p. 335; Lynn Etheridge Davis, *The Cold War Begins: Soviet-American Conflict over Eastern Europe* (Princeton: 1974), pp. 11–37.

[23] *FR: 1941*, I, 368. For a discussion of Roosevelt's war aims, see John Lewis Gaddis, *The United States and the Origins of the Cold War, 1941–1947* (New York: 1972), pp. 1–31.

[24] Ulam *Expansion and Coexistence*, p. 348.

the view that Hitler was more dangerous than Stalin, and even if they had not, public opinion in neither Britain nor the United States would have tolerated dealings with the Germans. The furor set off by General Dwight Eisenhower's relatively innocent discussions with Admiral Darlan of Vichy France in November 1942, gives some clue to what the reaction would have been had Roosevelt and Churchill tried to deal with the Germans at Soviet expense.[25]

Furthermore, there was always the danger that the Russians might play the same game. Not having public opinion to worry about, Stalin could have carried off such an arrangement far more easily than could his Western colleagues, as indeed his 1939 actions had demonstrated. In an effort to guard against this possibility and to reassure public opinion, Roosevelt and Churchill proclaimed the doctrine of unconditional surrender at Casablanca in January 1943. Despite this, the evidence indicates that Stalin did authorize tentative contacts with the Germans the following summer, a low point in Russian relations with the West because of the delay in creating the second front. It was his own increasingly frequent military successes, not his allies' assurances, which kept him from pursuing these initiatives.[26]

Another way of avoiding the expansion of Soviet power into central Europe would have been to organize military operations in such a way as to interpose British and American forces between the Russians and the Germans. An Anglo-American invasion of the Balkans was the most frequently mentioned possibility, but one which carried with it overwhelming difficulties. Logistical and topographical obstacles were so great there could be no assurance of reaching Germany ahead of the Russians. And, although Stalin from time to time suggested such a plan,[27] it seems unlikely that he would have welcomed large-scale Western military operations in the Balkans, an area he regarded as within his postwar sphere of influence. Such an operation also would have encountered stiff opposition from the Ameri-

---

[25] Ibid., p. 349; Arthur Layton Funk, *The Politics of TORCH* (Lawrence, Kansas: 1974), pp. 249–255.
[26] Vojtech Mastny, "Stalin and the Prospects of a Separate Peace in World War II," *American Historical Review*, LXXVII(December, 1972), 1365–1388.
[27] Harriman and Abel, *Special Envoy*, p. 379.

can military, already impatient with Churchill's "indirect" strategy of attrition, suspicious of him (unjustly, as it turned out) for seeking to substitute in place of the cross-Channel attack operations which would promote British political objectives in the eastern Mediterranean.[28]

Still another way of attempting to ensure Russian postwar cooperation might have been to impose political conditions on the Lend-Lease aid which the United States was sending, in increasing quantities, to the USSR. By the spring of 1943, several of Roosevelt's top advisers were recommending such a course of action.[29] But there were problems with this strategy too. Although aid to Russia did speed military operations against the Germans, the tide of battle on the eastern front had largely been reversed before aid had begun to arrive in quantity. The Russians at no point were so dependent on Lend-Lease that they would have been willing to compromise, in any significant way, their postwar plans.[30] Then, too, even if promises had been made, there was no way of ensuring that the Russians would keep them, as American officials had learned to their dismay during the years following the Roosevelt-Litvinov agreements of 1933.

Other problems as well inhibited direct opposition to Stalin's program. Washington officials attached great importance to securing Soviet participation in the war against Japan, which projections indicated would last at least a year and a half after Germany's defeat and would cost at least as many casualties.[31] Similarly, Moscow's cooperation was deemed essential in the organization of the United Nations, which many Americans expected to be the major instrument for maintaining world order after the war. It is significant that when Ambassador Harriman proposed raising the question of Poland at the Moscow Foreign

---

[28] See, on this point, Richard M. Leighton, "OVERLORD Revisited: An Interpretation of American Strategy in the European War, 1942–1944," *American Historical Review*, LXVIII(July, 1963), 919–937.

[29] Herring, *Aid to Russia*, pp. 80–109.

[30] Ulam, *Expansion and Coexistence*, pp. 330; Herring, *Aid to Russia*, pp. 139–140.

[31] See Ernest R. May, "The United States, the Soviet Union, and the Far Eastern War, 1941–1945," *Pacific Historical Review*, XXIV (May, 1955), 153–174; and Louis Morton, "Soviet Intervention in the War with Japan," *Foreign Affairs*, XL(July, 1962), 653–662.

Ministers' Conference in October 1943, Secretary of State Cordell Hull rejected the idea: "I don't want to deal with these piddling little things," he complained. "We must deal with the main issues."[32] As it turned out, the USSR probably would have entered both the Far Eastern war and the United Nations without inducements from the United States, simply because Stalin considered both moves advantageous to the Soviet Union's position as a great power. The Kremlin autocrat was shrewd enough to appear reluctant, though, thereby further limiting his allies' ability to contest his postwar claims.

This complex of considerations convinced Roosevelt that there was no feasible way to employ Anglo-American strategic flexibility to block Soviet expansion. Instead, he concluded that the only way to achieve both military victory and a favorable postwar settlement would be to try to integrate Stalin's war aims with those of his Western allies. This would not be, Roosevelt thought, an impossible task. Proceeding on the assumption that insecurity, not ideology, drove Stalin's expansionism, the president reasoned that if the Soviet dictator's fears could be relieved, his motives for seeking to project influence beyond his borders would disappear and a settlement agreeable to all might be reached. Roosevelt sought to accomplish this end: (1) by ensuring the total destruction of German and Japanese power; (2) by meeting, where possible, Stalin's legitimate security needs in Europe and the Far East; and (3) by seeking to build an atmosphere of mutual trust between the Soviet leader and his Western allies which would assure him that he had nothing to fear.

Unconditional surrender had been part of that strategy; so too had been the president's insistence, over the objections of the State Department, on the postwar partition of Germany. On Eastern Europe, Roosevelt had at first opposed Stalin's proposed boundary changes, on grounds that they would have violated the spirit of the Atlantic Charter. But by the spring of 1943 he had come to the conclusion that the West lacked the means of denying Stalin the gains he wanted, and that his own efforts should be directed toward arranging the best possible

---

[32] Harriman and Abel, *Special Envoy*, p. 236.

compromise. Accordingly, he worked to restore relations between Moscow and the staunchly anti-Soviet Polish government-in-exile, located in London. He also hoped to convince Stalin to hold plebiscites in the Baltic states in order to make their incorporation into the USSR palatable to American and world opinion.[33] But Roosevelt's chief priority was to arrange a personal meeting with the Soviet dictator, in the expectation that the feeling of trust which had come to characterize the Roosevelt-Churchill relationship could be expanded to include Stalin as well. After several delays, occasioned by the president's unsuccessful attempts to exclude Churchill and by Stalin's reluctance to leave Moscow, the Big Three finally agreed to meet in Teheran at the end of November 1943.

The conference was, to all appearances, a great success. Roosevelt and Churchill made the final commitment to Stalin to launch a second front in the spring of 1944, and the Soviet leader promised in turn to enter the war against Japan three months after Germany's surrender. The president also indicated to Stalin that he would not oppose territorial changes in Eastern Europe, although the Russians must not expect public acknowledgment until after the 1944 election. Roosevelt appealed to Stalin to handle Eastern European issues in such a way as not to offend world opinion and urged upon him, without success, the idea of a plebiscite for the Baltic states. Stalin enthusiastically seconded Roosevelt's advocacy of harsh treatment for Germany, though no final agreements were reached on specifics.[34] Most important, the conference took place in the atmosphere of hearty good-fellowship which Roosevelt considered essential if his goal of integrating Stalin's war aims with those of the Western allies was to be achieved.

---

[33] This analysis of Roosevelt's views follows Gaddis, *The United States and the Origins of the Cold War*, pp. 6–7, 64–65, 100–101, 136–137. See also Davis, *The Cold War Begins*, pp. 76–80.

[34] The record of the Teheran Conference can be traced in *Foreign Relations: The Conferences at Cairo and Tehran, 1943* (Washington: 1961). For the Soviet version of these events, see Robert Beitzell, ed., *Tehran, Yalta, Potsdam: The Soviet Protocols* (Hattiesburg, Mississippi: 1970); and Valentine Berezhkov, "The Teheran Meeting," *New Times*, #48 (November 29, 1967), pp. 16–21, #49 (December 6, 1967), pp. 27–34.

IV

It seems likely that the Big Three left Teheran with differing ideas of what had been accomplished. To Stalin, the fact that his Anglo-American colleagues had not objected to the Eastern European boundary changes he wanted probably suggested that they viewed the Atlantic Charter as window dressing; Roosevelt and Churchill, he believed, had tacitly recognized the Soviet Union's right to have subservient governments along its borders. After all, the British prime minister himself had proclaimed that in the postwar world the big powers must be satisfied, like rich, happy men.[35] Roosevelt, on the other hand, believed that by demonstrating that he had found Stalin's requests reasonable, he had thereby won the Soviet leader's trust. Stalin, he thought, would not presume upon this relationship to press extreme demands. Provided the Poles could be made to see the futility of their anti-Russian position, there was no reason why free elections could not be held throughout Eastern Europe which would, in turn, produce governments friendly to the Soviet Union.

That there was a considerable gap between these perceptions quickly became apparent, most obviously with regard to Poland. While Roosevelt and Churchill had reluctantly accepted Stalin's position on boundaries, they were not prepared to see the independence of what remained of that country compromised. Britain had gone to war in 1939 on Poland's behalf, and, in the United States, a large and vociferous Polish-American community ensured that any East European settlement would be strictly tested against the principles of the Atlantic Charter. Stalin, however, took advantage of the Red Army's entry onto Polish soil to establish the nucleus of a new government, subservient to the Soviet Union, independent of the Polish government-in-exile in London, unrecognized by either the British or the Americans. George Kennan noted the significance of these developments in his diary on August 1: "The jealous and intolerant eye of the Kremlin can distinguish, in the end, only vassals and enemies; and the neighbors of Russia, if

---

[35] *FR: Tehran,* p. 568. See also Ulam, *Expansion and Coexistence,* p. 360; and Vojtech Mastny, "Soviet War Aims at the Moscow and Teheran Conferences of 1943," *Journal of Modern History,* XLVII(September, 1973), 503.

they do not wish to be the one, must reconcile themselves to being the other."[36]

The same day Kennan wrote those lines, the Polish underground organization in Warsaw, knowing that the Red Army was approaching the city and encouraged by Soviet broadcasts to take action, launched an uprising against the Germans. To the horror of Western observers, Stalin refused to order an advance to help the Poles, or to allow British and American planes to land at Soviet airfields after dropping supplies. It is to this day unclear whether Stalin's behavior was based solely on military considerations or was a calculated move to decimate the pro-Western Polish underground.[37] The latter was clearly the effect, however, and from this point many of Roosevelt's advisers came strongly to doubt Soviet willingness to allow anything but satellite governments in Eastern Europe. Kennan himself thought that the time had come to cut off all aid to the Soviet Union until Moscow became more cooperative. Ambassador Harriman was not willing to go that far, but he did warn Washington that "unless we take issue with the present policy there is every indication the Soviet Union will become a world bully wherever their interests are involved."[38]

By this time, problems had developed in other areas as well. Citing the Anglo-American occupation of Italy as a precedent, Stalin refused to allow his allies anything more than a token role in the occupation of Rumania, Bulgaria, and Hungary, into which the Red Army also marched in 1944. Attempts to arrange the exchange of military information for the coming joint effort against Japan produced little fruit, while the Russians insisted on terminating a plan for the shuttle-bombing of Germany, using Ukrainian air bases, after only a few missions. The Russians had, by the fall, expressed reservations about voting procedures in the United Nations; they also persistently refused, despite repeated requests, to distinguish between Lend-Lease aid intended for military purposes and that to be used for post-

---

[36] Kennan, *Memoirs: 1925–1950*, p. 209.

[37] Werth, *Russia at War*, pp. 869–883; Ulam, *Expansion and Coexistence*, pp. 361–363; Seaton, *The Russo-German War*, pp. 453–456.

[38] Kennan, *Memoirs: 1925–1950*, p. 211; Harriman and Abel, *Special Envoy*, p. 344; Bohlen, *Witness to History*, p. 161.

war reconstruction. Wartime collaboration brought no change in the policies of harassment to which Westerners in Moscow had long been subject. And, finally, Roosevelt and his principal military advisers had evidence, by this time, of a sustained effort by Soviet intelligence to penetrate the security of the top-secret Anglo-American project to develop the atomic bomb.[39]

Roosevelt refused, however, to interpret these events as evidence that his policy of winning Stalin's trust had failed. Himself a realist when it come to international affairs, the president saw little surprising or reprehensible in the Soviet leader's desire to have friendly governments in Eastern Europe. He still nursed the hope that, with Germany's defeat and demilitarization, Stalin's demands would become less severe[40] —such sentiments may well have influenced his brief support for the punitive Morgenthau Plan in the fall of 1944. At the same time, though, as a realist in domestic politics, Roosevelt could not allow Stalin a completely free hand. Eastern Europe had the potential of becoming a major campaign issue in the 1944 election; it might also generate sufficient opposition within the Senate to block American participation in the United Nations.[41] Accordingly, the president tried throughout 1944 to keep the issue as quiet as possible, in the hope of achieving some kind of compromise between the legitimate security interests of the USSR and the principles of the Atlantic Charter.

Roosevelt was not wholly without resources in seeking such a compromise. The president rejected his advisers' recommendation that he impose political conditions on future Lend-Lease aid, but he did make clear his intention not to grant postwar credits to the Russians "until we get what we want." In a reversal from his previous support for the Morgenthau Plan, Roosevelt had also come, by the end of 1944, to accept the State Department's argument that United States and Great Britain should retain as much control as possible over the flow of reparations from Germany to the Soviet Union. He had further de-

---

[39] Gaddis, *The United States and the Origins of the Cold War*, pp. 80–91; Herring, *Aid to Russia*, pp. 126–138; Harriman and Abel, *Special Envoy*, pp. 295–300, 308–309, 341–342; Martin J. Sherwin, *A World Destroyed: The Atomic Bomb and the Grand Alliance* (New York: 1975), pp. 102–103.

[40] See, on this point, Robert Murphy, *Diplomat Among Warriors* (Garden City, New York: 1964), p. 227.

[41] Gaddis, *The United States and the Origins of the Cold War*, pp. 139–157.

cided, by this time, not to inform the Russians of the atomic bomb project, even though he knew they were aware, through espionage, of the program's existence.[42] While the president's motives in making these decisions are not entirely clear, there is reason to believe that he may have anticipated the possibility, at some point in the future, of trading reconstruction aid and information about the bomb for political concessions. His chief resource in winning Stalin's cooperation, however, remained his own belief in his ability to "get through" to the Soviet leader in face-to-face negotiations. To this end, he attached great importance to arranging another meeting of the Big Three, which took place at Yalta, in the Crimea, in February 1945.

Like Teheran, Yalta produced surface conviviality and surface agreements. The Big Three agreed that the Lublin Polish government, which Stalin had recognized the month before, would "be reorganized on a broader democratic basis with the inclusion of democratic leaders from Poland itself and from Poles abroad." Elections for a permanent government, Stalin promised, would be held soon, possibly within a month. Roosevelt, Churchill, and Stalin also signed a "Declaration on Liberated Europe," calling for the creation of governments in Eastern Europe "broadly representative of all democratic elements in the population and pledged to the earliest possible establishment through free elections of governments responsible to the will of the people." No final agreements were reached on Germany, other than to accept, "as a basis for negotiations," a Soviet request for reparations in the amount of $10 billion. In the Far East, Roosevelt and Churchill promised Stalin, in return for his agreement to enter the war against Japan after Germany's defeat, the Kurile Islands, lower Sakhalin, leases at Port Arthur and Dairen, control of the Chinese Eastern and South Manchurian railroads, and recognition of the independence from China of Outer Mongolia.[43]

---

[42] Herring, *Aid to Russia,* pp. 169–170; Gaddis, *The United States and the Origins of the Cold War,* pp. 86–88, 126–127; Sherwin, *A World Destroyed,* pp. 108–135; Barton J. Bernstein, "The Quest for Security: American Foreign Policy and International Control of Atomic Energy, 1942–1946," *Journal of American History,* LX(March, 1974), 1003–1010.

[43] The fullest record of the Yalta Conference is *Foreign Relations: The Conferences at Malta and Yalta, 1945* (Washington: 1955). See also Diane Shaver Clemens, *Yalta* (New York: 1970), *passim.*

Contrary to charges made in later years, Roosevelt gave up nothing at Yalta not already under Stalin's actual or potential control. His chief concern was cosmetic: to put the best possible face on a bad situation in order to make palatable to the American people the postwar expansion of Soviet influence. Otherwise, he feared, the gap between the ideals for which the war had been fought and its very realistic outcome would be so great as to render peacetime Soviet-American cooperation impossible. The president relied heavily on Stalin's cooperation in this process: the Soviet leader, he hoped, would be discreet in projecting power beyond his borders, operating behind the facade of democratic procedures wherever possible. Perhaps, in time, Soviet insecurity might decline to the point that illusion might approach reality. Yalta, Roosevelt told the Congress in his final appearance before that body, was not a perfect peace. "But it can be a peace—and it will be a peace—based on the sound and just principles of the Atlantic Charter."[44]

Stalin would not cooperate, however, in conveying even the appearance of action consistent with Western ideals. Within two weeks of signing the Declaration on Liberated Europe, he violated it by forcing a subservient government on Rumania. Tedious negotiations to broaden the Soviet-sponsored government of Poland got nowhere. In March, reports began reaching Washington that the Russians were mistreating American prisoners-of-war liberated from the Germans; that same month, Moscow announced that Foreign Minister Molotov would be too busy to attend the San Francisco Conference on the organization of the United Nations. "Our gallant allies," Ambassador Harriman's daughter noted in a letter from Moscow, "are being most bastard-like." Worst of all, Stalin chose to interpret an abortive Anglo-American effort to arrange the surrender of German forces in Italy as a plot, coordinated with Berlin, to keep the Red Army out of Central Europe. "I cannot avoid a feeling of bitter resentment," Roosevelt fumed, "toward your informers, whoever they are, for such vile misrepresentations of my actions and those of my trusted subordinates."[45]

---

[44] Rosenman, ed., *Roosevelt Public Papers*, XIII, 579.

[45] Roosevelt to Stalin, April 4, 1945, *FR: 1945*, III, 746. See also Harriman and Abel, *Special Envoy*, pp. 419–428.

There are indications that Roosevelt was reassessing his policy toward the Soviet Union at the time of his death. "Averell [Harriman] is right," he told a friend on March 23. "We can't do business with Stalin. He has broken every one of the promises he made at Yalta." Roosevelt remained firm in his refusal to consider a postwar loan until Russian intentions had become clearer, nor did he object when Congress that month prohibited the use of Lend-Lease for reconstruction purposes. Nor did the president alter his policy of withholding information about the atomic bomb. "We must not permit anybody to entertain a false impression that we are afraid," he wrote to Churchill on April 6. "Our armies will in a very few days be in a position that will permit us to become 'tougher' than has heretofore appeared advantageous to the war effort."[46]

None of this means that Roosevelt had abandoned his hope of cooperating with the Russians to build a new postwar order. "I would minimize the general Soviet problem as much as possible," he observed in his last cable to Churchill, "because these problems, in one form or another, seem to arise every day and most of them straighten out."[47] It does seem likely, however, that events since Yalta had convinced Roosevelt of the futility of trying to win Stalin's trust and of the need to place dealings with the Russians henceforth on the strict *quid-pro-quo* basis that Harriman and the other Soviet specialists had been recommending for more than a year.

Critics would charge, in retrospect, that Roosevelt had been naive to the point of irresponsibility by persisting in the belief that he could win Stalin's trust through personal cordiality, political appeasement, and unconditional aid. In fact, however, his approach was more realistic than that. A policy which withheld the second front for two years, tied reconstruction aid to political concessions, and rejected the sharing of atomic bomb information can hardly be regarded as one of timid acquiescence. When Roosevelt did make concessions, it was generally in areas where Anglo-American power could not feasibly be

---

[46] Ibid., p. 444; Herring, *Aid to Russia,* pp. 174–178; Sherwin, *A World Destroyed,* pp. 136–139; Francis J. Loewenheim, Harold D. Langley, and Manfred Jonas, eds., *Roosevelt and Churchill: Their Secret Wartime Correspondence* (New York: 1975), p. 705.

[47] Ibid., p. 709.

brought to bear to deny the Russians what they wanted. The president saw more clearly than most observers that insecurity, not world revolutionary ambitions, drove Soviet expansionism; he was also correct in his perception that only Stalin was in a position to modify the tradition of institutionalized suspicion which separated Russia from the West.

Roosevelt's mistakes, it would appear, were three: (1) He underestimated the depth of Stalin's paranoia—not until after Yalta did he see that the Soviet dictator's distrust of his allies had been just as great as his fear of the Germans. (2) He overestimated the intensity of American isolationism, thus discounting the United States' capacity to project political influence in the postwar world—it is significant that he told Stalin at Yalta that public opinion would not tolerate the retention of American troops overseas for more than two years after the war.[48] (3) He failed, whether because of want of insight or energy, to use his own considerable persuasive powers to prepare the American people for the kind of realistic postwar settlement his own instincts told him would be inevitable. It was Roosevelt's fate to live just long enough to see that these mistakes had been made; devising strategies to correct them would be up to his diligent but ill-informed and inexperienced successor.

V

Harry S. Truman knew very little of the deterioration that had taken place in Soviet-American relations when he came into office because Roosevelt had not kept him informed. He quickly sought recommendations from the late president's advisers, most of whom had long favored a firmer policy than Roosevelt had been prepared to implement. Unsure of himself, yet eager to appear decisive, Truman quickly accepted their advice to "get tough," a course of action consistent with his own favorite method of handling crises. He was not afraid of the Russians, the new president told Harriman; after all, "the Soviet Union needed us more than we needed them." He would not expect to get 100% of what the United States wanted, but "we should be able to get 85 percent." He was going ahead with plans for the

---

[48] *FR: Yalta,* p. 617.

San Francisco conference, and if the Russians disapproved, "they could go to hell."[49]

The president's first opportunity to demonstrate his toughness came on April 23, 1945, when Soviet Foreign Minister Molotov stopped off in Washington on his way to San Francisco (Stalin had reversed his earlier decision and ordered Molotov to attend, as a mark of respect for Roosevelt's memory.) The Soviet diplomat's reception at the White House was not warm, however: Truman lectured him in the manner of a World War I artillery captain shaping unruly troops into line. An agreement had been made at Yalta, the president stated, and all that remained was for Stalin to carry it out. When Molotov tried to explain that the Soviet government was carrying out what it considered to be the correct interpretation of the Yalta agreements, Truman cut him off. The United States wanted cooperation with Russia, he snapped, but not as a one-way proposition. The usually imperturbable Molotov emerged from this experience badly shaken. "I gave it to him straight," Truman later bragged, "one-two to the jaw."[50]

Some historians have seen this as the moment at which the Cold War began.[51] Certainly the new president's truculence upset the Russians, who had grown used to the smooth and slippery platitudes of his predecessor. In fact, however, Truman had no intention of reversing Roosevelt's Russian policy; he had reason to believe he was continuing it. Roosevelt himself had come to see the need for a tougher approach by the time of his death, and the new president's advisers were almost unanimous in urging a firm stand. In his eagerness to appear decisive Truman probably overreacted, as he himself later realized,[52] but he did so in an effort to solidify his own authority, not to wreck chances for postwar accommodation with the USSR.

---

[49] *FR: 1945,* V, 232–233, 253.

[50] Joseph E. Davies Diary, April 30, 1945, Joseph E. Davies Papers, Library of Congress. See also *FR: 1945,* V, 256–258; and Harry S. Truman, *Year of Decisions* (Garden City, New York: 1955), pp. 79–82.

[51] See, for example, Clemens, *Yalta,* pp. 268–274; D. F. Fleming, *The Cold War and Its Origins, 1917–1960* (Garden City, New York: 1961), I, 265–269; Gar Alperovitz, *Atomic Diplomacy: Hiroshima and Potsdam* (New York: 1965), pp. 12–13: Alexander Werth, *Russia: The Postwar Years* (New York: 1971), pp. 56–61, 117–118.

[52] Jonathan Daniels, *Man of Independence* (Philadelphia: 1950), pp. 269–270.

During this period, Truman made other decisions which had the effect of avoiding, rather than encouraging, conflict with the Soviet Union. He agreed to support Roosevelt's Yalta pledge that the Russians could have three seats in the United Nations General Assembly, even though he himself disapproved of this arrangement. He turned down Winston Churchill's proposal that Allied troops in Central Europe remain in the advanced positions they had attained by V-E Day, not withdrawing into previously agreed-upon occupation zones until the Russians had become more cooperative. He made no change in the Far Eastern agreement Roosevelt had concluded with Stalin at Yalta whereby the Russians would receive political concessions in return for entering the war against Japan.[53]

By mid-May 1945, Truman had nonetheless begun to fear that the Russians had misunderstood his intentions. The fate of Poland remained unsolved. The San Francisco Conference seemed to be turning into a forum for the airing of differences instead of their resolution. Shortly after V-E Day, overzealous subordinates ordered ships transporting Lend-Lease supplies to Russia to return to port if the material they carried was not intended for use against Japan. Truman, who had intended a more gradual curtailment of Lend-Lease, immediately countermanded this order, but not before the Russians had complained bitterly. The incident convinced the president of the extreme anti-Soviet hostility that existed among some Washington officials and of the need to make a new effort to settle differences with Moscow.[54]

Truman entrusted this delicate responsibility to Roosevelt's favorite unofficial emissary, Harry Hopkins, who went to Moscow in late May. "I told Harry he could use diplomatic language or he could use a baseball bat if he thought that was the proper approach," Truman wrote.[55] Hopkins' sympathetic attitude toward the Russians was no secret, though; Truman knew very well that his approach would be conciliatory. The Hopkins-Stalin conversations did much to clear the air. They produced a

---

[53] Gaddis, *The United States and the Origins of the Cold War*, pp. 206–215; Lisle A. Rose, *Dubious Victory: The United States and the End of World War II* (Kent, Ohio: 1973), pp. 126–170.

[54] Herring, *Aid to Russia*, pp. 180–211; Margaret Truman, *Harry S. Truman* (New York: 1972), p. 255.

[55] Ibid., p. 252.

compromise on Poland which preserved Soviet influence there but allowed the West to save face; Stalin reiterated his promise to enter the war against Japan and helped resolve a stalemate at San Francisco by accepting the American formula on voting in the United Nations Security Council; and, finally, the Russian leader agreed to meet Truman and Churchill in July at Potsdam, just outside Berlin.[56]

Potsdam was the longest of the wartime summits—two and a half weeks—but it produced the fewest agreements. With Poland's difficulties resolved, however unsatisfactorily from the viewpoint of London and Washington, the German question moved to center stage. The need for joint occupation and demilitarization provoked no disagreement, but there were serious differences over the question of German reparations. The Russians, eager to use German resources for reconstruction, sought the right to extract up to $10 billion in reparations from the country as a whole, regardless of the effect such removals would produce on the German economy. Truman and Churchill strongly opposed this course of action, recalling the effect arbitrary reparations demands had had on Germany in the 1920s, reluctant to have to employ British and American resources to prevent economic collapse there. In the end, the Big Three reached a complicated accord giving each occupying power the authority to take what it wanted from its own zone and promising the Russians such additional deliveries from the industrialized Western zones as were not vital to the German economy. This arrangement placed London and Washington in a position to control the flow of reparations to Russia, but only at the expense of undermining prospects for central administration of the defeated state.[57]

On other issues, little was accomplished. The Big Three agreed to set up a Council of Foreign Ministers to begin work on peace treaties with former Axis satellites. Attempts to secure stronger Soviet compliance with the Yalta Declaration on Liberated Europe failed, though, as the Russians insisted on equating

---

[56] For the Hopkins-Stalin negotiations, see Robert E. Sherwood, *Roosevelt and Hopkins: An Intimate History* (New York: 1948), pp. 887–912.
[57] Bruce Kuklick, *American Policy and the Division of Germany* (Ithaca: 1972), pp. 114–177.

the situation in Eastern Europe with that in Italy and Greece. Stalin did renew his promise to enter the war against Japan and obligingly provided the Americans with news of peace feelers from Tokyo. Other matters, including the disposition of Italian colonies, revision of the Montreux Convention governing access to the Turkish Straits, troop withdrawals from Iran, and an American proposal for the internationalization of strategic waterways, had to be referred to the foreign ministers for further consideration.[58]

One week after the Potsdam Conference ended, on August 6, 1945, the United States dropped the first atomic bomb on Hiroshima. Two days later, on August 8, the Soviet Union declared war against Japan, three months to the day after Germany's defeat, as had been promised. The second bomb followed on August 9, and on August 14 the Japanese government announced its acceptance of Allied surrender terms. Stalin, as startled as anyone by this swift series of events, nonetheless seized the occasion to request participation by Soviet troops in the occupation of Japan. Truman in an equally peremptory manner rejected this claim. "I . . . had not anticipated that such would be your reply," Stalin complained. But Truman's position on Japan, together with another decision, made at the same time, to have American troops occupy southern Korea, simply reflected Washington's acceptance of a proposition Stalin himself had asserted repeatedly in Europe: that "this war is not as in the past; whoever occupies territory also imposes his own social system as far as his army can reach. It cannot be otherwise."[59]

The atomic bomb's effect on the Soviet-American relationship has been the subject of intense speculation and debate. There is no doubt that the bomb's political implications had concerned American officials since the early days of its development: both

---

[58] For the Potsdam Conference, see *Foreign Relations: The Conference of Berlin (The Potsdam Conference), 1945* (Washington: 1960); also Rose, *Dubious Victory*, pp. 270–304; Herbert Feis, *Between War and Peace: The Potsdam Conference* (Princeton: 1960), pp. 155–324; and Charles L. Mee, Jr., *Meeting at Potsdam* (New York: 1975), *passim*.

[59] Milovan Djilas, *Conversations with Stalin* (New York: 1962), p. 114. See also Truman, *Year of Decisions*, pp. 440–443; Herbert Feis, *Contest Over Japan* (New York: 1967), pp. 19–20; and, on Korea, James F. Schnabel, *Policy and Direction: The First Year* (Washington: 1972), pp. 9–10.

the Roosevelt and Truman administrations expected the new weapon to strengthen considerably the American bargaining position in future negotiations with the Soviet Union.[60] But this fact does not justify charges that Truman's motives in using the bomb were as much to intimidate the Russians as to defeat the Japanese.[61] Despite the fact that American cryptographers had long since cracked the Tokyo government's codes, no conclusive evidence existed indicating an immediate willingness on Japan's part to surrender. An invasion of Kyushu, with anticipated casualties of up to 500,000 men, appeared to be the only alternative to use of the bomb. Given conditions of almost total war, given the expenditure of time and resources that had gone into its production, given the prospect of saving thousands of American lives, the decision to use the bomb took on a logic of its own, never entirely separated from considerations of postwar international politics but never dominated by them either.[62]

To the extent that these considerations did play a role, it was with the expectation that a combat demonstration of the new weapon's effectiveness would facilitate, not impair, chances for an amicable resolution of differences with the Soviet Union. The simple fact that the United States possessed the bomb would make possible a firmer American negotiating position, something Truman and his advisers increasingly regarded as necessary if talks with the Russians were to succeed. The bomb would also give the United States a bargaining chip, in the sense that information regarding its production—or a commitment to seek its control by an international agency—might be exchanged for Soviet political concessions. Finally, much in the minds at least of several of the scientists involved in the bomb project was the conviction that only a graphic illustration of what the new weapon could do would shock the world into taking those measures necessary to prevent its future use. As one of them

---

[60] Sherwin, *A World Destroyed, passim.* See also Bernstein, "The Quest for Security," pp. 1003–1015; and Barton J. Bernstein, "Roosevelt, Truman, and the Atomic Bomb, 1941–1945: A Reinterpretation," *Political Science Quarterly,* XC(Spring, 1975), 23–69.

[61] See, for example, Alperovitz, *Atomic Diplomacy, passim.*

[62] Rose, *Dubious Victory,* pp. 305–355; Sherwin, *A World Destroyed,* pp. 198–200; Walter Smith Schoenberger, *Decision of Destiny* (Athens, Ohio: 1969), pp. 285–307.

noted, "Without a military demonstration it may be impossible to impress the world with the need for national sacrifices to gain lasting security."[63]

These hopes never materialized; plans for the international control of atomic energy foundered on the mutual distrust with which Russians and Americans had come, by the end of the war, to regard each other. In time, however, once both sides had perfected nuclear weapons and the means of delivering them, mutual deterrence would come to discourage the use of such devices as efficiently as proposed schemes for their international control might have done. It may be in this respect that the decision to end World War II with atomic weapons has had its most beneficial, if wholly unforeseen, effect: without the awesome demonstrations Hiroshima and Nagasaki provided of the consequences of failure, it is difficult to imagine how the "balance of terror" could have been maintained with the success that it has during the past quarter-century.

VI

The Grand Alliance represented a triumph of interests over ideologies in a moment of shared peril; without its potent combination of Russian manpower and Western technology, it is difficult to see how Hitler's defeat, not to mention that of the Japanese, could have been accomplished in less than four years. At no point during that conflict, though, were politics adjourned, whether in Washington, London, or Moscow: military strategy on each side reflected visions of a postwar settlement not always congruent with what the other side had in mind. As a result, seeds of future conflicts began to grow, even as fruits of victory were being harvested. In whatever particular Hell he inhabited, the Austrian corporal must have enjoyed a fleeting moment of consolation, for the coalition he had inadvertently forged had now, through the act of destroying him, begun to destroy itself.

---

[63] Arthur H. Compton to Henry L. Stimson, June 12, 1945, quoted in Bernstein, "Roosevelt, Truman, and the Atomic Bomb," p. 60n. See also Sherwin, *A World Destroyed*, pp. 200, 212, 218; and Gaddis, *The United States and the Origins of the Cold War*, p. 267.

CHAPTER VII

The Origins of the Cold War: 1945–1953

I T IS, OF COURSE, A TRUISM that coalitions tend not to survive their enemies' defeat. Certainly during World War II most observers of the international scene had expected differences eventually to arise among the victors. The hope had been, though, that a sufficiently strong framework of common interests—whether the United Nations or some mutually acceptable agreement on spheres of influence—would develop which could keep these differences within reasonable limits. This did not happen. While both sides sought security, while neither side wanted a new war, disagreements over how to achieve those goals proved too great to overcome. With a rapidity that dismayed policymakers in both Washington and Moscow, allies shortly before united against the Axis found themselves in a confrontation with each other which would determine the shape of the postwar world. Russian-American relations, once a problem of rarely more than peripheral concern for the two countries involved, now became an object of rapt attention and anxiety for the entire world.

I

It is no simple matter to explain why the concepts of postwar security held by national leaders in the United States and the Soviet Union proved to be so dissimilar. Certainly there existed, in the history of the two countries' encounters with one another, ample basis for mutual distrust. But there were ʔso strong motives for cooperation, not the least of which was that, had they been able to act in concert, Russians and Americans might have achieved something close to absolute security in an insecure world. Their failure to do so may be attributed, ultimately, to irreconcilable differences in four critical areas: perceptions of history, ideology, technology, and personality.

Clearly the divergent historical experiences of the two countries conditioned their respective views of how best to attain security in the postwar era.[1] The Russians tended to think of security in terms of space—not a surprising attitude, considering the frequency with which their country had been invaded, or in view of the way in which they had used distance to defeat their adversaries. That such a concept might be outmoded in an age of atomic weapons and long-range bombers appears not to have occurred to Stalin; Hitler's defeat brought no alteration in his determination to control as much territory along the periphery of the Soviet Union as possible. "He regarded as sure only whatever he held in his fist," the Yugoslav Communist Milovan Djilas has written. "Everything beyond the control of his police was a potential enemy."[2]

Americans, on the other hand, tended to see security in institutional terms: conditioned by their own atypical historical experience, they assumed that if representative governments could be established everywhere, together with a collective security organization capable of resolving differences between them, peace would be assured. That such governments might not always harbor peaceful intentions toward their neighbors, that the United Nations, in the absence of great power agreement, might lack the means of settling disputes, occurred to only a few informed observers. The general public, upon whose support foreign policy ultimately depended, tended to accept Cordell Hull's vision of a postwar era in which "there will no longer be need for spheres of influence, for alliances, for balance of power, or any of the special arrangements through which, in the unhappy past, the nations strove to safeguard their security or to promote their interests."[3]

There was, of course, room for compromising these conflict-

---

[1] See, on this point, Louis J. Halle, *The Cold War as History* (New York: 1967), pp. 10–29.

[2] Djilas, *Conversations with Stalin*, p. 82.

[3] *Congressional Record*, November 18, 1943, p. 9679. See also Michael Donelan, *The Ideas of American Foreign Policy* (London: 1963), p. 36.

ing viewpoints. Neither the United States nor its British ally had been prepared wholly to abandon spheres of influence as a means of achieving their own postwar security; both accepted the premise that the USSR was entitled to have friendly countries along its borders. The great difficulty was that, unlike the expansion of American and British influence into Western Europe and the Mediterranean, the Soviet Union's gains took place without the approval of most of the governments and most of the people of the areas involved. The Anglo-Americans simply did not find it necessary, in the same measure as did the Russians, to ensure their own security by depriving people within their sphere of influence of the right to self-determination. Given Western convictions that only the maximum possible diffusion of democratic institutions could guarantee peace, given Hitler's all-too-vivid precedent, this kind of forcible expansion could not help but appear ominous, whatever its motives. Stalin found himself able to implement his own vision of security only by violating that of the West. The result was to create for the Soviet Union new sources of hostility and, ultimately, insecurity in the world

Ideological differences constituted a second source of antagonism. Stalin had deliberately downplayed the Soviet commitment to communism during the war, even to the point of abolishing the Comintern in 1943. Some Americans concluded that the Russians had abandoned that ideology altogether, if on no other grounds than that a nation which fought Germans so effectively could not be all bad.[4] The European communist movement remained very much the instrument of Soviet policy, however, and the Russians used it to facilitate their projection of influence into Eastern Europe. This development raised fears in the West that Soviet collaboration against the Axis had been nothing but a marriage of convenience and that, victory having been achieved, the Kremlin was now embarking upon a renewed crusade for world revolution.

This was, it now appears, a mistaken view. Stalin had always placed the security of the Soviet state above the interests of international communism; it had been the former, not the latter,

---

[4] Gaddis, *The United States and the Origins of the Cold War*, pp. 32–42.

that had motivated his expansion into Eastern Europe. Far from encouraging communists outside the Soviet Union to seize power, Stalin initially advised restraint, especially in his dealings with such movements in France, Italy, Greece, and China.[5] But the Soviet leader's caution was not all that clear in the West. Faced with the sudden intrusion of Soviet power into Europe, faced with a revival of anticapitalist rhetoric among communists throughout the world,[6] faced with painful evidence from the recent past of what happened when dictators' rhetoric was not taken seriously, observers in both Western Europe and the United States jumped to the conclusion that Stalin, like Hitler, had insatiable ambitions, and would not stop until contained.

Technological differences created a third source of tension. The United States alone emerged from World War II with an industrial plant superior to what it had possessed before that conflict started; the Soviet Union, in turn, had come out of the war with its land ravaged, much of its industry destroyed, and some twenty million of its citizens dead. The resulting disparity of power caused Americans to exaggerate their ability to influence events in the rest of the world; it simultaneously produced in the Russians deep feelings of inferiority and vulnerability.[7]

This problem manifested itself most obviously with regard to Russian reconstruction. Stalin had hoped to rebuild with the help of Lend-Lease and a postwar loan from the United States; his conviction that Americans would soon be facing a postwar depression led him to believe that Washington would have no choice but to provide such aid as a means of generating foreign markets for surplus products. His surprise was great when the United States passed up the economic benefits it would have derived from granting a loan in favor of the political concessions it hoped to obtain by withholding it. Nor would Washington

---

[5] On this point, see Djilas, *Conversations with Stalin,* pp. 27, 74, 132, 182; Ulam, *Expansion and Coexistence,* pp. 457, 486–487; and Roy A. Medvedev, *Let History Judge: The Origins and Consequences of Stalinism* (New York: 1971), pp. 473–474.

[6] John C. Campbell, *The United States in World Affairs, 1947–48* (New York: 1948), pp. 4–7.

[7] Thomas G. Paterson, *Soviet-American Confrontation: Postwar Reconstruction and the Origins of the Cold War* (Baltimore: 1973), pp. 8–14. For a recent Soviet view, see B. Ponomaryov, A. Gromyko, and V. Khvostov, eds., *History of Soviet Foreign Policy, 1945–1970* (Moscow: 1974), pp. 15, 29, 160–161.

allow the use of Lend-Lease for reconstruction; to compound the offense, the Truman administration also cut off, in 1946, the flow of reparations from the American zone in Germany. Whether more generous policies on these matters would have produced better relations with the Soviet Union is impossible to prove—certainly the Russians were never in such need of this aid as to make substantial political concessions. There is no doubt, though, that they bitterly resented their exclusion from these fruits of Western technology.[8]

Another "fruit" of Western technology which impressed the Russians was, of course, the atomic bomb. Although Soviet leaders carefully avoided signs of concern about this new weapon, they did secretly accelerate their own bomb development project while simultaneously calling for the abolition of all such instruments of mass destruction.[9] After much debate within the government, the United States, in the summer of 1946, proposed the Baruch Plan, which would have transferred control of all fissionable materials to the United Nations. In fact, however, neither the Russians nor the Americans had sufficient faith in the world organization to entrust their security completely to it. Washington at no point was willing to surrender its bombs until the control system had gone into effect, while Moscow was unwilling to accept the inspection provisions which would allow the plan to operate. Both sides had concluded by 1947 that they would find greater security in an arms race than in an unproven system of international control.[10]

Finally, accidents of personality made it more difficult than it might otherwise have been to achieve a mutually agreeable settlement. The Russians perceived in the transition from Roosevelt to Truman an abrupt shift from policies of cooperation to those of confrontation. "The policy pursued by the US ruling circles after the death of Franklin D. Roosevelt," a recent Soviet history has noted, "signified a total renunciation of the loyal, mutually beneficial co-operation with the Soviet Union which

---

[8] Paterson, *Soviet-American Confrontation*, pp. 54–56, 260–264.

[9] Nikita S. Khrushchev, *Khrushchev Remembers: The Last Testament* (Boston: 1974), pp. 58–59.

[10] See, on this point, PPS/7, "General United States Policy With Respect to International Control of Atomic Energy," August 21, 1947, *FR: 1947*, I, 607.

had been so fruitful during the Second World War."[11] In fact, though, Roosevelt's policy had been firmer than Stalin realized; Truman's on the other hand, was not as uncompromising as his rhetoric suggested. What was different was style: where Roosevelt had sought to woo Stalin by meeting his demands wherever possible, Truman, like a good poker player, tried to deal from positions of rhetorical, if not actual, strength. The new chief executive's tough talk was designed to facilitate, not impede negotiations—any appearance of weakness, he thought, would only encourage the Russians to ask for more.

What Truman failed to take into account, however, was the possibility that Stalin also might be bluffing. Given the history of Western intervention to crush Bolshevism, given the Soviet Union's economic and strategic inferiority, it seems likely that the aging Soviet dictator was as frightened of the West as the West was of him. Truman's tough rhetoric, together with Hiroshima's example of what the atomic bomb could do, may well have reinforced Stalin's conviction that if *he* showed any signs of weakness, all would be lost. Both leaders had learned too well the lesson of the 1930's: that appeasement never pays. Prospects for an amicable resolution of differences suffered accordingly.

There was nothing in this set of circumstances to make conflict inevitable—few things ever are inevitable in history. But a situation such as existed in Europe in 1945, with two superpowers separated only by a power vacuum, seems almost predestined to produce hostility, whether either side willed it or not. As a result, the United States, the Soviet Union, and much of the rest of the world as well would have to suffer through that prolonged period of insecurity which observers at the time, and historians since, have called the "Cold War."

II

The evolution of United States policy toward the Soviet Union between 1945 and 1947 can be seen as a three-stage process of relating national interests to national capabilities. From V-J Day

---

[11] Ponomaryov, *et al.*, eds., *History of Soviet Foreign Policy, 1945–1970*, p. 32. See also Nikita S. Khrushchev, *Khrushchev Remembers* (Boston: 1970), p. 232.

through early 1946, there existed genuine confusion in Washington as to both Soviet intentions and appropriate methods for dealing with them. Coordination between power and policy was, as a result, minimal. By early 1946, a consensus had developed favoring resistance to further Soviet expansion, but little effort had been made to determine what resources would be necessary to accomplish that goal or to differentiate between areas of primary and secondary concern. It was not until the spring of 1947 that there began to emerge an approach to the Soviet Union which bore some reasonable relationship to American capabilities for projecting influence in the world.

There appeared to be no lack of power available to Washington for the purpose of ordering the postwar world as it saw fit, but the task of transforming technological superiority into political influence proved frustratingly difficult. Secretary of State James F. Byrnes had hoped to trade reconstruction assistance and a commitment to the international control of atomic energy for Soviet concessions on such outstanding issues as implementation of the Yalta Declaration on Liberated Europe, peace treaties with former German satellites, and, ultimately, a final resolution of the German question itself. But the Russians maintained a posture of ostentatious unconcern about the atomic bomb, nor would they yield on significant issues to obtain reconstruction assistance. Congressional skepticism regarding Russian intentions ensured that any loan to the Soviet Union would carry a political price far beyond what the Russians would willingly pay, while liberal opinion pushed Truman into a premature decision to seek United Nations control of atomic energy before Byrnes had made any attempt to extract concessions from the Russians in return. Economic and strategic superiority thus won the United States surprisingly few practical benefits in its early postwar dealings with the USSR. [12]

There still existed in Washington, moreover, a substantial number of officaials who viewed Soviet hostility as the product of misunderstandings and who expected that, with restraint on both sides, a mutually satisfactory resolution of differences

---

[12] Gaddis, *The United States and the Origins of the Cold War*, pp. 244–276; Lisle A. Rose, *After Yalta: America and the Origins of the Cold War* (New York: 1973), pp. 113–146.

might still occur. It is significant that as late as November 1945, a State Department representative could rebuke the Joint Chiefs of Staff for confidentially suggesting that the wartime alliance might not survive victory. "We must always bear in mind," a Department memorandum noted the following month, "that because of the differences between the economic and political systems [of the United States and the Soviet Union], the conduct of our relations requires more patience and diligence than with other countries." President Truman, despite his tough rhetoric, shared this view. Differences with the Russians were to be expected once the common bond of military necessity had been removed, he told advisers; in time, these differences would disappear, because "Stalin was a fine man who wanted to do the right thing."[13]

But events made this position increasingly difficult to sustain. The Russians remained adamant in their determination to exclude Western influence from Eastern Europe and the Balkans, while continued Soviet presence in Iran and Manchuria raised fears that Moscow might try to impose control over those territories as well. Russian interest in the eastern Mediterranean seemed to be growing, with demands for trusteeships over former Italian colonies, boundary rectifications at Turkey's expense, and a revision of the Montreux Convention governing passage through the Dardanelles. And in February 1946, news of Soviet atomic espionage became public for the first time with the revelation that the Canadian government had arrested a group of Russian agents for trying to steal information about the bomb. That same month, Stalin in his first major postwar foreign policy speech stressed the incompatibility between communism and capitalism, implying that future wars were inevitable until the world economic system was restructured along Soviet lines.[14]

It was at this point that there arrived at the State Department a dispatch from George F. Kennan, now *chargé d'affaires* at the

---

[13] *FR: 1946*, I, 1126–1127, 1139; Thomas M. Campbell and George C. Herring, eds., *The Diaries of Edward R. Stettinius, Jr., 1943–1946* (New York: 1975), p. 437; John Morton Blum, ed., *The Price of Vision: The Diary of Henry A. Wallace, 1942–1946* (Boston: 1973), p. 490.

[14] *Vital Speeches*, XII(March 1, 1946), 300–304. See also Gaddis, *The United States and the Origins of the Cold War*, pp. 299–302.

American embassy in Moscow, which did much to clarify official thinking regarding Soviet behavior. Russian hostility toward the West, Kennan argued, stemmed chiefly from the internal necessities of the Stalinist regime: the Soviet dictator required a hostile outside world in order to justify his own autocratic rule. Marxism provided leaders of the Soviet Union with

> justification for their instinctive fear of the outside world, for the dictatorship without which they did not know how to rule, for cruelties they did not dare not to inflict, for sacrifices they felt bound to demand. . . . Today they cannot dispense with it. It is the fig leaf of their moral and intellectual respectability.

It followed that Stalin was, by nature, incapable of being reassured. "Nothing short of complete disarmament, delivery of our air and naval forces to Russia and resigning of the powers of government to American Communists would even dent this problem," Kennan noted in a subsequent dispatch, "and even then Moscow would smell a trap and would continue to harbor the most baleful misgivings." The solution, Kennan suggested, was to strengthen Western institutions in order to render them invulnerable to the Soviet challenge while simultaneously awaiting the eventual mellowing of the Soviet regime.[15]

There was little in Kennan's analysis which he and other career Soviet experts had not been saying for some time. What was new was Washington's receptivity to the message, a condition brought about both by frustration over Soviet behavior and by growing public and Congressional resistance to further concessions. In contrast to its earlier optimism about relations with Moscow, the State Department now endorsed Kennan's analysis as "the most probable explanation of present Soviet policies and attitudes." The United States, it concluded, should demonstrate to the Kremlin "in the first instance by diplomatic means and in the last analysis by military force if necessary that the present course of its foreign policy can only lead to disaster for the Soviet Union."[16]

The spring and summer of 1946 did see a noticeable toughen-

---

[15] Kennan to Byrnes, February 22 and March 20, 1946, *FR: 1946*, VI, 696–709, 721–723. See also Kennan, *Memoirs: 1925–1950*, pp. 292–295.

[16] H. Freeman Matthews to the State-War-Navy Coordinating Committee, April 1, 1946, *FR: 1946*, I, 1167–1169.

ing of United States policy toward the Soviet Union. In early March, Truman lent public sanction to Winston Churchill's strongly anti-Soviet "iron curtain" speech by appearing on the platform with him at Fulton, Missouri. That same month Secretary of State Byrnes insisted on placing the issue of Iran before the United Nations, even after the Russians had agreed to withdraw their troops from that country. The termination of German reparations shipments came in May; three months later, Byrnes publicly committed the United States to support German rehabilitation, with or without Russian help. In July, Truman endorsed the continued presence of American troops in southern Korea on the grounds that that country constituted "an ideological battleground upon which our whole success in Asia may depend." Soviet pressure on Turkey for bases produced a decision in August to maintain an American naval presence indefinitely in the eastern Mediterranean. In September, White House aide Clark Clifford submitted a report to the president, prepared after consultation with top military and diplomatic advisers, arguing that "this government should be prepared . . . to resist vigorously and successfully any efforts of the U.S.S.R. to expand into areas vital to American security."[17]

But these policies were decided upon without precise assessments of whether the means existed to carry them out. The atomic bomb was of little use for such purposes, given the strong inhibitions American officials felt about brandishing their new weapon in peacetime, given the limited number of bombs, and properly equipped bombers, available if war came.[18] Nor could the administration hold out the prospect of economic aid as a means of inducing more cooperative Russian behavior, in the face of continued Congressional reluctance to appropriate funds for such purposes.[19] Such conventional military power as the United States possessed was rapidly melting away under

---

[17] Truman to Edwin Pauley, July 16, 1946, *FR: 1946*, VIII, 713; Clifford report, "American Relations with the Soviet Union," September, 1946, printed in Arthur Krock, *Memoirs: Sixty Years on the Firing Line* (New York: 1968), p. 477. See also Gary R. Hess, "The Iranian Crisis of 1945–46 and the Cold War," *Political Science Quarterly*, LXXXIX(March, 1974), 117–146.

[18] See, on this point, George H. Quester, *Nuclear Diplomacy: The First Twenty-Five Years* (New York: 1973), pp. 1–9.

[19] Paterson, *Soviet-American Confrontation*, pp. 51–54.

the pressures of demobilization, and while most Americans supported firmer policies toward the Soviet Union, the election of an economy-minded, Republican-controlled Congress in November suggested that few were prepared to assume the burdens, in the form of high taxes and military manpower levels, such policies would require.

Shortly thereafter a severe economic crisis, the product of remaining wartime dislocations and an unusually harsh winter, hit Western Europe. This development caused the British to announce their intention, in February 1947, of terminating economic and military aid to Greece and Turkey, countries which had, up to that point, been regarded as within London's sphere of responsibility. It also raised the longer-range but even more frightening prospect that economic conditions in Western Europe generally might deteriorate to the point that communist parties there could seize power through coups or even free elections. Suddenly the whole European balance of power, which the United States had gone to war to restore, seemed once again in peril.

This situation, which appeared so to threaten European stability, was one the Russians had done little if anything to instigate; it was rather the product primarily of internal conditions within the countries involved. But there could be small doubt of Moscow's ability to exploit the European economic crisis if nothing was done to alleviate it. And action was taken, with such energy and dispatch that the fifteen weeks between late February and early June 1947, have come to be regarded as a great moment in the history of American diplomacy, as a rare instance in which "the government of the United States operat[ed] at its very finest, efficiently and effectively."[20]

Such encomiums may be too generous. Certainly the language Truman used to justify aid to Greece and Turkey ("at the present moment in world history nearly every nation must choose between alternative ways of life. . . . I believe that it must be the policy of the United States to support free peoples who are resisting attempted subjugation by armed minorities or

---

[20] Joseph M. Jones, *The Fifteen Weeks (February 21–June 5, 1947)* (New York: 1955), p. vii.

by outside pressures")[21] represented a projection of rhetoric far beyond either the administration's intentions or capabilities.[22] Whatever its usefulness in prying funds out of a parsimonious Congress, the sweeping phraseology of the "Truman Doctrine" would cause problems later on as the president and his foreign policy advisers sought to clarify distinctions between vital and peripheral interests in the world. That such distinctions were basic to United States policy became apparent with the announcement, in June 1947, of the Marshall Plan, an ambitious initiative which reflected, far more than did the Truman Doctrine, the careful calibration of ends to means characteristic of the administration's policy during this period.

The European Recovery Program, to use its official title, proposed spending some $17 billion for economic assistance to the non-communist nations of Europe over the next four years. (Aid was offered to the Soviet Union and its East European satellites as well, but with the expectation, which proved to be correct, that it would be turned down.) It was a plan directed, not against Soviet military attack, a contingency United States officials considered remote, but against the economic malaise which had sapped self-confidence among European allies, rendering them vulnerable to internal communist takeovers. It involved no direct military commitments; rather its architects assumed, much as had advocates of the "arsenal of democracy" concept before World War II, that the United States could most efficiently help restore the balance of power in Europe by contributing its technology, not its manpower. It represented a deliberate decision to focus American energies on the recovery of Europe at the expense of commitments elsewhere: it is significant that the spring of 1947 also saw the Truman administration move toward liquidating its remaining responsibilities in China and Korea.[23] What took place in Washington during the famous

---

[21] *Public Papers of the Presidents: Harry S. Truman, 1947* (Washington: 1963), pp. 178–179.

[22] See, on this point, John Lewis Gaddis, "Was the Truman Doctrine a Real Turning Point?" *Foreign Affairs*, LII(January, 1974), 390–393.

[23] See Tang Tsou, *America's Failure in China, 1941–50* (Chicago: 1963), pp. 443–446; Robert W. Patterson to Dean Acheson, April 4, 1947, *FR: 1947*, VI, 626; JCS 1769/1, "United States Assistance to Other Countries from the Standpoint of National Security," April 29, 1947, ibid., I, 737–738.

"fifteen weeks," then, was not so much a proliferation of commitments as a reordering of priorities, executed with a sharp awareness of what the United States would have to accept in the world and what, given limited resources, it could realistically expect to alter.

Unfortunately, rhetoric again obscured the point, this time by way of a mysterious article, entitled "The Sources of Soviet Conduct," which appeared in the July 1947 issue of *Foreign Affairs*. Attributed only to a "Mr. X," it advanced the notion that

the main element of any United States policy toward the Soviet Union must be that of a long-term, patient but firm and vigilant containment of Russian expansive tendencies. . . . Soviet pressure against the free institutions of the Western world is something that can be contained by the adroit and vigilant application of counter-force at a series of constantly shifting geographical and political points, corresponding to the shifts and maneuvers of Soviet policy.[24]

Then, as now, nothing remained secret for very long, and word soon leaked out that "Mr. X" had been none other than Kennan, who had recently become head of the State Department's new Policy Planning Staff. This information imparted to the "X" article the character of an official document, and it quickly came to be viewed as the definitive expression of administration policy toward the Soviet Union.

In fact, Kennan had not intended his article as a comprehensive prescription for future action; it was, rather, an elaboration of the analysis of Soviet behavior he had submitted in his February 1946 telegram to the State Department. Such policy recommendations as Kennan did include reflected only in the most approximate and incomplete way the range of his thinking on Soviet-American relations. The article implied an automatic commitment to resist Russian expansion wherever it occurred; there was in it little sense of the administration's preoccupation with limited means and of the consequent need to distinguish between primary and secondary interests. Nor did the piece make it clear that economic rather than military methods were to be employed as the chief instrument of containment.[25] The

---

[24] "X", "The Sources of Soviet Conduct," *Foreign Affairs*, XXV (July, 1947), 575–576.
[25] For Kennan's own critique of the "X" article, and an account of the circumstances surrounding its publication, see his *Memoirs: 1925–1950*, pp. 354–367.

safest generalization that can be made about the "X" article is
that, like the Truman Doctrine, it was an outstanding demonstration of the obfuscatory potential of imprecise prose. It was
not an accurate description of the policies the United States was,
at that moment, in the process of implementing.

Kennan provided a much clearer explanation of what he
meant by "containment" in a secret review of the world situation prepared for Secretary of State George C. Marshall in
November 1947. Soviet efforts to fill power vacuums left by
German and Japanese defeats had largely been halted, Kennan
argued, but this accomplishment had dangerously strained
American resources: "The program of aid to Europe which we
are now proposing to undertake will probably be the last major
effort of this nature which our people could, or should,
make. . . . It is clearly unwise for us to continue the attempt to
carry alone, or largely singlehanded, the opposition to Soviet
expansion." Further dispersal of resources could be avoided
only by identifying clearly those parts of the world upon whose
defense American security depended. Aside from the Western
Hemisphere, Kennan's list included only non-communist
Europe, the Middle East, and Japan. In China there was little the
West could do, although there were as well "definite limitations
on both the military and economic capabilities of the Russians in
that area." Since Korea was "not of decisive strategic importance to us, our main task is to extricate ourselves without too
great a loss of prestige." All in all, Kennan concluded, "our best
answer is to strengthen in every way local forces of resistance,
and persuade others to bear a greater part of the burden of
opposing communism."[26]

"Containment," then, involved no indiscriminate projection
of commitments around the world; it was, instead, a policy precise in its identification of American interests, specific in its assessment of threats to those interests, frugal in its calculation of
means required to ward off those threats, vague only in its public presentation. But this very vagueness would, in time, corrupt
the concept, for where gaps between policy and rhetoric exist, it
is often easier to bring the former into line with the latter than

---

[26] PPS/13, "Resumé of World Situation," November 6, 1947, *FR: 1947*, I, 770–777.

the other way around. The result would be the eventual prom-
ulgation of policies under the rubric of "containment" far removed from what that doctrine had been originally intended to
mean.

III

Despite its limited character, the vigor of the American response to Soviet postwar probes apparently caught Stalin by
surprise. His response was to try to strengthen further the security of his own regime, first by increasing safeguards against
Western influences inside the Soviet Union; second, by tighten-
ing control over Russia's East European satellites; and finally by
working to increase central direction of the international communist movement. By a perverse kind of logic, each of these
moves backfired, producing consequences which made more
difficult of attainment the security Stalin sought.

Soviet leaders had always faced a dilemma regarding contacts
with the West. Such associations might carry substantial
benefits—certainly this had been true of collaboration with
Great Britain and the United States during World War II. But
there were also costs, not the least of which was the possibility
that prolonged exposure to Western ideas and institutions
might erode the still vulnerable base of the Soviet regime. It is
an indication of the seriousness with which Stalin viewed this
problem that he shipped hundreds of thousands of returning
prisoners-of-war off to labor camps in 1945, much to the horror
of Americans who had forcibly repatriated many of them.[27] By
1947, Moscow's campaign against Western influences had extended to literature, music, history, economics, and even gene-
tics. As a result, Soviet prestige suffered throughout the world;
the effect of these policies on science, and, in turn, on the ad-

---

[27] The classic account is Alexander Solzhenitsyn, *The Gulag Archipelago* (New
York: 1973), especially pp. 237–276; but also see Russell D. Buhite, "Soviet-
American Relations and the Repatriation of Prisoners of War, 1945," *The His-
torian*, XXXV(May, 1973), 394–397; and Mark Elliott, "The United States and
Forced Repatriation of Soviet Citizens, 1944–47," *Political Science Quarterly*,
LXXXVIII(June, 1973), 253–275.

vancement of Russian military capabilities, can only be guessed at.[28]

Even more striking in its impact on the West, though, was Stalin's harsh effort to consolidate his control over Eastern Europe. Subservience to Moscow, not ideological uniformity, had been the chief Soviet priority in that area until 1947, but in June of that year the Russians imposed a communist-dominated government in Hungary, a country in which relatively free elections had been held in the fall of 1945. "I think it's an outrage," President Truman told a press conference on June 5. "The Hungarian situation is a terrible one." In February 1948, the Communist Party of Czechoslovakia overthrew the duly-constituted government of that country—an event which produced the death, either by murder or suicide, of the popular Czech foreign minister, Jan Masaryk. It would be difficult to exaggerate the impact of this development in the West, where there still existed guilty consciences over what had been done to the Czechs at Munich ten years before. One immediate effect was to ensure Congressional passage of the Marshall Plan; another was to provoke Britain, France, and the Benelux countries into forming the Western Union, the first step toward a joint defensive alliance among the non-communist nations of Europe. Yet another was the stimulation of something approaching a war scare in the United States, an administration request for Universal Military Training and the reinstitution of Selective Service, and a public condemnation by Truman of the Soviet Union as the "one nation [which] has not only refused to cooperate in the establishment of a just and honorable peace, but—even worse—has actively sought to prevent it."[29]

Meanwhile, attempts to resolve the question of divided Germany had produced no results, despite protracted and tedious negotiations. In February 1948 the three Western occupying powers, plus the Benelux countries, met in London and decided

---

[28] Ulam, *Stalin*, pp. 643–652; Barghoorn, *The Soviet Image of the United States*, pp. 103–124; Marshall D. Shulman, *Stalin's Foreign Policy Reappraised* (Cambridge, Massachusetts: 1963), pp. 57–58.

[29] Truman press conference, June 5, 1947, *Truman Public Papers, 1947*, p. 265; Truman address to Congress, March 17, 1948, *Public Papers of the Presidents: Harry S. Truman, 1948* (Washington: 1964), p. 183. For the impact of the Czech crisis, see Herbert Feis, *From Trust to Terror: The Onset of the Cold War, 1945–1950* (New York: 1970), pp. 291–305.

to move toward formation of an independent West German state. Stalin's response, after intitial hesitation, was to impose a blockade on land access to Berlin, which the World War II settlement had left a hundred miles inside the Soviet zone. The Berlin crisis brought the United States and the Soviet Union as close to war as they would come during the early postwar years. Truman was determined that Western forces would stay in the beleaguered city, however untenable their military position there, and to reinforce this policy he ostentatiously transferred to British bases three squadrons of B-29 bombers, apparently capable of carrying atomic weapons.[30] Fortunately, however, the Russians did not interfere with air access rights, and through this means the United States and its allies were able to keep West Berlin supplied for almost a year. By May of 1949, the Russians had agreed to lift the blockade, but not before they had approached a distinction they had won in the Russo-Finnish War a decade earlier—of simultaneously projecting the appearance of brutality and incompetence.

The Berlin blockade had two important effects, both of which were detrimental from the Soviet point of view. It provided the impetus neccessary to transform the Western Union into the North Atlantic Treaty Organization, a defensive alliance linking the United States, Canada, and ten West European nations, established in April 1949. Simultaneously, the blockade lessened prospects for a settlement of the German problem in collaboration with the Russians; the result was to accelerate implementation of the London program, a goal accomplished with the formation, in September 1949, of the Federal Republic of Germany.

Stalin's efforts to tighten control over the international communist movement also produced unintended consequences. As part of his reaction to the Marshall Plan, the Soviet leader, in September 1947, authorized the revival of a central directorate for the communist movement, this time to be known as the Cominform. It is doubtful that Stalin had anything more in mind by this action than to make international communism a more reliable instrument of Soviet foreign policy, but the effect in the West was to confirm lurking suspicions that world revolution had, all along, been his major goal. As Elbridge Durbrow,

---

[30] Quester, *Nuclear Diplomacy*, pp. 49–52.

the American *chargé d'affaires* in Moscow put it, the move was "patently a declaration of political and economic war against the U.S. and everything the U.S. stands for in world affairs."[31]

Establishment of the Cominform substantially weakened the position of communist parties in Western Europe, whose success, up to that point, had been based largely on their ability to demonstrate some degree of independence from Moscow's control. Even worse, from the Soviet point of view, the effort to enforce ideological uniformity provoked an open split with Tito's Yugoslavia, heretofore the Kremlin's most reliable satellite. In Washington, the State Department's Policy Planning Staff immediately saw the importance of this development:

For the first time in history we may now have within the international community a communist state . . . independent of Moscow. . . . A new factor of fundamental and profound significance has been introduced into the world communist movement by the demonstration that the Kremlin can be successfully defied by one of its own minions.[32]

Winning support from within the government and from Congress for a policy of actually aiding a communist regime took time, but by 1949 the United States was supporting Tito's position in the United Nations and providing economic assistance. After the outbreak of the Korean War, military aid would follow as well.[33] Stalin's effort to enforce monolithic unity had the ironic effect of producing the first crack in the monolith—an error of which the United States was quick to take advantage.

Through his policies, Stalin had thus brought about many of the things he most feared: an American commitment to defend Western Europe; a revived West German state, closely tied to his adversaries; the beginnings of fragmentation within the international communist movement. It was a sobering demonstration of the consequences which can follow from a chronic inability to anticipate the impact of one's own actions; it also

---

[31] Durbrow to Marshall, October 6, 1947, *FR: 1947*, IV, 596. For Stalin's motives in creating the Cominform, see Ulam, *Expansion and Coexistence*, pp. 449–450; and Vladimir Dedijer, *The Battle Stalin Lost: Memoirs of Yugoslavia, 1948–1953* (New York: 1971), pp. 118–119.

[32] PPS/35, "The Attitude of This Government Toward Events In Yugoslavia," June 30, 1948, *FR: 1948*, IV, 1079–1080.

[33] John C. Campbell, *Tito's Separate Road: American and Yugoslavia in World Politics* (New York: 1967), pp. 10–27.

provides evidence for the view that one of the West's major, if unsuspected, assets during the early days of the Cold War was the persistent ineptitude of the Soviet dictator himself.[34]

IV

By 1949, containment had largely achieved its primary objective—restoration of a balance of power in Europe. A sense of self-confidence had begun to reappear; simultaneously fears of further Soviet expansion, whether by military attack or internal subversion, had begun to subside. In tacit acknowledgment that its previous policies had failed, the Soviet Union in the spring of that year launched a massive "peace campaign," the precursor, as it turned out, of the shift from the doctrine of "inevitable conflict" between communism and capitalism to that of "peaceful coexistence."[35] But success in international relations is an elusive, sometimes undetectable quality, and the Truman administration in 1949 felt anything but buoyant. Perversely, containment's very achievements raised problems of such magnitude as to prevent Washington from taking advantage of that policy's successes.

Kennan himself had never believed that the United States should remain content simply with limiting Soviet expansion in Europe and the Far East. His concept of containment, as worked out in the Policy Planning Staff during 1947 and 1948, had two additional goals, to be sought once the original objective of geographically restricting Soviet power had been achieved: (1) to encourage a split between the Soviet Union and its chief instrument for projecting influence beyond its borders, the international communist movement; and (2) to negotiate a mutual withdrawal of Soviet and American forces from the advanced positions they had occupied since the end of World War II.

The idea of exploiting differences between the Soviet Union and international communism had been based on the assumption that the Russians would not indefinitely be able to control that movement, partly because of their own inability to tolerate

---

[34] On this point, see Townsend Hoopes, *The Devil and John Foster Dulles* (Boston: 1973), p. 285.

[35] Shulman, *Stalin's Foreign Policy Reappraised*, pp. 81–103.

diversity, and partly because the very act of coming to power in foreign countries would tend to make communist leaders less dependent on Moscow. Kennan and his associates on the Policy Planning Staff saw Soviet expansionism as a new form of colonialism, subject to all the frailties, vulnerabilities, and self-destructive tendencies of that earlier phenomenon. "Conditions are therefore favorable," a staff paper noted in August 1948,

to a concentrated effort on our part designed to take advantage of Soviet mistakes and of the rifts that have appeared, and to promote the steady deterioration of the structure of moral influence by which the authority of the Kremlin has been carried to peoples far beyond the reach of Soviet police power.[36]

In time, it was thought, two opposing blocs might develop in the communist world—one dominated by the Soviet Union, the other made up of communists defiant of Moscow's leadership. As a report to the National Security Council observed in 1949, "a situation of this description might eventually provide us with an opportunity to operate on the basis of a balance in the communist world, and to foster the tendencies toward accommodation with the West implicit in such a state of affairs."[37]

Efforts were made, between 1947 and 1949, to implement this strategy. The offer of Marshall Plan aid to the Soviet Union and Eastern Europe in 1947 had been made in the hope that a Soviet rejection would reveal the nakedness of Moscow's control and place strains on its relations with its satellites.[38] In February 1948, Kennan recommended tying United States military operations in the eastern Mediterranean to the level of communist activity in Italy and Greece. If the Russians came to realize that increased communist militancy would bring about an increased American military presence in the area, then "a conflict would be produced in the Kremlin councils between the interests of the Third Internationale, on the one hand, and those of the sheer

---

[36] PPS/38, "United States Objectives With Respect to Russia," August 18, 1948, pp. 390–391, Policy Planning Staff Files, Department of State. See also NSC 58, "United States Policy Toward the Soviet Satellite States in Eastern Europe," September 14, 1949, pp. 9–10, National Security Council Files, Division of Modern Military Records, National Archives.

[37] Ibid., p. 15.

[38] PPS/38, August 18, 1948, p. 386. See also Kennan, *Memoirs: 1925–1950*, p. 342.

military security of the Soviet Union, on the other."[39] The Policy Planning Staff moved rapidly to exploit Tito's split with Moscow in the summer of 1948, and saw that event as a precedent for what might happen elsewhere: "The possibility of defection from Moscow, which has heretofore been unthinkable for foreign communist leaders, will from now on be present in one form or another in the mind of every one of them."[40]

Unfortunately, the administration made few attempts to explain the distinction between Soviet expansionism and international communism to the American people. In part, this failure reflected the belief of many in Washington that only the prospect of an undifferentiated global threat could shake Americans out of the isolationist tendencies which remained latent among them. "The only way we can sell the public on our new policy," one official had written at the time of the Truman Doctrine speech, "is by emphasizing the necessity of holding the line: communism vs. democracy should be the major theme."[41] In part, lack of clarity on this issue reflected genuine confusion on the part of many in Washington as to whether ideology motivated, or was the instrument of, Kremlin policy: Kennan's analyses themselves had not been entirely clear on that point.[42] In part, it reflected also domestic political expediency: in a period characterized by an unrelenting, sometimes hysterical, search for subversive elements at home, it was no easy task to justify the necessity of distinguishing between varieties of communism overseas.

The result was to institutionalize, in American thinking about the communist world, what one political scientist has called "casual ascription"—the tendency to picture "all Communist moves, with whatever party or state they originate, as manifestations of . . . Soviet strategy."[43] This phenomenon had its most obvious effect on United States policy in the Far East,

---

[39] PPS/23, "Review of Current Trends: U.S. Foreign Policy," February 24, 1948, *FR: 1948*, I, 519.

[40] PPS/35, June 30, 1948, p. 1080.

[41] Jones, *The Fifteen Weeks*, p. 151.

[42] See, on this point, Charles Gati, "What Containment Meant," *Foreign Policy*, #7(Summer, 1972), p. 25.

[43] William Welch, *American Images of Soviet Foreign Policy* (New Haven: 1970), p. 83.

where, by the end of 1949, efforts to leave the way open for possible dealings with Mao Tse-tung's new communist government in China had generated strong opposition in Congress; after the onset of the Korean War, such approaches would become almost impossible.[44] "Casual ascription" produced perceptions of unity among adversaries where it either did not exist or would not last; the consequence was an unnecessary proliferation of enemies in the world, an outcome very different from what the original concept of containment had intended.

Kennan had also repeatedly stressed the importance of eventually negotiating a settlement of differences with Moscow in both Europe and the Far East. Neither the Russians nor the Americans could indefinitely man World War II truce lines, he believed; United States interests would best be served by encouraging the emergence of independent centers of power in the world, particularly in Germany and Japan. To be achieved peacefully, such an objective required the voluntary contraction of Soviet power; this, in turn, necessitated an American willingness to talk with the Russians and, ultimately, arrange for mutual troop withdrawals.[45]

American officals at this time, however, tended to view such negotiations as involving almost unacceptable risks. Hence, when on Kennan's recommendation word was passed to Moscow in April 1948 that the United States stood prepared "for full discussion and composing of our difficulties," the Russians were able to torpedo the initiative by simply making public the fact that it had taken place. Six months later, during the final days of the 1948 presidential campaign, Secretary of State Marshall publicly vetoed a hastily contrived scheme put together by

---

[44] See, on this point, PPS/39, "United States Policy Toward China," September 7, 1948, *FR: 1948*, VIII, 147–149; NSC 48/1, "The Position of the United States with Respect to Asia," December 23, 1949, U.S. Department of Defense, *U. S. – Vietnam Relations, 1945–1967* (Washington: 1971), VIII, 225–264; Acheson's National Press Club speech, January 12, 1950, *Department of State Bulletin*, XXII(January 23, 1950), 111–118; and his executive session testimony before the Senate Foreign Relations Committee, U.S. Congress, Senate, Committee on Foreign Relations, *Reviews of the World Situation, 1949–1950* (Washington: 1974), pp. 272–277.

[45] PPS/23, February 24, 1948, p. 522; PPS/37, "Policy Questions Concerning a Possible German Settlement," August 12, 1948, *FR: 1948*, II, 1287–1297. See also Kennan, *Memoirs: 1925–1950*, p. 365.

Truman's political advisers to send Chief Justice Fred Vinson to Moscow for talks with the Russians.[46] Behind both of these responses was the fear that anything approaching substantive discussions would undermine the morale of American allies, convey to Moscow an impression of weakness, and raise in the minds of the general public images of another "Yalta," a symbol of appeasement now almost as potent as "Munich."[47]

As a result, no real effort was made to determine what possibilities existed for a joint reduction of forces of the kind Kennan had recommended. Instead, the energies of American diplomats went into building up such anti-Russian bastions as NATO, an independent West Germany, and, by 1951, a postoccupation Japan closely linked to the United States by security treaty. Kennan had definite reservations about the wisdom of these moves: "There is no logical stopping point in the development of a system of anti-Russian alliances," he wrote in late 1948, "until that system has circled the globe and has embraced all the non-communist countries of Europe, Asia, and Africa."[48] But in the absence of any concrete assurances that negotiations would bear fruit, in the presence of the understandable tendency within the administration to prefer safety over risk, Kennan's recommendations no longer carried the weight they once had.

The announcement, in September 1949, that the Russians had exploded their first atomic bomb further set back prospects for negotiations by producing in the West fears of military inferiority. The United States and its allies had never equaled the Russians in terms of conventional manpower, but Washington's monopoly over the atomic bomb, it had been thought, would deter Moscow from taking advantage of its numerical superiority. News of the Soviet atomic test led to arguments that the American deterrent would have to be bolstered if it was to remain effective; these considerations produced the decision,

---

[46] Ibid., pp. 346–347; Robert A. Divine, *Foreign Policy and U.S. Presidential Elections: 1940–1948* (New York: 1974), pp. 254–260.

[47] John C. Campbell, *The United States in World Affairs: 1948–49* (New York: 1949), p. 28; Coral Bell, *Negotiation From Strength: A Study in the Politics of Power* (New York: 1963), pp. 15–16.

[48] PPS/43, "Considerations Affecting the Conclusion of a North Atlantic Security Pact," November 24, 1948, *FR: 1948*, III, 286.

early in 1950, to construct a hydrogen bomb. They also contributed to a growing conviction in Western capitals that until the United States could regain its nuclear superiority over the Russians, Washington and its NATO allies would have to try to counterbalance, for the first time, Soviet conventional force levels in Europe.[49] Restoration of confidence—the original goal of containment—would in time require not only economic aid but also military assistance, the long-term stationing of United States forces in Europe, and, eventually, the rearmament of West Germany.

"The issues that face us are momentous, involving the fulfillment or destruction not only of this Republic but of civilization itself." So ran the introduction to NSC-68, a comprehensive review of American policy toward the Soviet Union conducted by the National Security Council early in 1950. There was much in this important document which paralleled Kennan's thinking: it associated American interests in the world with diversity, not uniformity; it viewed Soviet expansionism as stemming more from internal insecurities than from ideological compulsions; it recommended dealing with that threat "by developing the moral and material strength of the free world [so] that the Soviet regime will become convinced of the falsity of its assumptions and that the pre-conditions for workable agreements can be created."[50]

But Kennan had based his prescriptions for action on the assumption that, while the Russians were fully capable of starting a war, they would not in fact do so, except by miscalculation. Such judgments, based on what Kennan admitted was "the unfirm substance of the imponderables,"[51] were not enough to satisfy those in Washington responsible for national security policy, especially after the Soviet Union's demonstration of an atomic capability. These analysts, among them Secretary of State Dean Acheson, argued that the only safe way to proceed

---

[49] Quester, *Nuclear Diplomacy*, pp. 59–63.

[50] NSC 68, "United States Objectives and Programs for National Security," April 14, 1950, *Naval War College Review*, XXVII(May-June, 1975), 55, 57, 60–61. See also Paul Y. Hammond, "NSC-68: Prologue to Rearmament," in Warner R. Schilling, Paul Y. Hammond, and Glenn H. Snyder, *Strategy, Politics, and Defense Budgets* (New York: 1962), pp. 267–378.

[51] Kennan diary note, July 12, 1950, Kennan, *Memoirs: 1925–1950*, p. 499.

was to base United States planning, not on what the Russians were likely to do, but on what they *could* do—on Soviet capabilities rather than Soviet intentions. Viewed in this light, the drafters of NSC-68 calculated that the Russians had the *immediate* capability

a. To overrun Western Europe, with the possible exception of the Iberian and Scandinavian Peninsulas; to drive toward the oil-bearing areas of the Near and Middle East; and to consolidate Communist gains in the Far East;

b. To launch air attacks against the British Isles and air and sea attacks against the lines of communications of the Western Powers in the Atlantic and the Pacific;

c. To attack selected targets with atomic weapons, now including the likelihood of such attacks against targets in Alaska, Canada, and the United States.[52]

"No need to ask *why* [the adversary] should be moved to take certain hostile actions, or whether he would be likely to take them," Kennan noted years afterward, in describing the kind of thinking that went into NSC-68; "that he has the capability of taking them suffices."[53]

Measured against that standard, NSC-68 found the military position of the United States dangerously inadequate, leaving Washington officials in many situations with "no better choice than to capitulate or precipitate a global war." The solution, the document argued, was "a build-up of military strength by the United States and its allies to the point at which the combined strength will be superior . . . to the forces that can be brought to bear by the Soviet Union and its satellites." Such a program would require a significant increase in expenditures: "Budgetary considerations will need to be subordinated to the stark fact that our very independence as a nation may be a stake." It would mean postponing negotiations with the Russians until the build-up had been completed: "The present world situation . . . is one which militates against successful negotiations with the Kremlin—for the terms of agreement . . . would reflect present realities and would therefore be unacceptable, if not disas-

---

[52] NSC 68, April 14, 1950, p. 65.
[53] George F. Kennan, "The United States and the Soviet Union, 1917–1976," *Foreign Affairs*, LIV(July, 1976), 682.

trous." It would require recognition "by this Government, the American people, and all free peoples, that the cold war is in fact a real war in which the survival of the free world is at stake."[54]

"Containment" had thus evolved, in the course of three years, from the assumption that international stability required only the limited application of economic power in a few key areas to the conviction that such equilibrium depended upon willingness to wield military force wherever Western interests were threatened. "The assault on free institutions is world-wide now," NSC-68 had argued. "In the . . . present polarization of power a defeat of free institutions anywhere is a defeat everywhere."[55] It was a proposition to be tested sooner than anyone had expected—in the mountains and rice paddies of Korea.

V

There is, to this day, no entirely adequate explanation of why North Korean forces crossed the 38th parallel on June 25, 1950. Circumstantial evidence indicates that Stalin had given general authorization for an invasion sometime that summer but that the Pyongyang government "jumped the gun," catching the Russians off guard and thus unable to veto United Nations participation in the defense of South Korea (the Russians had walked out of the Security Council some months earlier as a protest against that body's failure to seat Communist China.)[56] Whatever the facts surrounding its origins, Stalin probably did not regard his Korean gambit as a departure from his usual policy of avoiding direct confrontations with the West. It seems, rather, to have been intended as a "probe by proxy" in an area the United States had publicly declared not vital to its security, designed perhaps to recoup lost prestige resulting from the Berlin blockade's failure; perhaps to strengthen the Soviet position against Mao Tse-tung, of whom Stalin was already suspicious;

---

[54] NSC 68, April 14, 1950, pp. 80, 98–100, 107–108.
[55] Ibid., p. 56.
[56] See, on this point, Robert R. Simmons, *The Strained Alliance: Peking, Pyongyang, Moscow and the Politics of the Korean Civil War* (New York: 1975), pp. 102–136.

perhaps also to compound the security problems of Japan, a country in which American troops appeared likely to remain stationed for the indefinite future.

To the Russians' astonishment, Truman quickly ordered United States troops to defend South Korea. The reasons for this decision are not hard to grasp, even in the light of the administration's relative inaction in China between 1947 and 1949 and Secretary of State Acheson's explicit exclusion of Korea from the American "defensive perimeter" some months earlier.[57] The attack across the 38th parallel was far more blatant than anything that had happened in China; it resembled nothing so much as the Japanese invasion of Manchuria in 1931, an uncomfortable precedent with obvious implications. It also represented a direct challenge to the authority of the United Nations, a consideration whose importance to Truman would be difficult to overrate. NSC-68 had only recently sensitized administration officials to the dangers of "piecemeal aggression"—to the prospect of "gradual withdrawal under the direct or indirect pressure of the Soviet Union, until we discover one day that we have sacrificed positions of vital interest."[58] Finally, Korea was one of the few places in the world where the United States could respond quickly, thanks to the presence in and around Japan of the Eighth Army and the Seventh Fleet. As General J. Lawton Collins later noted, "Nowhere else abroad did we have such forces of all arms immediately available for employment."[59]

"The attack on Korea makes it plain beyond all doubt," Truman told the nation on June 27, "that communism has passed beyond the use of subversion to conquer independent nations and will now use armed invasion and war."[60] This widely shared but inaccurate impression, foreshadowed in NSC-68, led to three important developments: (1) It brought about the approval and implementation of that document, with the result that the fiscal 1951 defense budget shot up from an original

[57] Acheson National Press Club speech, January 12, 1950, p. 116. See also Gaddis Smith, *Dean Acheson* (New York: 1972), pp. 175–176.

[58] NSC 68, April 14, 1950, pp. 80, 93.

[59] J. Lawton Collins, *War in Peacetime: The History and Lessons of Korea* (Boston: 1969), p. 4.

[60] *Public Papers of the Presidents: Harry S. Truman, 1950* (Washington: 1965), p. 492.

request for $13.5 billion to a final authorization of $48.2 billion.[61] (2) It transformed NATO from a traditional mutual defense alliance into a integrated military structure, involving the appointment of an American supreme commander and the stationing of United States troops in Europe.[62] (3) Finally, by speeding decisions to rearm West Germany and to sign, with or without Soviet participation, a peace treaty with Japan, it accelerated the process by which former enemies became future allies. Stalin's Korean adventure thus demonstrated once again his uncanny ability, through his own actions, to rally his adversaries against himself.

That the Truman administration was capable of similar accomplishments becomes clear when one considers the consequences of its decisions, made within hours of the North Korean attack, to neutralize the Taiwan Strait and to step up aid to French forces in Indochina. These two actions had been directed more against the Russians than the Chinese Communists: concern over Taiwan reflected fears of what might happen if Mao should grant the Russians air and naval bases there,[63] while support of counterinsurgency efforts in Indochina had been decided upon, even before Korea, as a means of facilitating a more substantial French contribution to NATO.[64] The new Peking government could regard neither move with equanimity, however; its resulting suspicion of Washington's motives goes far toward explaining Mao's decision to intervene in the Korean War following MacArthur's crossing of the 38th parallel in the fall of 1950. Hopes for driving a wedge between Moscow and Peking never totally disappeared in Washington—as late as May 1951, a National Security Council paper could still list this as a

---

[61] NSC 68/2, "United States Objectives and Programs for National Security," September 30, 1950, National Security Council Files, Modern Military Records Division, National Archives; Hammond, "NSC-68," p. 351.

[62] Bohlen, *Witness to History*, pp. 303–304; Robert E. Osgood, *NATO: The Entangling Alliance* (Chicago: 1962), pp. 68–74.

[63] See, on this point, General Douglas MacArthur to the Joint Chiefs of Staff, June 14, 1950, and Major General Charles L. Bolté to Secretary of the Army Frank Pace, June 28, 1950, both in the *Declassified Documents Reference System* (Arlington, Virginia: 1975), 75: 28E and 64D. See also Schnabel, *Policy and Direction*, pp. 50–51.

[64] Smith, *Acheson*, pp. 313–316.

major objective of United States Far Eastern policy.[65] But most officials, and probably most Americans, would have agreed with President Truman when he told British Prime Minister Clement Attlee in December 1950 that the Chinese "are satellites of Russia and will be satellites as long as the present Peiping regime is in power. . . . The Russians cannot dominate them forever, but that is a long-range view and does not help us just now."[66]

There is, thus, both irony and justification in the argument that the United States, far from exploiting latent Sino-Soviet antagonism, may have inadvertently moderated it.[67] Admittedly, it was difficult for Washington officials at that time to know the exact nature of the Moscow-Peking relationship; outward appearances, at least, did project an impression of unity. But the original strategy of containment had based itself on the assumption that, in the end, national differences would prove more decisive than ideological similarities in shaping relations between Russia and China. It was an acute and farsighted judgment, amply borne out by subsequent events.

That it did not become the basis for American policy during the Korean War may be attributed to the triumph of short-term military considerations over long-term political ones, to the administration's conviction that generalization in the public identification of threats more often produced popular and Congressional support than did precision, and to the peculiar American tendency, destined to manifest itself time and time again in the future, to rely excessively on ideology as an instrument with which to predict the behavior of adversaries. As a consequence, the United States fell into the paradoxical error of treating international communism as a monolith at almost exactly the moment that it ceased to be one.

By May of 1951, Stalin apparently was ready to accept what had become a military stalemate in Korea. Informal soundings

---

[65] NSC 48/5, "United States Objectives, Policies and Courses of Action in Asia," May 17, 1951, *U.S. - Vietnam Relations,* VIII, 428, 431.

[66] Minutes, Truman-Attlee meeting of December 4, 1950, *Declassified Documents Reference System,* 75: 29E.

[67] See, on this point, Franz Schurmann, *The Logic of World Power* (New York: 1974), pp. 242–243.

produced indications that the Russians would be willing to arrange armistice negotiations with the North Koreans and the Chinese Communists,[68] and in July of that year, these talks got underway. They would take no less than two years to complete, during which time the fighting in Korea continued unabated. It did so, however, with some assurance on the part of the major powers involved that the conflict would be kept limited—that the small war many had thought might be the prelude to World War III would not, in fact, become so.

Nonetheless, the Korean War had exposed a fundamental contradiction in the original concept of containment. That strategy had sought to achieve its objective by means ultimately psychological in nature: the restoration of self-confidence in areas threatened by Soviet expansionism. It had also stressed the need, though, to distinguish carefully between those interests which were vital and those which were not; only in this way, it was thought, could limited resources be applied with maximum effectiveness. What Korea showed was that interests once considered peripheral could become vital if attacked, that victories for communism in peripheral areas could undermine self-confidence in vital ones, unless resisted. The need to choose between the competing claims of credibility and economy, to avoid the twin dangers of inaction on the one hand and dispersal of resources on the other, would constitute a central dilemma for American policymakers for years to come.

VI

On December 21, 1951, President Truman announced the nomination of George F. Kennan to be the next United States ambassador to the Soviet Union. Kennan's appointment sailed through the Senate with no difficulty—he was, after all, the country's most prominent Soviet expert, a man whose experience with the USSR stretched back beyond the establishment of diplomatic relations in 1933, a man who, more than any other single individual, had shaped the strategy of containment. It was, Kennan recalled in his *Memoirs*, "a task for which my

---

[68] George F. Kennan, *Memoirs: 1950–1963* (Boston: 1972), pp. 35–38.

whole career had prepared me, if it had prepared me for any-thing at all."[69]

Unfortunately for Kennan, however, Soviet-American ten-sions had moved beyond the point at which diplomacy could play any meaningful role. Kennan found himself wholly with-out instructions from either the White House or the State De-partment; upon inquiry, he discovered that the administration's priorities lay more in the direction of solidifying alignments against the Russians than in negotiating differences with them. "So far as I could see, we were expecting to be able to gain our objectives . . . without making any concessions whatsoever to the views and interests of our adversaries." It was a position justifiable, Kennan thought, only "if we were really all-powerful, and could hope to get away with it. I very much doubted that this was the case."[70]

Upon proceeding to Moscow, Kennan found the atmosphere there even more stifling and confining than on previous tours of duty. The American embassy had come to resemble a prison, with floodlit walls and fences on all sides, patrolled by armed guards. Plainclothes police guards followed Kennan every-where, discouraging contacts with Soviet citizens. The embassy, as always, was bugged; the servants even more surly and un-friendly than before:

Looking out the window, I could see the Soviet citizens piously cros-sing the street to avoid walking in the dangerous proximity of our fence. I could hear, night after night, the testing of jet engines some-where off across the Moscow River. Sometimes I would wander around the building without turning the lights on, go down into the great, dimly lit white ballroom and play the grand piano, or, having no one with whom to speak Russian, establish myself in one of the gilded chairs of the several living rooms and read Russian aloud to myself just to indulge my love of the language. . . . So I wandered securely in my gilded prison, comforting myself with the reflection that if this venera-ble building, with its unhappy history, had a ghost, the ghost was unquestionably I.

Diplomatic contacts with Soviet officials were confined to una-voidable formalities; the new ambassador was not invited, and

---

[69] Ibid., p. 106.
[70] Ibid., pp. 107–110.

never tried, to see Stalin. Soviet propaganda was full of charges about American preparations for future war; charges that Kennan, out of sympathy with much of the administration's policy, could not wholly dismiss: "I began to ask myself whether . . . we had not contributed, and were not continuing to contribute—by the overmilitarization of our policies and statements—to a belief in Moscow that it was war we were after."[71]

While passing through Germany, in September 1952, Kennan, in answer to a press conference question, compared the conditions of diplomats in Moscow to those he had encountered while interned in Berlin during the first months of World War II. Bristling at this implied analogy with Hitler's regime, the Soviet government declared Kennan *persona non grata* and refused to allow him to reenter the country. It was, Kennan acknowledged in retrospect, "an extremely foolish thing for me to have said."[72] Yet his statement was neither untrue nor unprecedented: his frustrations had been felt by American diplomats in Russia for more than a century. The problem was not so much Kennan's qualifications as a diplomat (although he would later judge himself severely on that score) as it was the general invulnerability of Soviet-American hostility to the usages of traditional diplomacy. As such, Kennan's abortive ambassadorship may stand as a fitting symbol of what the Cold War had become.

CHAPTER VIII

From Confrontation to Confrontation: 1953–1962

"T HE GOVERNMENT OF THE UNITED STATES tenders its official condolences to the Government of the U.S.S.R.
on the death of Generalissimo Joseph Stalin, Prime Minister of
the Soviet Union." Such, in its entirety, was the Eisenhower
administration's public response to the passing of the Soviet
autocrat on March 5, 1953. The White House had, the day before, taken the occasion to express sympathy for the Russian
people "regardless of the identity of government personalities";
significantly, however, even this innocuous pronouncement
raised doubts among some presidential advisers, notably Secretary of State John Foster Dulles, who thought it might be read
as an invitation to revolution.[1]. These cautious statements having been placed on the record, the new administration turned its
attention to the problems of dealing with the Soviet Union in a
post-Stalin era. Rhetoric to the contrary notwithstanding, it
brought to this task attitudes more conducive to continuity than
to change.

I

Diplomacy and politics are never completely separate from
one another, of course, but the quadrennial process of running
for president in the United States does seem to generate, with
unusual frequency, public commitments on foreign policy

---

[1] *Public Papers of the Presidents: Dwight D. Eisenhower, 1953* (Washington: 1960),
pp. 75, 91. See also Dwight D. Eisenhower, *The White House Years: Mandate for
Change, 1953–1956* (Garden City, New York: 1963), pp. 143–144.

which tend to restrict candidates' options once in office.[2]. The campaign of 1952 was no exception. Dwight D. Eisenhower, faced not so much with the problem of winning the election as with securing the Republican Party's nomination, felt obliged to assure conservatives in that party that he would change the policy of containment which the Truman administration had pursued in its dealings with the Soviet Union during the previous five years. Eisenhower did not keep that promise; his policies in the end confirmed more than they repudiated those of his predecessor. But political necessity impelled the president and his secretary of state to minimize this fact as much as possible, a circumstance which in turn limited their flexibility in responding to the shifts in Soviet foreign policy that followed Stalin's death.

Critics of containment had made four basic charges against it: (1) that it risked dispersing scarce resources by relying too heavily on American manpower and not enough on American technology; (2) that it accepted too willingly the status quo, thereby condemning millions behind the iron curtain to permanent "enslavement"; (3) that it concentrated too heavily on resisting Soviet expansionism in Europe, when the balance of power could as easily be upset in Asia as well; and (4) that it had been administered, in part, by individuals sympathetic, or possibly even subservient, to the interests of the Soviet Union.[3] Not all opponents of containment endorsed all of these charges; not all of the charges themselves were consistent. But they did all arise, in one form or another, during the 1952 campaign; the new administration accordingly found it difficult to ignore them.

Fears that containment would lead to a dispersal of resources were nothing new. Kennan's original strategy had assumed only limited means and had insisted, as a consequence, on a rigid differentiation between peripheral and vital interests. Korea had demonstrated, though, how a country of what appeared to be marginal importance to American security interests could become vital once attacked. The Truman administration's

---

[2] See, on this point, Robert A. Divine, *Foreign Policy and U.S. Presidential Elections: 1952–1960* (New York: 1974), p. ix.

[3] Norman A. Graebner, *The New Isolationism* (New York: 1956), pp. 18–30; James T. Patterson, *Mr. Republican: A Biography of Robert A. Taft* (Boston: 1972), pp. 476–496.

response had been to improvise the concept of limited war —conventional military operations tightly controlled both in geographical scope and levels of violence. But how such operations could be sustained over protracted periods of time, given their costs, given growing public impatience, given the need simultaneously to protect other more vital areas, was a problem the Truman administration had not resolved at the time it left office.

The Eisenhower administration's answer was what came to be known as the "New Look," a strategy first proposed by Dulles during the 1952 campaign. Containment, Dulles argued, had left decisions as to the time, place, and method of aggression up to the enemy; the United States had been saddled, as a result, with the impossible task of organizing resistance on all fronts. What was needed instead was a determination on the part of the West "to retaliate, instantly, by means and at places of our own choosing." By allowing the United States and its allies to select their own weapons and the appropriate circumstances for emloying them, Dulles' strategy would produce "maximum protection at bearable cost."[4]

There was both more, and less, to this "New Look" strategy than met the eye. Certainly it did imply a greater reliance than in the past on air power, and this, in turn, suggested an increased willingness to use nuclear weapons. But what critics quickly dubbed the doctrine of "massive retaliation" did not mean automatic escalation to nuclear war in every crisis; rather, the idea was to create uncertainty in the minds of potential adversaries in hopes of deterring them from taking aggressive action.[5] Nor did the strategy exclude employing local forces of resistance when appropriate, an important nuance Dulles' public explanations left unclear.[6] Nor was the "New Look" as dramatic a departure

---

[4] Speech to the Council on Foreign Relations, January 12, 1954, *Department of State Bulletin,* XXX(January 25, 1954), 107–110. See also John Foster Dulles, "A Policy of Boldness," *Life,* XXXII(May 19, 1952), 146–160.

[5] Glenn H. Snyder, "The 'New Look' of 1953," in Schilling, Hammond and Snyder, *Strategy, Politics and Defense Budgets,* pp. 463–470; Hoopes, *Dulles,* pp. 273–274; Alexander L. George and Richard Smoke, *Deterrence in American Foreign Policy: Theory and Practice* (New York: 1974), pp. 246–247.

[6] Seyom Brown, *The Faces of Power: Constancy and Change in United States Foreign Policy from Truman to Johnson* (New York: 1968), pp. 74–75.

as it seemed from the Truman administration's strategic concepts: seared by the experience of Korea, Truman and his advisers had already decided not to allow "privileged sanctuaries" should war break out again in Asia and to rely on air and naval power to accomplish American objectives there.[7] What was new about the "New Look" was its public announcement—a maneuver Dulles performed in a more bellicose manner than was necessary, the rigidity with which it tied defense policy to budgetary considerations, and, most important, its attempt to achieve security through a deliberate effort to blur, rather than clarify, distinctions between primary and secondary interests.

"Liberation" was not a new concept either. As early as December 1949, President Truman had approved a National Security Council paper calling for efforts "to foster a heretical drifting-away process on the part of the [East European] satellite states." This document had stressed the need to avoid provoking Soviet retaliation, however, and had cautioned against taking actions beyond United States capabilities to support.[8] Privately, Dulles had no quarrel with this approach; his view, like Kennan's, was that the West could do little other than to wait for fissures within the Soviet Union's sphere of influence to manifest themselves.[9] But Dulles went out of his way in public to emphasize the difference between the Truman administration's "purely defensive policy" and his own more active "liberation policy" for Eastern Europe. The Republican platform of 1952 went even further, condemning "the negative, futile and immoral policy of 'containment' which abandons countless human beings to . . . despotism and Godless terrorism," and calling for the repudiation of "all commitments contained in secret un-

[7] See NSC 118/2, "United States Objectives and Courses of Action in Korea," December 20, 1951, National Security Council Files, Modern Military Records Division, National Archives; and NSC 124/2, "United States Objectives and Courses of Action with Respect to Southeast Asia," June 25, 1952, *U.S. - Vietnam Relations*, VIII, 531–534.

[8] NSC 58/2, "United States Policy Toward the Soviet Satellite States in Eastern Europe," December 8, 1949, National Security Council Files, Modern Military Records Division, National Archives.

[9] Hoopes, *Dulles*, pp. 127–133; Michael A. Guhin, *John Foster Dulles: A Statesman and His Times* (New York: 1972), pp. 170–180.

derstandings such as those of Yalta which aid Communist enslavements."[10]

Events soon made it clear, however, that "liberation" had been aimed more toward freeing the government in Washington from Democratic control than toward contesting Soviet influence in Eastern Europe. A challenge to Moscow's authority there did arise in June 1953, when riots broke out in East Germany, but the Eisenhower administration had no plans for exploiting such a situation and was reduced, in the end, to the role of a passive spectator as the Russians crushed the revolt. Nor did Eisenhower honor campaign pledges to repudiate the Yalta agreements, fearing that any such unilateral disavowal might call into question United States rights in the occupied cities of Berlin and Vienna.[11] Even more than had been the case on matters of strategic doctrine, then, the new administration's policies regarding Eastern Europe constituted a tacit endorsement, rather than a rejection, of the principles of containment.

Another charge made against Truman's foreign policy had been that it concentrated too heavily on Europe, neglecting events in Asia. It is true that the original containment concept had seen Europe as the most vital area of concern for United States foreign policy, but Japan had also rated high on Washington's list of priorities, and the Korean War had focused attention on much of the rest of Asia as well. By the time Truman left office, the United States had security treaties with Japan, the Philippines, Australia and New Zealand, and had begun providing military and economic aid to the French in Indochina as well. The major difference between the Truman and Eisenhower administrations as far as the Far East was concerned was the latter's willingness to associate itself openly with Chinese Nationalist aspirations to reconquer the mainland, a move that Truman and Acheson had carefully avoided. Here, once again, domestic politics came into play: by promising early in 1953 to "unleash" Chiang Kai-shek, Eisenhower and Dulles sought to placate the right wing of the Republican Party, which had been vociferous in its support of the Nationalists since

---

[10] Arthur M. Schlesinger, Jr., ed., *History of American Presidential Elections, 1789–1968* (New York: 1971), IV, 3284.

[11] Eisenhower, *Mandate for Change,* p. 211.

China's "fall" to communism in 1949. The price of "releashing" Chiang during the delicate Quemoy-Matsu crisis a year and a half later was an explicit American commitment to defend Taiwan if attacked.[12]

Finally, containment had become a target for attacks by Senator Joseph R. McCarthy and his followers, on the grounds that it had been formulated and implemented by officials disloyal to to the United States. Again, this was not a new charge: the Truman administration had, since 1947, maintained its own loyalty program designed to screen out security risks, at times on a less than discriminating basis.[13] The program had not prevented Republicans from making "communism in government" a major campaign issue in 1952, however, and, as a consequence, Senator McCarthy gained an indirect veto over almost all State Department appointments during the first year of the Eisenhower administration. This situation produced the resignation, either forcibly or voluntarily, of a number of career Foreign Service officers associated with the doctrine of containment, including Kennan himself.[14] The administration did insist, to its credit, on supporting Charles E. Bohlen's nomination as ambassador to the Soviet Union in 1953, but the fact that an appointee of such unquestionable qualifications could not be confirmed without a major Senate fight illustrates the extent to which indiscriminate anticommunism had come, by that time, to affect the conduct of American foreign policy.[15]

The Truman and Eisenhower versions of containment, then, differed more in matters of nuance and emphasis than in substance. Such variations as did occur stemmed, not from foreign policy considerations at all, but from what Eisenhower and Dulles perceived to be the requirements of domestic politics. What seems odd about this in retrospect is not that a political party

---

[12] George and Smoke, *Deterrence in American Foreign Policy*, pp. 269–272; Foster Rhea Dulles, *American Foreign Policy Toward Communist China, 1949–1969* (New York: 1972), pp. 150–156.

[13] Alan D. Harper, *The Politics of Loyalty: The White House and the Communist Issue, 1946–1952* (Westport, Connecticut: 1969), pp. 232–254; Richard M. Fried, *Men Against McCarthy* (New York: 1976), pp. 23–29.

[14] Kennan, *Memoirs: 1950–1963*, pp. 168–189; E. J. Kahn, Jr., *The China Hands* (New York: 1975), pp. 246–263.

[15] Bohlen, *Witness to History*, pp. 309–336.

should make extravagant promises in the heat of a campaign, but that an administration with such a strong base of popular support as Eisenhower's should have felt called upon to try, however briefly, to implement its pledges in so literal a manner. The effect was to discourage any significant reexamination of American policy toward the Soviet Union at a time when innovative thinking was badly needed.

II

Soviet policy did, of course, change dramatically after Stalin's death. The new collective leadership of the USSR seemed to welcome, rather than discourage, friendly ties with the West; it also partially dismantled Stalin's secret police apparatus, emphasized the production of consumer goods, relaxed controls over Eastern Europe, and advanced cautious but increasingly frequent denunciations of the "cult of personality." It renewed, as well, an intriguing offer Stalin himself had made in 1952: to consider the establishment of a reunified, partially rearmed, but neutral Germany.[16] The problem, for Washington officals, was to determine whether the congenial appearance which Malenkov, Khrushchev, and their associates presented to the world did, in fact, represent a fundamental shift in the Soviet concept of international relations, or was merely another in a long series of tactical modifications designed to further the ultimate aim of world revolution.

John Foster Dulles had, at an earlier stage of his career, acknowledged the possibility that Soviet ideology might change in the face of new circumstances, but he also believed deeply that Western unity depended upon the existence of a credible external threat.[17] For this reason, Dulles viewed the new Kremlin regime with extreme wariness, fearing that any lessening of Cold War tensions might induce dangerous complacency both inside the United States and among its allies. Domestic political considerations reinforced this conviction. To a degree not yet

---

[16] On this point, see James L. Richardson, *Germany and the Atlantic Alliance* (Cambridge, Massachusetts: 1966), pp. 25–27; and Ronald Bitzer, "Soviet Policy on German Reunification in 1952," *World Affairs*, CXXXII(1969), 245–255.

[17] Guhin, *Dulles*, pp. 136–138, 143–149. See also John Foster Dulles, *War, Peace, and Change* (New York: 1939), p. 90.

adequately recognized, the new secretary of state was a strong partisan, prone to frame foreign policy as much in terms of what looked good at home as to what effect it would produce on the international scene.[18] Having campaigned on a platform of vigorous resistance to an implacable foe, he found himself unprepared when confronted instead by an apparently reasonable and humane rival, eager for negotiations. In this sense, as one biographer has noted, Stalin did Dulles a profound disservice by dying too soon.[19]

Eisenhower, on the other hand, inclined toward somewhat measured optimism. Stalin's death might well clear the way for fundamental changes in the Soviets' view of the world, he thought. "Consequently, a major preoccupation of my mind throughout most of 1953 was the development of approaches to the Soviet leaders that might be at least a start toward the birth of mutual trust."[20] The president's most notable effort in this regard was a speech made over Dulles's objections in April 1953, in which he drew a clear distinction between Stalin and the new Soviet leadership and offered, if the Russians would make concrete gestures toward resolving outstanding differences, to begin negotiations looking toward a mutual reduction of armaments.[21] Eisenhower held out no great hope that the Russians would accept this approach, but he did attach a higher priority than did Dulles to clearing the way for negotiations should negotiable issues prove to exist.

Conciliatory gestures of the kind Eisenhower had requested were not long in coming. In an unusual step, *Pravda* reprinted the full text of the president's address; shortly thereafter, Soviet officials began seeking informal social contacts with American diplomats in Moscow for the first time in years.[22] More important, the Russians in the spring of 1953 began applying pressure on the Chinese Communists and the North Koreans to end the

[18] Hoopes, *Dulles*, pp. 82, 124–125; Herbert S. Parmet, "Power and Reality: John Foster Dulles and Political Diplomacy," in Theodore A. Wilson and Frank Merli, eds., *Makers of American Diplomacy* (New York: 1974), pp. 596–601.

[19] Hoopes, *Dulles*, p. 171.

[20] Eisenhower, *Mandate for Change*, p. 144. See also Brown, *The Faces of Power*, pp. 86–90.

[21] Speech of April 16, 1953, *Eisenhower Public Papers, 1953*, pp. 179–188.

[22] Bohlen, *Witness to History*, pp. 348–352, 359–362.

fighting in Korea. It was not clear at the time, nor is it completely clear today, whether the July 1953 armistice agreement resulted primarily from internal developments in China, Soviet influence, or veiled threats by Eisenhower and Dulles to use nculear weapons in Korea if the fighting did not stop.[23] But, whatever brought it about, the Russians had not been unhelpful in arranging the cease-fire, and this was an encouraging sign.

Pressures, especially from the British, had begun to build as early as the summer of 1953 for a summit conference with Stalin's successors, but Dulles had strongly discouraged this course of action. Negotiations, he feared, might suggest to the Russians lack of resolve on the part of the West. They might also weaken NATO, an organization whose internal cohesion seemed to require existence of a strong external threat, particularly if French opposition to the integration of West German forces into a European defense structure was to be overcome. Finally, negotiations might cause difficulties at home, where repeated Republican invocations of "Yalta" as a symbol of appeasement made it no easy task, even for as popular an administration as Eisenhower's, to initiate the first top-level contacts with Kremlin officials since World War II.[24]

By early 1955, however, even Dulles was finding it difficult to hold out. The Soviet leadership, now increasingly dominated by the irrepressible Khrushchev, agreed in May to sign a long-delayed peace treaty with Austria, thus bringing to an end the four-power occupation of that country. That same month the Russians offered, for the first time, to consider disarmament plans involving limited on-site inspection within the USSR. McCarthyism in the United States had lost much of its potency by then; in Europe the French had agreed, if not to the integration of West German forces into an all-European army, at least to the Bonn government's membership in NATO. With public opinion in both the United States and Western Europe coming to favor summit talks, Eisenhower overrode Dulles' objections and agreed to meet with the leaders of Great Britain, France, and the Soviet Union at Geneva in July 1955.

---

[23] George and Smoke, *Deterrence in American Foreign Policy*, pp. 237–241.
[24] Hoopes, *Dulles*, pp. 173–177.

Substantive progress at Geneva was minimal. The Russians backed away from discussions of German reunification because, as Khrushchev candidly admitted, the East Germans had not yet had time "to be educated to the great advantage of Communism."[25] Eisenhower rejected Russian disarmament proposals as inadequate, suggesting instead the mutual aerial surveillance of all Soviet and American military installations. This "open skies" plan won the Americans propaganda points but had little chance of acceptance, given the disproportionate benefits it would have provided the United States, an open society with few secrets to give up, as compared to the Soviet Union.

Atmospherics are sometimes more important than accomplishments, though, and the sight of capitalist and communist leaders amiably agreeing to disagree had a curiously reassuring effect on world opinion, leading to newspaper headlines about something called "the spirit of Geneva." If such a spirit existed, it lay in the personal relationships formed during the five days of the conference. Khrushchev found Eisenhower to be "a good man," if very much under Dulles' influence. Eisenhower jokingly assured the Russians of his relief at finding them not to be fourteen feet high, with horns and a tail.[26] The conference thus established an unspoken assumption which would underlie much subsequent summit diplomacy: that nations whose leaders had dealt with each other face to face would find it difficult to be enemies. It was a simplistic view of international relations, but to the extent that direct acquaintance could free Soviet and American leaders from the tendency to explain each other's behavior in narrow ideological terms, perhaps not an entirely inaccurate one.

The Twentieth Party Congress, which met in Moscow in February 1956, provided striking confirmation of the changes which had taken place in the Soviet Union since Stalin's death. In a long, rambling, emotional speech, Khrushchev condemned the dead dictator and most of his works, thereby acknowledging fallibility, an unexpected trait in a system based on the "scien-

---

[25] Eisenhower, *Mandate for Change,* p. 523.
[26] *Khrushchev Remembers,* p. 434; Peter Lyon, *Eisenhower: Portrait of the Hero* (Boston: 1974), p. 660. See also Eisenhower, *Mandate for Change,* p. 527.

tific" application of theory to human events. The concept of "peaceful coexistence," employed on and off in the past for tactical purposes, now became a fixed principle of Soviet foreign policy; simultaneously the new leadership officially repudiated the Stalinist doctrine of inevitable conflict between states of differing social systems.[27]

From the perspective of two decades, it seems clear that these developments marked a turning point of fundamental importance in the history of Soviet foreign policy—an adaptation of ideology to fit reality much along the lines of what Kennan had predicted some years earlier.[28] But there ensued no immediate improvement in relations with the West, a fact for which both sides must bear some responsibility.

American policy, influenced more, on balance, by Dulles than by Eisenhower, continued to treat ideology as the determinant rather than the reflection of Soviet state interests, and so found it difficult to account for Moscow's conciliatory gestures in terms of anything other than deliberate deception. Compounding this tendency was an excessive preoccupation with maintaining the credibility of American commitments which made the costs of negotiations appear to outweigh their benefits.[29] It may well be that there was little to negotiate about: distrust on both sides was high and would remain so for years to come. Still, the Soviet leadership did undergo a period of uncertainty following Stalin's death which the West might have exploited to its advantage, particularly on the issues of disarmament and German unification, had it been more confident of its own strength and more willing to employ the normal processes of diplomacy.[30]

After 1955, such a course of action would become considerably more difficult. The integration of West Germany into NATO, together with the creation, in the East, of the Warsaw Treaty Organization, institutionalized the division of Europe into two hostile camps. De-Stalinization, which should have improved

[27] Wolfgang Leonhard, *The Three Faces of Marxism* (New York: 1974), pp. 144–154. See also Ulam, *Expansion and Coexistence,* pp. 574–580.

[28] See, on this point, William Zimmerman, *Soviet Perspectives on International Relations, 1956–1967* (Princeton: 1969), pp. 4–6.

[29] Bell, *Negotiation From Strength,* pp. 219, 235–236.

[30] Bohlen, *Witness to History,* p. 371; Adam B. Ulam, *The Rivals: America and Russia since World War II* (New York: 1971), pp. 230–232.

relations with the West, had precisely the opposite effect when the Russians chose, late in 1956, to suppress by brutal means the dissension in Eastern Europe created thereby. Within a year, the perfection of long-range missiles would tempt Khrushchev into a strategy of seeking negotiations through intimidation, an approach no more successful in relating intent to effect than had been Dulles' attempts to promote stability by avoiding negotiations. The Cold War had taken on a peculiar dynamic of its own, with indications of restraint on one side producing, not a corresponding response, but a hardening of position on the part of the other.

III

It is, by now, commonplace to note that the geographical scope of Soviet-American competition expanded, during the 1950s, from Europe and Northeast Asia into East and Southeast Asia, the Middle East, and Latin America. Nor are the reasons for this development hard to grasp: they are connected, most obviously, with the acceleration of decolonization brought about by World War II, together with the efforts of Stalin's successors to profit from the antagonism toward the West which this process generated. Less clear is why the United States responded to these events in the way that it did: why it so consistently exaggerated the strength of communism in the "Third World" and, correspondingly, neglected what would prove to be the more durable ideology there—nationalism.[31]

The Eisenhower administration sought to apply containment in that part of the world in three ways: by employing covert operations to overthrow governments suspected of promoting, either consciously or unconsciously, the interests of international communism; by working to stimulate and support nationalism in those parts of the world where it could be expected to assume a reliably anti-communist orientation; and, finally, by attempting to build safeguards against both external attack and internal subversion through the construction of a worldwide network of multilateral defense pacts, modeled on NATO.

---

[31] See, on this point, James K. Nathan and James K. Oliver, *United States Foreign Policy and World Order* (Boston: 1976), pp. 208, 220.

The United States is on record as having attempted, through the Central Intelligence Agency, at least four major covert operations against foreign governments during the Eisenhower administration: the successful overthrow of Prime Minister Mohammed Mossadeqh in Iran in August 1953; the equally efficient dispatch of President Jacobo Arbenz Guzman's left-wing regime in Guatemala in June 1954; an unsuccessful effort to undermine the position of Indonesian President Sukarno in 1958; and the abortive attempt to organize a rebellion against Fidel Castro's government in Cuba, planned during the final months of Eisenhower's term, but actually implemented in April 1961, three months after President Kennedy took office.[32] What these four targets of American intervention had in common was not communism—none of the four had openly expressed adherence to the doctrines of Marxism-Leninism—but rather anti-Americanism; that such sentiments might not automatically mean subservience to the Soviet Union appears not to have occurred to administration officials. Nor, in planning these operations, did they weigh fully the long-term costs of covert action, successful or not, in evoking suspicion of American motives both at home and abroad.

Covert action was not the administration's preferred method of operation, however; instead it sought, where possible, to encourage governments which would be both nationalist *and* anti-communist. In many parts of the world this was not an unreasonable objective: the examples of South Korea, the Philippines, Pakistan, Iran (after Mossadeqh's overthrow), Saudi Arabia, and much of Latin America come to mind. But there were regions where nationalism was indissolubly linked with communism, despite the best efforts of the United States to drive them apart. One such area was Indochina, where by 1954, France's long effort to suppress Ho Chi Minh's communist insurgency had come close to collapse. Although Ho had, in recent years, been receiving considerable amounts of military and economic assistance from Moscow and Peking, there was little doubt in Washington about the genuinely national base of his

---

[32] David Wise and Thomas B. Ross, *The Invisible Government* (New York: 1964), pp. 8–90, 110–114, 137–146, 169–183.

movement.[33] The Eisenhower administration found it impossible to align the United States with nationalism in this case, though, for the simple reason that it proceeded under the rubric of "communism." Instead, following the Geneva Conference on Indochina in 1954, Washington embarked on a long, costly, and ultimately unsuccessful effort to develop an anticommunist variety of Vietnamese nationalism through support of the Ngo Dinh Diem regime in Saigon, a course of action destined ultimately to involve the United States in its most protracted war.

In other parts of the world, regimes which were both nationalist and anti-communist existed, but the administration did not always recognize or support them. The most conspicuous example was Egypt, where the United States initially endorsed the strongly nationalist government of Gamal Abdel Nasser but backed off when in 1955 Nasser demonstrated a determination to maintain close ties with the Soviet Union and Communist China as well. Suspecting, incorrectly in this case, that association with communists meant control by them (and motivated as well by Congressional skepticism and a desire to expose as a bluff Soviet offers of aid[34]), Dulles in the summer of 1956 withdrew an earlier offer to fund construction of Nasser's pet project, the Aswan Dam. This action led in turn to Egyptian seizure of the Suez Canal, an abortive Anglo-French-Israeli military operation to take it back, and the odd sight of the United States and the Soviet Union cooperating in the United Nations to restore order in that part of the world.

By all logic, the United States should have emerged from the Suez crisis with an enhanced reputation in the Middle East for having resisted the last major effort by colonial powers to impose their will there. That it did not may be attributed, in large part, to the workings of a third administration approach to the problem of communism and nationalism—the extension of multilateral, bilateral, and, at times, unilateral security guarantees to those areas of the Third World seen as vulnerable to the expansion of Soviet or Chinese influence.

It had been the Eisenhower administration's role in organiz

---

[33] Eisenhower, *Mandate for Change*, p. 372.
[34] Guhin, *Dulles*, pp. 267–277; Hoopes, *Dulles*, pp. 338–344.

ing the 1955 Baghdad Pact (made up of Great Britain, Turkey, Iraq, Iran, and Pakistan) which had provoked Nasser into improving his relations with Moscow and Peking in the first place; now, in early 1957, Dulles asked Congress to approve the "Eisenhower Doctrine," a declaration of intent by the United States to defend the entire Middle East against "overt armed aggression from any nation controlled by International Communism."[35] Dulles had expected this statement to deter Soviet efforts to exploit Western weakness in the Middle East after Suez; paradoxically it had the effect of raising doubts, both in Congress and in the country at large, regarding the administration's ability to gauge threats precisely or to formulate appropriate responses. Reaction in the Middle East was largely negative, a trend which intensified the following year when the United States, acting under terms of the doctrine, landed troops in Lebanon to protect that country's government against a coup attempt that turned out to have been instigated more by forces of Arab nationalism (and Nasserism) than by machinations of the Kremlin.[36]

The Eisenhower Doctrine was but the final link in a chain of security commitments the administration had assumed since taking office—the South East Asian Treaty of 1954, the Formosa Treaty of 1955, and the Baghdad Pact (with which the United States was closely associated, even though it did not formally join). By 1958, Washington had taken on explicit obligations to defend some forty-three countries against attack, and, by implication, several more. This "pactomania," as critics called it, was a logical outgrowth of the Eisenhower administration's strategy of seeking maximum deterrence at minimum cost: it sought to convey the impression that while not all commitments could be met, enough might be to render aggression unprofitable. If aggressive ambitions did exist in either Moscow or Peking, this approach may well have discouraged attempts to fulfill them. What it could not deter, however, was the process of revolutionary change going on within many of the countries involved.[37]

---

[35] *Department of State Bulletin,* XXXVI(January 21, 1957), 86.

[36] George and Smoke, *Deterrence in American Foreign Policy,* pp. 309–358.

[37] See Stephen J. Genco, "The Eisenhower Doctrine: Deterrence in the Middle East, 1957–1958," in ibid., pp. 355–358.

The Eisenhower administration persistently ascribed such developments to its adversaries, thus exaggerating both their unity and capabilities while simultaneously offending that sense of nationalism which probably afforded Third World countries their best long-term protection against hegemonial aspirations from the outside.

In retrospect, though, the most significant developments in the evolving relationship between communism and nationalism during this period were taking place, not in the "nonaligned" world at all, but in the increasingly uneasy partnership between the two giants of the communist world, the Soviet Union and the Peoples' Republic of China. Indications of growing tension were not difficult to find. As early as September 1953, a Central Intelligence Agency analysis had concluded that "there is a real, albeit latent, area of disagreement between the Chinese and the Soviets."[38] Within four years, oblique but persistent differences on major issues had begun to creep into the public rhetoric of the two governments; after Khrushchev failed to support Mao's position during the second Quemoy-Matsu crisis in 1958, the exchange of polemics became too obvious to ignore. By the time of his death in 1959, even Dulles had come around to the view that while both Moscow and Peking were under the domination of "international communism," the mainland Chinese government could no longer be considered a satellite of the Soviet Union.[39]

But, beyond an agreement to hold informal talks with Chinese representatives, the Eisenhower administration made no effort during this period to improve its relations with Peking, or to exploit growing Sino-Soviet antagonism to the advantage of the United States. Dulles adamantly refused to consider diplomatic recognition or China's admission to the United Nations; he also opposed cultural exchanges, the reciprocal visits of newsmen, and, in one case, the acquisition of a Chinese panda for an American zoo.[40] Domestic politics in large part motivated this

---

[38] Philip Bridgham, Arthur Cohen, and Leonard Jaffe, "Mao's Road and Sino-Soviet Relations: A View from Washington, 1953," *China Quarterly*, #52(October/December, 1972), p. 695.

[39] Donald S. Zagoria, *The Sino-Soviet Conflict, 1956–1961* (Princeton: 1962), pp. 154–168, 217–221; Dulles, *American Foreign Policy Toward Communist China*, p. 185.

[40] Hoopes, *Dulles*, pp. 415–423.

policy: Mao's intervention in Korea had given his government, in the eyes of many Americans, a reputation for evil surpassing even that of the Soviet Union. The resulting vociferously anti-Chinese atmosphere provided little incentive for those within the government who perceived the depth of Sino-Soviet antagonism to seek to have their assessments of the split translated into policy.[41]

There was, throughout the Eisenhower administration's attempts to deal with problems of communism and nationalism in the Third World, a curious pessimism regarding the ability of the latter ideology to sustain itself against the former. It was this lack of faith in the "staying power" of nationalism which caused the administration to offer security guarantees with what appeared to be a sweeping disregard for American capabilities. The same phenomenon made Eisenhower and Dulles less sensitive than they might have been to the backlash such efforts would produce in the nonaligned world, where perfervid American attempts to recruit allies appeared at least as intrusive and destabilizing as anything the Russians were doing. It also caused Washington to lose sight of the distinction between revolutions its adversaries had instigated and those upon which they were merely trying to capitalize. Finally, it may have delayed by some years exploitation of the Sino-Soviet split, the most important alteration in the global balance of power since the end of World War II.

The early strategists of containment had taken a very different view: that in any competition between communism and nationalism, the latter would, in the end, prevail; that this had already happened inside the USSR, where communism had become the instrument of Soviet national interests; that by discreetly encouraging nationalism elsewhere in the world, the Kremlin's ability to project influence beyond its borders might be significantly reduced.[42] The Eisenhower administration was not completely unsympathetic to this approach: it continued to support communist Yugoslavia on the basis of its demonstrated independence from Moscow, and one of Dulles' chief concerns in the Middle East was to disassociate United States policies

---

[41] See Bernard S. Morris, *International Communism and American Policy* (New York: 1966), pp. 133–140.

[42] See Chapter VII, above.

from the activities of former colonial regimes there.[43] But the domestic political costs of dealing with governments which, though nationalist, were also communist, neutralist, or in some other way not inclined to follow Washington's wishes, proved in most cases greater than the administration was willing to pay. As a result, containment, a strategy originally designed to work with the forces of nationalism to restrain Soviet expansion, now took on the appearance of a crusade against nationalism itself, an approach very different from what its original architects had intended.

IV

If the 1950s witnessed an expansion of the Cold War into geographical areas previously untouched by it, these years also saw an unprecedented intrusion of that conflict into the realm of technology. Up to that point, the chief impact of technology on the Cold War had been to confirm the superior power of the United States over the Soviet Union. Lend-Lease, the atomic bomb, the European Recovery Program, and development of a strategic bombing force capable of reaching the USSR—all had been, in one way or another, the products of sophisticated American technology, much resented by the Russians but also, one suspects, much envied.[44] This situation changed dramatically, at least insofar as appearances were concerned, when, on October 4, 1957, the Soviet Union successfully launched "Sputnik," the first artificial earth satellite. Russian scientists seemed to have made a major breakthrough, carrying with it the potential for a major shift in the strategic balance of power.

Obtuse though he was in many ways, Stalin must be given credit for having had a clearer vision than did his Western counterparts of the course developments in strategic weapons technology were going to take during the 1950s. Thanks to programs he initiated, the Soviet Union actually achieved an operational hydrogen bomb capability before the United States did—the first such device dropped from an airplane was a Russian

---

[43] Guhin, *Dulles*, pp. 266, 288.

[44] See, for example, *Khrushchev Remembers: The Last Testament*, pp. 11, 35, 58–59, 220.

weapon, successfully tested in 1955.[45] Stalin also decided, at some point after World War II, that the USSR would not try to counter the rapidly growing American strategic bombing force, but would instead concentrate its energies on developing long-range missiles capable of carrying nuclear weapons.[46] Stalin's successors, kept in the dark regarding much of this, found a missile development program well underway at the time of the dictator's death. The new leadership had a great deal to learn: "We were like peasants in a marketplace," Khrushchev later recalled, describing the occasion upon which members of the Politburo were shown a long-range missile for the first time. "We walked around and around the rocket, touching it, tapping it to see if it was sturdy enough—we did everything but lick it to see how it tasted."[47] Whatever their lack of sophistication, however, Khrushchev and his associates were not slow to take advantage of the technological lead their unlamented predecessor had given them.

"It always sounded good to say in public speeches that we could hit a fly at any distance with our missiles," Khrushchev subsequently admitted,[48] but, in fact, problems of guidance and cost prevented the Soviet Union, at any point during his leadership, from deploying a sufficient number of launchers to obtain an assured first-strike capability against the United States. Instead, the Russians accepted strategic inferiority while simultaneously working to convince the West that *it* was operating from a position of weakness. This massive bluff (resembling as nothing else the old Chinese tactic of building paper forts, then painting bellicose but impotent dragons on them to ward off aggressors) depended for its success on Moscow's ability to conceal from outsiders the nature and extent of Soviet military deployments, and on the Kremlin's confidence that the United States would not take advantage of its actual strategic superioity to attack the USSR.

The first requirement could, for the moment, be taken for granted: overhead reconnaissance, whether by high-altitude

---

[45] Quester, *Nuclear Diplomacy*, pp. 91–92.

[46] Thomas W. Wolfe, *Soviet Power and Europe, 1945–1970* (Baltimore: 1970), pp. 36–37; Shulman, *Stalin's Foreign Policy Reappraised*, pp. 24–26.

[47] *Khrushchev Remembers: The Last Testament*, p. 46

[48] Ibid., p. 47

aircraft or satellites, was not yet a reality; Western observers were reduced to gleaning what knowledge they could of Soviet military capabilities from weapons displays in May Day parades, occasional closely guarded trips around the country, and the scraps of information that appeared in the official press. The limitations of this process became evident following Moscow Aviation Day ceremonies in July 1955, when the Russians managed to set off a major "bomber gap" scare in the West, and a substantial acceleration in the production of American B-52s, through the simple expedient of flying a single squadron of their own "Bison" bombers past the reviewing stand several times.[49]

Soviet leaders could be somewhat less sure of Washington's peaceful intentions: there is evidence that the Eisenhower administration's talk of "massive retaliation" frightened them, setting off debates within the Kremlin on how best to deter the Americans. The 1955 Geneva summit appears to have lessened fears of an American attack, however, while the West's failure to support the uprising in Hungary the following year may well have confirmed impressions that the Eisenhower-Dulles version of containment would differ little from what had gone before.[50] It is significant that Khrushchev's first public threat to rain rockets on European capitals, delivered in reaction to the Anglo-French-Israeli invasion of Egypt, occurred just as Soviet troops were beginning the successful reoccupation of their unfortunate East European satellite.

The summer of 1957 saw two important developments which facilitated exploitation of a "strategic deception" strategy. One was the elimination, in June, of Khrushchev's remaining rivals for power in the Kremlin, an event which left him, for the time being, in full control of Soviet foreign policy. The other was the first successful test, in August, of an intercontinental ballistic missile. Claims regarding this test were greeted with incredulity in the outside world, until in October the Russians demonstrated their capability for all to see by launching *Sputnik*. There followed in the West a condition approaching panic and, on

[49] Quester, *Nuclear Diplomacy*, pp. 126–139; Allen Dulles, *The Craft of Intelligence* (New York: 1963), p. 149; Arnold L. Horelick and Myron Rush, *Strategic Power and Soviet Foreign Policy* (Chicago: 1966), pp. 27–28.

[50] Ibid., pp. 18–29, 211–212. See also Wolfe, *Soviet Power and Europe*, pp. 133–135.

Khrushchev's part, a gradually escalating series of carefully worded claims designed to imply, if not overtly assert, the Soviet Union's ability to destroy the United States in any future war.[51]

Khrushchev did not at first tie his assertions regarding ICBM development to specific political issues, but in November 1958, he abruptly threatened to turn over control of Berlin access routes to the East Germans if the Western powers did not agree to terminate their occupation rights in West Berlin within six months. Shortly thereafter, Soviet Foreign Minister Andrei Gromyko warned that should fighting break out over Berlin, "modern military technology" would make it certain that the flames of war "would inevitably spread to the continent of America."[52] Khrushchev's decision to instigate a new Berlin crisis almost certainly reflected fears that the West Germans might gain access, through NATO, to tactical nuclear weapons and intermediate-range ballistics missiles—such devices had already been sent to West Germany under American control, ironically in response to fears the Russians themselves had provoked of a "missile gap." Then, too, West Berlin's continued existence as a bastion of capitalism deep within communist East Germany remained a perpetual irritant. Khrushchev may also have hoped to impress the Chinese, who had raised questions about Soviet resolve as a result of Moscow's cautious attitude during the second Quemoy-Matsu crisis earlier that year.[53] But whatever his objectives, Khrushchev clearly expected Soviet achievements in missile and space technology to help him attain them.

Significantly, Khrushchev coupled his demands on Berlin with a series of conciliatory gestures aimed apparently at re-creating the "spirit of Geneva." These included an invitation for Eisenhower to visit the Soviet Union, trips by subordinates Anastas Mikoyan and Frol Kozlov to the United States, a return trip by Vice-President Richard Nixon to Moscow (the occasion of a spirited debate between Nixon and Khrushchev, held in the

---

[51] Horelick and Rush, *Strategic Power and Soviet Foreign Policy*, pp. 42–49.

[52] Quoted in ibid., pp. 119–120.

[53] Ulam *The Rivals*, pp. 287–295; Jack M. Schick, *The Berlin Crisis, 1958–1962* (Philadelphia: 1971), p. 233.

unlikely setting of a model kitchen in an American exhibition then visiting the Soviet capital), and, finally, an agreement to hold a foreign ministers' meeting on the subject of Berlin. Eisenhower, who following Dulles' death in May 1959, had decided to play a more active personal role in the conduct of Soviet-American relations, responded by inviting Khrushchev to visit the United States if the foreign ministers' meetings in Geneva produced progress on Berlin. They did not, but through a misunderstanding the president's precondition was not made clear to the Russians, and Khrushchev, to Eisenhower's chagrin, decided to come anyway.[54]

The Soviet leader attached great importance to this visit—"we had finally forced the United States to recognize the necessity of establishing closer contacts with us." To all appearances, he enjoyed himself hugely, bantering with reporters, sipping champagne with leading capitalists in Averell Harriman's apartment, debating methods of corn production with Iowa farmers, allowing himself to be scandalized by a cancan dance on a Hollywood sound stage, and working himself up into a considerable tantrum over not being allowed, for security reasons, to visit Disneyland. Talks between Eisenhower and Khrushchev at the president's Maryland mountain retreat led inevitably to press speculation about the "spirit of Camp David" (it is a sign of how spotty the Russians' information about the United States was at this time that Khrushchev and his entourage had some difficulty in determining what Camp David was, and in reassuring themselves that their invitation to this out-of-the-way place had not been meant as an insult),[55] but beyond Eisenhower's acknowledgment that the Berlin situation was "abnormal" and Khrushchev's agreement not to press for a settlement until after a four-power summit the following spring, practical results of the Khrushchev visit appeared minimal.

Meanwhile, alarm within the administration over Soviet missile developments had begun to subside. The United States had, by the end of 1959, convincingly demonstrated its own satellite

[54] Dwight D. Eisenhower, *The White House Years: Waging Peace, 1956–1961* (Garden City, New York: 1965), pp. 405–408.

[55] See Khrushchev's lengthy and revealing account of this trip in *Khrushchev Remembers: The Last Testament*, pp. 368–416.

and ICBM capability. Even more important, secret means of detection had begun to reveal evidence that Soviet missile deployments had come nowhere close to anticipated projections. High-altitude U-2 reconnaissance aircraft, developed by the Central Intelligence Agency, had been overflying the Soviet Union since late 1956. The information they produced could not be conclusive because of the limited frequency and coverage of the flights,[56] but it was enough, when combined with Eisenhower's own deeply-felt concern about inflation, to cause him to resist calls for massive increases in the defense budget following *Sputnik*.[57]

The U-2 also became the occasion of a major crisis, though, when in May 1960 one crashed, or was shot down, near Sverdlovsk in central Russia two weeks before the Paris summit. Khrushchev gave Eisenhower the opportunity to disavow responsibility for the overflight, but the president, in an unprecedented acknowledgment of a covert action operation, refused to do so, announcing that he had indeed authorized the mission and that others like it had been going on for three and a half years. This left Khrushchev little choice: "[Eisenhower] had, so to speak, offered us his back end, and we obliged by kicking it as hard as we could."[58] The Soviet leader traveled to Paris but, once there, cancelled the summit (and the president's invitation to visit the Soviet Union) in an outburst of offended rhetoric: "We shall not tolerate insults, we have our pride and our dignity. We represent a mighty socialist state."[59]

Whether the Paris summit would have produced progress on Berlin is difficult to say. Khrushchev clearly had staked his personal reputation on talks with Eisenhower—if the Chinese are to be believed, he had even repudiated an agreement to share nuclear weapons with them as a means of facilitating the discussions at Camp David.[60] Certainly he gave the president every

---

[56] Philip J. Klass, *Secret Sentries in Space* (New York: 1971), pp. 30–31, 47–48, 50–51, 79.

[57] See, on this point, Richard A. Aliano, *American Defense Policy from Eisenhower to Kennedy* (Athens, Ohio: 1975), pp. 6–8, 47–60.

[58] *Khrushchev Remembers: The Last Testament*, p. 448.

[59] Khrushchev press conference, Paris, May 18, 1960, *Documents on International Affairs, 1960* (London: 1961), p. 34.

[60] See, on this point, Schurmann, *The Logic of World Power*, pp. 302–303, 308–309.

chance to sweep the U-2 incident under the rug. On the other hand, Khrushchev was already under considerable pressure, from both within his own government and from the Chinese, for yielding too much.[61] The U-2 episode gave him a convenient excuse for avoiding negotiations—an excuse all the more important since, presumably, recovered photographs from the downed plane had given the Russians some indication of how good American intelligence on Soviet missile deployments was. What is clear is that Eisenhower made his decision to accept public responsibility for the overflight, and thus risk the summit, more for reasons of personal honesty and a desire to avoid the appearance of not controlling his own administration[62] than from any sensitivity to Khrushchev's internal problems or the way in which these might affect future Soviet-American relations.

The United States had to give up U-2 overflights, but this meant only a brief gap in the flow of intelligence before a new and even better source became available—satellite reconnaissance. This new instrument quickly confirmed what had been suspected for some time—that the Soviet missile buildup had been more rhetorical than real and that the Russians had deployed only a fraction of the number of ICBMs they could have built had they chosen to do so.[63] That they did not can be seen both as evidence of efficient budgetary management—it made sense to delay deployment of clumsy, first-generation, liquid-fueled rockets until more reliable solid-fueled versions had come along—and as an attempt by Khrushchev to implement his own "new look" strategy of maximum deterrence at minimum cost. The practice of "strategic deception" can also be taken, though, as reflecting a high degree of confidence on the Russians' part regarding Washington's peaceful intentions: the Kremlin leadership apparently decided that it could live com-

---

[61] Ulam, *The Rivals*, pp. 310–312; Michel Tatu, *Power in the Kremlin: From Khrushchev to Kosygin* (New York: 1969), pp. 41–122.

[62] Eisenhower, *Waging Peace*, pp. 552–553. For a less than convincing argument that the Eisenhower Administration deliberately engineered the U-2 crash in order to torpedo the Paris summit, see Nathan and Oliver, *United States Foreign Policy and World Order*, pp. 264–274.

[63] Klass, *Secret Sentries in Space*, pp. 100–105.

fortably with strategic inferiority because the United States was unlikely to put its strategic superiority to actual use.[64]

"Of course, we tried to derive maximum political advantage from the fact that we were the first to launch our rockets into space," Khrushchev recalled after his retirement from political life. "We wanted to exert pressure on American militarists—and also influence the minds of more reasonable politicians—so that the United States would start treating us better. However, . . . we had no intention of starting a war."[65] Not surprisingly, this approach backfired. The problem with any such effort to translate technological superiority into political benefits is that the very act of demonstrating that superiority is likely to impress potential adversaries more with the need to catch up than with the desirability of resolving differences. Certainly the United States had found this to be the case in its own sporadic attempts to exploit a technological edge over the Soviet Union after World War II. Khrushchev's "strategic deception" ploy represented at once a more ambitious and more blatant effort to obtain such political gains, on the basis of a technological advantage considerably less impressive than that which the United States had enjoyed a decade earlier. Such minimal dividends as his strategems did produce were largely the result, not of the skill or dexterity with which they were executed, but of the Eisenhower administration's reluctance to divulge the means by which it had discovered the fraudulent ground upon which they rested.

V

There is little reason to doubt Khrushchev's assertion that he did not want a war. Indeed, it now appears that a principal objective of Soviet foreign policy during the decade in which he controlled it was to improve relations with the West—a goal Khrushchev came, in the end, to regard as more important than maintaining the solidarity of the international communist movement. Nor is there much doubt as to what motivated this policy: the Soviet leader apparently meant it when he repeatedly warned his Chinese Communist critics that there could

---

[64] Horelick and Rush, *Strategic Power and Soviet Foreign Policy,* pp. 105–107.
[65] *Khrushchev Remembers: The Last Testament,* p. 53.

be no winners in a nuclear exchange.[66] Yet Khrushchev's methods for seeking a relaxation of tensions were distinctly odd. One historian has compared them to those of a man

who seeks to have a friendly chat with a man next door, . . . [but] instead of knocking politely on the door of the apartment, climbs on the window ledge outside, makes ferocious faces through his neighbor's window or loudly bangs at the door, threatening to break it open. In the interval, he explains that all he wants is friendship and neighborly comity.[67]

This strategy of seeking detente through intimidation reached its climax between 1960 and 1962.

It was a period which saw Khrushchev publicly threaten, in the wake of the abortive Paris summit, to "take the American imperialists by the scruff of their necks, [and] give them a good shaking."[68] It witnessed the Soviet leader making a spectacle of himself at the United Nations in September 1960, jeering speakers, pounding the desk with his fists and, in several instances, his shoe. ("Some people did not seem to understand this unparliamentary method," he admitted afterwards.)[69] In January 1961, Khrushchev made it clear that the Soviet Union's desire to avoid nuclear war in no way precluded support for "wars of national liberation" throughout the world. Eight months later, he shocked the world by ordering construction of a fortified wall separating East and West Berlin; there quickly followed a unilateral resumption of nuclear weapons tests in the atmosphere (by tacit understanding, there had been a moratorium on such tests since 1958) and a new barrage of threats based on Soviet space achievements:

The Soviet Union has worked out designs for creating a series of super-powerful nuclear bombs equivalent to 20, 30, 50 and 100 million tons of T.N.T., and powerful rockets . . . [which] can lift and deliver such nuclear bombs to any point on the globe. . . . It would be unjustifiable thoughtlessness not to draw appropriate conclusions.[70]

---

[66] Zagoria, *The Sino-Soviet Conflict*, pp. 156, 280–284, 290–294.

[67] Ulam, *The Rivals*, pp. 285–286.

[68] Khrushchev press conference, May 18, 1960, *Documents on International Affairs, 1960*, p. 36.

[69] *Khrushchev Remembers: The Last Testament*, p. 473.

[70] Soviet government statement of August 30, 1961, *Documents on International Affairs, 1961* (London: 1965), p. 463. For Khrushchev's January 6, 1961, speech on wars of national liberation, see ibid., pp. 259–273.

Finally, sometime in the spring of 1962, Khrushchev made the risky decision to place medium- and intermediate-range ballistic missiles in Cuba, a maneuver that would bring the world closer to a nuclear war than ever before, or since. These were policies more bellicose and provocative than anything Stalin had ever attempted. And yet they paralleled persistent efforts on Khrushchev's part to move toward detente with the West.

Khrushchev entertained high hopes that the coming of power of a new administration in Washington would produce such a result. The Soviet leader had quietly rooted for John F. Kennedy in his close 1960 contest with "that son-of-a-bitch Richard Nixon";[71] fortunately for the Democrats, however, he showed unaccustomed discretion and kept his sympathies to himself. Immediately after Kennedy's inauguration, Khrushchev ordered the release of two downed American airmen as a sign of goodwill and let it be known that he would welcome an opportunity to meet with the new president. Kennedy, less prone than his predecessor to explain Soviet behavior in ideological terms and consequently more optimistic about negotiations, agreed, and a meeting was scheduled for Vienna in early June 1961.[72] It was not, from Washington's point of view, the most auspicious moment for a summit—the month of April had brought an embarrassing American humiliation, with the failure of the Bay of Pigs operation against Castro, and a new Soviet space feat, Yuri Gagarin's successful orbit of the earth. Kennedy attempted to recoup what prestige he could by committing the United States to placing a man on the moon by the end of the decade; this lofty (and expensive) objective set, the president set off for Europe and his encounter with the unpredictable Soviet premier.

If there was a "spirit of Vienna," it was one very different from the temporarily optimistic moods generated by the earlier Geneva and Camp David summits. The responsibility, it would appear, lay on both sides. Khrushchev once again brought up the subject of Berlin, threatening to sign a peace treaty with the East Germans cutting off Western access rights by the end of the

---

[71] *Khrushchev Remembers*, p. 507.
[72] Theodore C. Sorensen, *Kennedy* (New York: 1965), pp. 541–543; Arthur M. Schlesinger, Jr., *A Thousand Days: John F. Kennedy in the White House* (New York: 1965), pp. 278–286.

year. Kennedy responded by insisting that the West would keep its commitments. The American president in turn berated the Soviet leader for his "wars of national liberation" strategy; Khrushchev struck back with a denunciation of American attempts to freeze the status quo. Arguments on both sides reflected reversion to ideological stereotypes: Kennedy appeared to be asserting that the Soviet Union was responsible for revolutionary movements everywhere, while Khrushchev charged that "monopolists" who could not afford to disarm ran the United 'States. The Vienna summit produced one unexpected agreement to work for the neutralization of Laos, but in general the effect was to increase rather than lower the level of tension. As Kennedy put it in a report to the American people: "We have wholly different views of right and wrong, of what is an internal affair and what is aggression, . . . of where the world is and where it is going."[73]

Two months later, following an announcement by Khrushchev of a large increase in the Soviet defense budget, Kennedy ordered a tripling of draft calls, asked Congress for authority to call up reserves, and endorsed implementation of a new and elaborate civil defense program.[74] If these moves were intended to impress Khrushchev, they apparently succeeded. It seems likely that his decision in August to erect the Berlin Wall, although it appeared at the time as a new provocation, was in fact an effort to defuse the crisis—it is significant (and typical) that Khrushchev coupled his announcement in October of a fifty-megaton nuclear test with yet another postponement of his deadline for a Berlin settlement.[75] It is also noteworthy that Khrushchev picked this period to initiate a personal exchange of correspondence with Kennedy outside normal diplomatic channels—a means of communication which was to prove of great value during the events that followed.[76]

---

[73] Kennedy television address of June 6, 1961, *Documents on International Affairs, 1961*, p. 283. See also Sorensen, *Kennedy*, pp. 543–550, 584–586, 646–647; Schlesinger, *A Thousand Days*, pp. 333–348.

[74] Kennedy television address of July 25, 1961, *Documents on International Affairs, 1961*, pp. 335–336.

[75] Khrushchev speech of October 17, 1961, ibid., pp. 224–225; Richard P. Stebbins, *The United States in World Affairs, 1961* (New York: 1962), p. 103.

[76] Sorensen, *Kennedy*, pp. 552–555.

Kennedy and his top advisers had known, since shortly after taking office, that the so-called "missile gap," which had figured so prominently in the 1960 campaign, was nonexistent. They chose not to make this information public, however, until late October of 1961, when Deputy Secretary of Defense Roswell Gilpatric, in a carefully worded public address, announced that "[the] Iron Curtain is not so impenetrable as to force us to accept at face value the Kremlin's boasts. . . . We have a second-strike capability which is at least as extensive as what the Soviets can deliver by striking first."[77] The administration's motives in making this and similar statements at that time are not wholly apparent: certainly there were domestic political advantages to dispelling once and for all the myth of the "missile gap"; there may also have been the expectation that such action would increase the credibility of the American deterrent.[78] Whatever its purposes, though, the effect of the Gilpatric speech was to challenge, openly and authoritatively, the inflated strategic claims upon which Khrushchev's policies of the past four years had been based.

Those policies had involved accepting a position of actual strategic inferiority as long as a facade of superiority could be maintained, if not with those Washington officials privy to U-2 and satellite intelligence, at least with the informed public in the West, the Soviet Union, and, significantly, China. The Gilpatric speech ripped away that facade, leaving the Soviet Union in an embarrassingly exposed strategic position, a condition made all the more alarming by the Kennedy administration's careful refusal to rule out, under certain circumstances, the possibility of initiating a nuclear exchange.[79] It was this uncomfortable situation which appears to have driven Khrushchev to take the risk of sending missiles to Cuba.

Such Soviet accounts as exist of the "Caribbean crisis" stress the defensive purposes of the missile deployment: it was intended, they argue, to protect Castro's regime from another

---

[77] *New York Times*, October 22, 1961.
[78] See, on the Gilpatric speech, Elie Abel, *The Missile Crisis* (New York: 1966), pp. 38–39; Horelick and Rush, *Strategic Power and Soviet Foreign Policy*, pp. 83–84; Klass, *Secret Sentries in Space*, pp. 69–70; and Quester, *Nuclear Diplomacy*, p. 232.
[79] See, on this point, Jerome H. Kahan, *Security in the Nuclear Age: Developing U. S. Strategic Arms Policy* (New York: 1975), pp. 90–92.

American invasion.[80] Khrushchev has added that a secondary objective was to "equalize" the balance of power: "The Americans had surrounded our country with military bases and threatened us with nuclear weapons, and now they would learn just what it feels like to have enemy missiles pointed at you."[81] While both objectives may well have been present, the weight of the evidence suggests that the latter one was in fact dominant. Missiles with ranges of from 1100 to 2200 nautical miles were hardly appropriate weapons for use against another Bay of Pigs-style landing; moreover the risks Khrushchev took in sending such weapons outside the Soviet Union for the first time seem far out of proportion to the gains envisaged had the defense of Cuba been his sole objective.[82]

A more satisfactory explanation is to view Khrushchev's action as a "post-strategic deception" maneuver, necessitated by the Kennedy administration's exposure of the "missile gap" myth. Although the Russians, despite Khrushchev's claims, had never produced enough ICBMs to obtain an assured first-strike capability against the United States, there was nothing fraudulent or illusory about their buildup of medium- and intermediate-range ballistic missiles targeted against Europe. Here the Russians went all out, producing some 700 such weapons by the end of 1962 as against less than 100 ICBMs capable of reaching the United States.[83] Although the Russians had at one point enjoyed a slight edge over the Americans in numbers of ICBMs,[84] this lead had long since been eclipsed by the assembly-line production of Atlas, Titan, and Minuteman rockets (almost 300 by the time of the missile crisis) and the submarine-launched Polaris (144 missiles by late 1962), all of

---

[80] A. A. Gromyko, "Karibskii krizis," *Voprosy istorii*, 1971, #7, pp. 135–144, #8, pp. 121–129; Iu. M. Mel'nikov, *Vneshnepoliticheskie doktriny SShA* (Moscow, 1970), pp. 383–384; A. A. Gromyko, *Through Russian Eyes: President Kennedy's 1036 Days* (Washington: 1973), pp. 169–171; Ponomaryov, et al., eds., *History of Soviet Foreign Policy, 1945–1970*, pp. 422–423.

[81] *Khrushchev Remembers*, p. 547.

[82] Graham T. Allison, *Essence of Decision: Explaining the Cuban Missile Crisis* (Boston: 1971), p. 49; Horelick and Rush, *Strategic Power and Soviet Foreign Policy*, pp. 127–128.

[83] Ibid., pp. 49, 94; Wolfe, *Soviet Power and Europe*, pp. 41–42, 98, 154, 183–184.

[84] Quester, *Nuclear Diplomacy*, p. 296.

which could reach targets inside the Soviet Union.[85] Cuba offered Khrushchev a quick means of redressing the unfavorable
balance to which the Kennedy administration had now called
attention—it provided an unsinkable platform from which
MRBMs and IRBMs, which the Russians possessed in abundance, could be aimed at American targets. The effect, had it
succeeded, would have been to double almost overnight the
Soviet Union's offensive missile capability against the United
States.[86]

Khrushchev was probably telling the truth when he asserted,
both at the time and subsequently, that he never intended to use
the missiles he dispatched to Cuba in an offensive capacity.[87]
What he apparently did hope to do was to reveal the missiles'
presence in a dramatic fashion and then demand, as the price
for removing them, concessions from the West, probably on
Berlin, possibly also on nuclear-free zones in Central Europe
and the Far East.[88] Such a maneuver would have been consistent with his repeated attempts, since the mid-1950s, to
bludgeon the West into a settlement of Cold War issues.

The actions the Kennedy administration took upon discover-
ing the Soviet missile deployment in Cuba—a "quarantine" of
the island, together with what was virtually a public ultimatum
to remove the weapons—have, in recent years, come under
considerable criticism. The president has been charged with
having exaggerated the strategic significance of the Soviet deployment; critics are fond of quoting Secretary of Defense
Robert S. McNamara's observation, made at the time, that "it
makes no great difference whether you are killed by a missile
fired from the Soviet Union or from Cuba." It has also been
argued that Kennedy made no effort to resolve the crisis
through diplomatic means but instead welcomed a public confrontation with the Russians; the implication is that he had

[85] Horelick and Rush, *Strategic Power and Soviet Foreign Policy*, pp. 35–36, 83;
Wolfe, *Soviet Power and Europe*, pp. 182–183; Robin Edmonds, *Soviet Foreign Policy, 1962–1973: The Paradox of Super Power* (London: 1975), p. 27.

[86] Allison, *Essence of Decision*, p. 54; Raymond L. Garthoff, *Soviet Military Policy:
A Historical Analysis* (New York: 1966), pp. 120–121.

[87] Khrushchev to Kennedy, October 26, 1962, *Department of State Bulletin*,
LXIX(November 19, 1973), 640; *Khrushchev Remembers*, p. 549.

[88] Tatu, *Power in the Kremlin*, pp. 231–233; Ulam, *The Rivals*, p. 329.

forthcoming Congressional elections much in mind. Finally, it has been asserted that the episode was not the finely orchestrated exercise in crisis management it is often pictured as having been; that what brought about its favorable resolution was not skill but simply, in Dean Acheson's words, "plain dumb luck."[89]

None of these arguments is wholly fallacious, but they do share a certain narrowness of perspective for which allowances should be made. A doubling of the number of launchers capable of reaching the United States was no insignificant event, even if it did leave unchanged the overall strategic balance. Shorter distances to targets meant improved accuracy and reduced warning time; moreover United States detection systems had not been designed to pick up missiles coming from the south.[90] It is true that the Russians would have had difficulty in coordinating simultaneous launches from the Soviet Union and Cuba, but Khrushchev could be sure that no such action was contemplated—Kennedy could not. No doubt the administration did want to avoid another humiliation like the Bay of Pigs, but this desire reflected more than mere partisan concerns. Appearances are by no means insignificant components of international power; as Kennedy himself noted, the fact that Khrushchev's maneuver would have altered only the *appearance* of power relationships gave no guarantee that very real, and undesirable, consequences might not flow from that development.[91]

Private diplomacy might well have accomplished the same end that was in fact achieved, but probably not as efficiently. The advantage of a public challenge to the Russians was that it made Kennedy's determination all the more credible by greatly increasing the price he would have to pay to back down. It also precluded any attempt by Khrushchev to reveal the missiles'

---

[89] Robert A. Divine, ed., *The Cuban Missile Crisis* (Chicago: 1971), *passim*. See also Nathan and Oliver, *United States Foreign Policy and World Order*, pp. 322–326; Richard J. Walton, *Cold War and Counterrevolution: The Foreign Policy of John F. Kennedy*, (New York: 1972), pp. 103–142; Louise FitzSimons, *The Kennedy Doctrine* (New York: 1972), pp. 126–172.

[90] Allison, *Essence of Decision*, p. 54; Horelick and Rush, *Strategic Power and Soviet Foreign Policy*, pp. 137–138.

[91] Sorensen, *Kennedy*, p. 678.

presence himself, in an effort to reap at least some of the dividends he had hoped for. It is true that Kennedy risked nuclear war by openly demanding that Khrushchev yield, but given the Soviet Union's inferiority, in this instance both in strategic *and* conventional capabilities, he would appear to have had better rational grounds on which to anticipate achieving his objectives peacefully than his Soviet counterpart did when he made his high-risk decision to install missiles in Cuba in the first place.

The crisis ended with an unsubtle hint, delivered through the president's brother, Robert Kennedy, that the United States would remove the missiles from Cuba forcibly if Russians did not immediately agree to withdraw them.[92] Khrushchev at this point agreed to do so, in return for a public no-invasion pledge from Kennedy. Both sides could thus emerge from the crisis claiming victory, but there was little doubt as to who the real winners and losers were. "I won't deny," Khrushchev later admitted, "that we were obliged to make some big concessions in the interests of peace."[93]

The United States had its way in the Cuban missile crisis because Kennedy was able to convince Khrushchev that American strategic power might actually be put to military use against the Soviet Union. It had been Khrushchev's skepticism on this point that had allowed him to tolerate actual strategic inferiority for the past five years while simultaneously claiming superiority. The Soviet leader's long and emotional message to Kennedy on October 26—the first real break in the crisis—reflects the degree to which his self-assurance had been shaken:

. . . [We] are normal people. . . . Consequently, how can we permit the incorrect actions which you ascribe to us? Only lunatics or suicides, who themselves want to perish and to destroy the whole world before they die, could do this. We, however, want to live and do not at all want to destroy your country.[94]

Several weeks later, in a long and self-serving explanation of his actions to the Supreme Soviet, Khrushchev reflected somewhat ruefully that while "imperialism today is no longer what it used

---

[92] Robert F. Kennedy, *Thirteen Days: A Memoir of the Cuban Missile Crisis* (New York: 1969), pp. 108–109.

[93] *Khrushchev Remembers*, p. 553.

[94] *Department of State Bulletin*, LXIX(November 19, 1973), 641.

to be," those who had described it as a "paper tiger" (meaning, of course, the Chinese) should know that "this 'paper tiger' has atomic teeth. It can use them and it must not be treated lightly."[95]

The Cuban missile crisis has been seen as having constituted a fundamental turning point in the history of the Cold War.[96] This may be to exaggerate its significance—the Cold War was, after all, a multifarious phenomenon; aspects of it had disappeared long before 1962, while others would persist long afterwards. What the missile crisis did do was to force Khrushchev to abandon once and for all his disruptive strategy of seeking detente through intimidation—the Soviet leader appears to have been genuinely shocked by the proximity with which the world had approached a nuclear holocaust. Paradoxically, however, the crisis also demonstrated, more clearly than any other single event since World War II, the beneficent effect of nuclear weapons development on the problem of maintaining world order. The level of tension in this crisis was sufficiently great that if both sides had not possessed such weapons, war almost certainly would have started. That it did not can be attributed, not so much to skilled diplomacy on each side, as to a sober realization on the part of both of what a failure of diplomacy would mean.

---

[95] Speech of December 12, 1962, *Documents on International Affairs, 1962* (London: 1971), p. 257.
[96] Halle, *The Cold War as History,* pp. 408–411.

CHAPTER IX

From Confrontation to Negotiation: 1962–1976

RELATIONS BETWEEN WASHINGTON AND MOSCOW, it sometimes appears, are conducted in a kind of acronymic short-hand—ICBM, SLBM, ABM, MIRV, MARV, MBFR, CSCE, MFN, even MAD—all have specific meanings, if not to laymen, at least to those responsible for monitoring developments in the frequently arcane fields which these abbreviations represent. There is yet another acronym, though, which might usefully be employed more often than it is: this is GRIT, or "graduated reciprocation in tension-reduction." Proposed by psychologist Charles E. Osgood in 1962, GRIT assumed that the process which had produced the Cold War—graduated, reciprocal increases in tension—could be reversed; that a "spiral of terror" could become a "spiral of trust."[1] It would be foolish to claim that in the ensuing decade and a half trust has in fact become the basis of relations among the super powers. Still, the relative importance of terror in that relationship has been reduced, in a manner roughly in accordance with Osgood's prescription. Both sides have at least shown a desire to avoid future confrontations on the scale of the Cuban missile crisis; as a result, there have gradually emerged more congruities of interest than either side thought existed. It is too early to say whether this means that the "Cold War" phase in Russian and American contacts with one another is drawing to a close. The relationship has, however, shifted to a less perilous level, and that fact offers grounds for at least limited optimism.

---

[1] Charles E. Osgood, *An Alternative to War or Surrender* (Urbana: 1962), pp. 86–87.

I

The Cuban missile crisis did not, as is sometimes popularly asserted, frighten Soviet and American leaders into embracing a policy of detente. Whatever their motives, both sides had for some time sought a relaxation of Cold War tensions, though by divergent methods. What the missile crisis did was to bring those methods into closer correspondence with one another. By far the greater movement took place on the Soviet side as Khrushchev now abandoned his obviously counterproductive strategy of seeking to bully the West into an easing of antagonisms. On the American side the change was less dramatic—the Kennedy administration made no significant alteration in its earlier policy of seeking agreements on such negotiable issues as existed while at the same time taking care not to convey to the Russians an appearance of weakness. Kennedy could pursue this approach with greater assurance of domestic support than in the past, however, thanks to the enhanced respectability the events of October 1962 had brought to the cause of detente.

Statements of Soviet leaders during the months following the missile crisis reflected what one observer at the time described as a "decidedly chastened spirit."[2] "It wasn't in the interests of socialism to allow the crisis over Cuba to develop into a thermonuclear war," Khrushchev told the Supreme Soviet with unconscious irony in December 1962: "Why should we invite ourselves to go to the Devil? . . . Nobody has yet returned from there to tell us that it is better there than it is on earth." Foreign Minister Gromyko blandly observed that if only the Americans had asked, he would gladly have told them of the Soviet missiles in Cuba. Less disingenuously, he congratulated Kennedy and his advisers for having "acted with circumspection, since it is dark, indeed, in this abyss and the bottom is not to be seen." Significantly, Gromyko also resurrected Lenin's 1921 call for friendly relations with the United States, observing that there were "sober voices" within that country "calling for . . . a policy which takes the interests of the Soviet Union and other socialist countries into consideration."[3]

---

[2] Richard P. Stebbins, *The United States in World Affairs, 1963* (New York: 1964), p. 10.

[3] *Documents on International Affairs, 1962*, pp. 260, 277–281.

The confrontation over Cuba had a sobering effect in the United States as well, though not in such an obvious way. With the conspicuous exception of the Bay of Pigs incident, each of the major foreign policy crises the Kennedy administration had faced since 1961 had been provoked by Khrushchev in pursuit of his "detente through intimidation" strategy. Renunciation of this approach would, in and of itself, have produced a considerable improvement in Soviet-American relations. Kennedy sought to hasten the process, though, with a carefully worded expression of willingness to move beyond ideological rigidities. "No government or social system is so evil that its people must be considered as lacking in virtue," he told an audience at American University in June 1963. "No nation in the history of battle ever suffered more than the Soviet Union suffered in the course of the Second World War." Kennedy then went on to assess realistically the prospects for detente:

Both the United States and its allies, and the Soviet Union and its allies, have a mutually deep interest in a just and genuine peace and in halting the arms race. Agreements to this end are in the interests of the Soviet Union as well as ours, and even the most hostile nations can be relied upon to accept and keep those treaty obligations, and only those treaty obligations, which are in their own interest.

"Our most basic common link," he concluded, "is that we all inhabit this planet. We all breathe the same air. We all cherish our children's future. And we are all mortal".[4]

It was a speech that could not have been given a year earlier without provoking outcries of "appeasement" and "softness toward communism," not just from Republicans but from members of the president's own party as well. As it was, criticism of the address was curiously muted, suggesting that the trauma of the missile crisis had at least expanded the range of politically feasible discourse within the United States on the subject of detente.[5] Khrushchev's reaction too was moderately favorable; there developed as a result a propitious atmosphere for talks which were about to begin in Moscow looking toward the conclusion of a limited nuclear test ban treaty.

---

[4] Richard P. Stebbins, ed., *Documents on American Foreign Relations, 1963* (New York: 1964), pp. 119–120.

[5] Sorensen, *Kennedy*, p. 733.

The "Treaty Banning Nuclear Weapons Tests in the Atmosphere, in Outer Space and Under Water," signed by representatives of the United States, the Soviet Union, and Great Britain on August 5, 1963, left open the possibility of underground weapons tests, and so represented a retreat from earlier Soviet attempts to achieve a comprehensive test ban treaty. Still, the agreement marked an important milestone for several reasons. It was the first formal undertaking between major Cold War antagonists to place some restraints, however limited, on the nuclear arms race. It avoided the problems of on-site inspection, upon which previous arms control discussions with the Russians had come to grief, by addressing itself only to those forms of testing capable of being monitored from outside the Soviet Union. It also constituted, for Khrushchev, a public endorsement of detente with the West at the expense of whatever appearance still remained of Sino-Soviet solidarity: his final attempt to resolve differences with the Chinese, vociferous critics of the treaty, had ended in failure five days before that document was initialed.[6] Finally, the steadily mounting enthusiasm with which the treaty was received in the United States, and the corresponding decline of opposition to it in the Senate, which gave its approval in September, suggested that suspicion of the Soviet Union was not so deep as to preclude taking some minimal risks to reduce the danger of war.[7]

The test ban treaty was only one of several accords reached with the Russians during the sudden flowering of mutual amiability that took place in 1963. An agreement establishing a Moscow-Washington "hot line" had been concluded in June —the purpose of this direct communications link was to avoid delays of the kind that held up exchanges between Kennedy and Khrushchev during the tense days of the missile crisis. In October, the United States and the Soviet Union agreed to endorse a United Nations resolution calling for a ban on the placement (as opposed to the testing, covered in the test ban treaty) of nuclear weapons in outer space. Prospects for

---

[6] John Gittings, *Survey of the Sino-Soviet Dispute, 1963–1967* (London: 1968), pp. 184–192.

[7] Stebbins, *The U.S. in World Affairs, 1963*, pp. 26–29. See also Sorensen, *Kennedy*, pp. 739–740.

economic contacts brightened noticeably that same month when President Kennedy approved the sale of some $250 million worth of surplus American wheat to the Soviet Union to help meet one of that country's chronic agricultural shortfalls. In none of these understandings did either side compromise anything approaching a vital national interest. But, as Kennedy noted in one of his last foreign policy addresses, delivered on October 19, the fact that agreements of even limited scope could be reached indicated how far Soviet-American relations had come since the dramatic events of a year before.[8]

John F. Kennedy's assassination in Dallas the following month occasioned a degree of sorrow in Moscow comparable only to that generated by Roosevelt's death eighteen years earlier. Khrushchev personally paid his respects at the American embassy; some years later he recorded this tribute in his oral reminiscences:

Kennedy was . . . someone we could trust. When he gave us public assurances that the US would not organize an invasion of Cuba, . . . we trusted him. We accepted the concession he was making and made a concession of our own by withdrawing our nuclear weapons from Cuba. . . . Despite the irreconcilability of our class antagonisms, . . . Kennedy and I found common ground and a common language when it came to preventing a military conflict. . . . He showed great flexibility and, together, we avoided disaster.[9]

Khrushchev, too, came to be regarded, during his last year in power, with a surprising degree of indulgence in the United States. When false rumors of his death swept Western capitals in April 1964, the *Washington Post* noted: "We felt a leap at the heart and a great concern that a man vital to the balance of the world had been lost".[10] The Soviet leader's abrupt deposition six months later brought more apprehension than rejoicing; it also elicited from Lyndon B. Johnson an assessment curiously parallel to Khrushchev's encomium on Kennedy:

---

[8] Stebbins, ed., *Documents on American Foreign Relations, 1963*, p. 164.

[9] *Khrushchev Remembers: The Last Testament*, pp. 513–514.

[10] Quoted in Abraham Brumberg, "The Fall of Khrushchev—Causes and Repercussions," in John W. Strong, ed., *The Soviet Union under Brezhnev and Kosygin* (New York: 1971), p. 2.

There were times when he was guilty of dangerous adventure. It required great American firmness and good sense—first in Berlin and later in the Cuban missile crisis—to turn back his threats and actions without war. Yet he learned from his mistakes, and he was not blind to realities. In the last 2 years, his Government has shown itself aware of the need for sanity in the nuclear age.[11]

Speculation as to the relative importance of men and circumstances in history tends to slide easily into the realm of the unverifiable. Still, it does not seem wholly irresponsible to suggest that the cause of peace was well served by the presence, during and immediately after a period of unprecedented tension, of leaders on both sides capable of perceiving shared interests through the distractions created by ideological differences, unwieldy bureaucracies, dissimiliar backgrounds, and the allurements of pride and prestige. Such had not always been the case in the history of Russian-American relations nor would it invariably be so in the future. Whatever their shortcomings as custodians of national power—and these are not difficult to point out—the unlikely "partnership" of Kennedy and Khrushchev must be given credit for having reversed, in however limited a fashion, the lockstep process of escalation and counter escalation that had characterized the first two decades of the postwar era.

II

Kennedy had felt obliged to caution shortly before his death, however, that "a pause in the cold war is not a lasting peace, and a *detente* does not equal disarmament."[12] This is a useful qualification to keep in mind in assessing the post-missile crisis "thaw" in Soviet-American relations, for while elements of change had clearly manifested themselves in the foreign policies of Washington and Moscow, there were also elements of continuity with what had gone before which placed definite limitations on how far the process of reconciliation could proceed.

One of these was the strategic arms race. It is becoming clear

---

[11] Statement of October 18, 1964, in Jules Davids, ed., *Documents on American Foreign Relations, 1964* (New York: 1965), p. 142.

[12] Speech of October 19, 1963, in Stebbins, ed., *Documents on American Foreign Relations, 1963*, p. 164.

in retrospect that among the Kennedy administration's most significant steps, in terms of its long-term consequences, was its decision to press on with the production of ICBMs and SLBMs after it had become clear that there was no missile gap. Eisenhower's final defense budget would have given the United States, by the mid-1960s, 19 missile-firing Polaris submarines and 450 silo-launched Minuteman missiles. Kennedy expanded this program, first to 29 submarines and 800 Minutemen, then, *after* public exposure of the "missile gap" myth late in 1961, to 41 submarines and 1000 Minutemen. This buildup reflected no quest for a first-strike capability against the USSR—American experts had, by 1963, ruled out any possibility of destroying all Soviet strategic weapons in a single attack. Rather, it was the product of interservice compromises within the Pentagon and a reluctance on the part of the administration to admit having overestimated the Soviet missile threat.[13] The effect, however, was to give the United States, by the time of Khrushchev's downfall, a considerable advantage over the Soviet Union in numbers of strategic weapons. As late as April 1965, Secretary of Defense McNamara could claim for the United States a superiority of three or four to one and could announce that the Russians had "lost the quantitative race."[14]

In its misreading of the future, this remark compares favorably with Neville Chamberlain's famous observation that Hitler had "missed the bus", for the year 1965 saw the Soviet Union begin a massive deployment of SS-9 and SS-11 ICBMs, together with improved missile-firing submarines, which would within five years bring it to the point of numerical parity with the United States.[15] To say that the Kennedy administration's missile buildup provoked this response would be to oversimplify —the strategic arms race has never been a straightforward cycle of action on one side and reaction of the other.[16] Still, it is clear

---

[13] Kahan, *Security in the Nuclear Age*, pp. 84–94; Harland B. Moulton, *From Superiority to Parity: The United States and the Strategic Arms Race, 1961–1971* (Westport, Connecticut: 1973), p. 79.

[14] "Interview with Robert S. McNamara, Defense Secretary: Is Russia Slowing Down the Arms Race?" *U.S. News and World Report*, LVIII(April 12, 1965), 52.

[15] Wolfe, *Soviet Power and Europe*, pp. 432–437.

[16] See, on this point, Albert Wohlstetter, "Is There a Strategic Arms Race?" *Foreign Policy*, #15(Summer, 1974), pp. 3–20, and #16(Fall, 1974), pp. 48–81.

that the new Soviet leadership of Leonid Brezhnev and Alexei Kosygin was not prepared to tolerate, as had Khrushchev, the prospect of indefinite strategic inferiority. This position involved no repudiation of Khrushchev's hopes for relaxing tensions with the West, but it did delay that process, since it proceeded from the assumption that the Soviet Union should not negotiate on arms control until rough strategic equivalency had been achieved. To the extent that Kennedy's program increased the number of weapons the Russians would have to build before reaching that point, it can be said to have contributed, as McNamara later admitted,[17] to some retardation in the progress of detente.

Another set of circumstances that threatened to affect detente was, of course, the growing American involvement in Indochina. Historians will long puzzle over what motivated the Kennedy and Johnson administrations to send United States forces to Vietnam; certainly the Russians must have marveled at the logic by which Washington could tolerate an avowed Soviet satellite ninety miles off Florida while expending vast amounts of money and blood halfway around the world to suppress an indigenous guerrilla movement whose deference to either Moscow or Peking was, at best, limited. Despite continued references, as if by reflex, to something called the "Sino-Soviet bloc," American officials had long since moved beyond regarding all communist movements everywhere as agents of the Kremlin. As Secretary of State Dean Rusk put it in February, 1964: "The Communist world is no longer a single flock of sheep following blindly behind one leader."[18] Still, administration spokesmen sought repeatedly to justify the war as one more stage in the long process of containment that had begun twenty years before. "The American people . . . have learned the great lesson of this generation," President Johnson told the Congress in May, 1965:

Wherever we have stood firm aggression has been halted, peace restored, and liberty maintained. This was true in Iran, in Greece and

---

[17] Robert S. McNamara, *The Essence of Security* (New York: 1968), pp. 57–59.
[18] Speech of February 25, 1964, in Davids, ed., *Documents on American Foreign Relations, 1964*, p. 146. See also Lyndon Baines Johnson, *The Vantage Point: Perspectives on the Presidency, 1963–1969* (New York: 1971), p. 470.

Turkey, and in Korea. It was true in the Formosa Strait and in Lebanon. It was true at the Cuban missile crisis. It will be true again in Southeast Asia.[19]

What had happened was that the process of containment had come to be regarded as of greater importance than precision as to who, or what, was being contained. As Johnson argued:

The aim in Vietnam is not simply the conquest of the South, tragic as that would be. It is to show that American commitment is worthless. Once that is done, the gates are down and the road is open to expansion and endless conquest.[20]

From a policy initially designed to rally forces of nationalism, even where communist, against the expanding power of the Soviet Union, containment had evolved into a program of resistance to communism, even where nationalist, for the purpose of preserving American credibility in the world. It is significant that George Kennan, more than anyone else the architect of the original concept of containment, now publicly condemned this application of it, noting that "there is more respect to be won in the opinion of this world by a resolute and courageous liquidation of unsound positions than by the most stubborn pursuit of extravagant and unpromising objectives."[21] Ironically, the Johnson administration came to place a considerable reliance, for its extrication from the Vietnam morass, on the original target of containment, the Soviet Union itself.

Johnson saw no reason why the Kremlin should not help arrange a Vietnam settlement: "We seek in southeast Asia an order and security that we think would contribute to the peace of the whole world," he announced in August 1966, "and in that, we think, the Soviet Union has a very large stake.[22] Not surprisingly, the Russians took a somewhat different view. Where Khrushchev had regarded the Indochina conflict with relative detachment, Brezhnev and Kosygin initiated a program

---

[19] Message to Congress, May 4, 1965, in Richard P. Stebbins, ed., *Documents on American Foreign Relations, 1965* (New York: 1966), p. 162.

[20] Ibid., p. 160.

[21] Quoted in Brown, *The Faces of Power*, p. 344.

[22] Speech of August 26, 1966, in Richard P. Stebbins, ed., *Documents on American Foreign Relations: 1966* (New York: 1967), p. 68.

of aid to North Vietnam which, while in no way comparable to American expenditures ($1.6 billion versus $99.2 billion for the period 1965–1971, by one estimate[23]), nonetheless did play a significant role in sustaining Hanoi's war effort. Nor did the Russians exert themselves unduly to speed an end to the fighting, although they did at several points serve as an intermediary between the Americans and the North Vietnamese. Clearly Washington's preoccupation with Southeast Asia served Soviet interests by distracting the attention of policymakers, dispersing men and resources in an area of peripheral importance, and isolating the United States from a considerable body of world opinion. As long as the struggle showed no signs of escalating beyond the region involved, the Russians were quite happy to have it continue.[24]

Still, Johnson was probably correct when he argued, in retrospect, that his Vietnam policy did not significantly impede the progress of detente.[25] The Russians have a long history of sacrificing allies' interests when in conflict with their own: even the systematic American bombardment of a "fraternal" socialist country, initiated with particularly graceless timing during Kosygin's February 1965 visit to Hanoi, was not enough to cause the Kremlin to give up its policy of avoiding direct confrontations with the United States. Certainly the war did not, as many had feared, drive the Russians and Chinese back together: arguments over who was doing more to help Ho Chi Minh provoked such bitterness that, by early 1967, Moscow and Peking were accusing each other of collusion with the Americans in Southeast Asia.[26] Furthermore, the war had the unanticipated effect of facilitating the Soviet drive for strategic parity: the Johnson administration decided not to try to stay ahead of the Russians in the quantitative ICBM race, as much because of budgetary pressures growing out of Vietnam as from informed

[23] International Institute for Strategic Studies, *Strategic Survey, 1972* (London: 1973), pp. 49–50.

[24] Edmonds, *Soviet Foreign Policy,* pp. 45–46; W. W. Kulski, *The Soviet Union in World Affairs: A Documented Analysis, 1964–1972* (Syracuse: 1973), pp. 240–241.

[25] Johnson, *The Vantage Point,* pp. 475–476.

[26] Edmonds, *Soviet Foreign Policy,* pp. 47–48; Gittings, *Sino-Soviet Dispute,* pp. 259–260.

judgments that the point of diminishing returns had been reached in long-range missile strength.[27]

The new American attitude toward the arms race became clear early in 1967 in response to indications that the Russians were constructing antiballistic missile emplacements around Moscow. While ostensibly defensive, the Soviet ABM deployment had definite offensive implications, for in the new and strange logic of stragic weapons competition, anything that might prevent one side's missiles from reaching their targets could be seen as tempting the other side into trying a first strike. Instead of seeking a comparable deployment of this expensive and unstable weapons system, Johnson proposed negotiations with the Russians to limit ICBMs, ABMs, and to conclude work on a treaty banning the further proliferation of nuclear weapons, on which exchanges had already taken place. Encouraged by the restraint the Russians had shown during the June 1967 Arab-Israeli War (during which the "hot line" had been used for the first time to defuse a crisis), Johnson agreed to meet with Kosygin while the Soviet premier was in New York for an emergency United Nations session on the Middle East. The ensuing three-day summit, held on a college campus in Glassboro, New Jersey at the end of June, produced generally friendly discussions but no agreement on negotiations to limit the strategic arms race. Yielding to growing domestic pressure, the administration later that year decided to go ahead with construction of a "thin" ABM system, officially described as directed against the Chinese.[28]

By the summer of 1968, however, the situation had changed in several respects. In quantitative terms, the Russians were approaching their goal of strategic parity. Johnson had limited the bombing of North Vietnam and had announced his forthcoming retirement from the presidency. Discussions on the Non-Proliferation Treaty had borne fruit, and as that document was signed, on July 1, the Russians announced their willingness to begin talks "in the nearest future" on the limitation of offensive and defensive weapons systems. On August 19, they proposed

---

[27] Moulton, *From Superiority to Parity*, pp. 283–287.

[28] Kahan, *Security in the Nuclear Age*, pp. 121–123. See also Johnson, *The Vantage Point*, pp. 297–301, 481–485.

starting the negotiations in Moscow in October and extended an invitation for Johnson to visit the Soviet capital on that occasion. The next day, however, Soviet ambassador Anatolii Dobrynin had to inform Johnson that

in connection with the further aggravation of the situation .. created by a conspiracy of the external and internal forces of aggression against the existing social order in Czechoslovakia . . ., the Government of the Czechoslovak Socialist Republic [has] approached the allied states, the Soviet Union among them, with a request of rendering direct assistance, including the assistance by military forces.

Much as Johnson had often done with regard to Vietnam, Dobrynin added his government's hope that "current events should not harm Soviet-American relations," but in fact the invasion of Czechoslovakia forced the administration to shelve, for the remainder of its term, plans for arms control talks with the Russians.[29]

The Czech crisis was at once the product of detente and an indication of its limitations. Both major European alliances —NATO and the Warsaw Pact—depended for their cohesion in large part on shared perceptions of external threat. As Soviet-American tensions began to decline after 1962, friction developed within each system. In the West, it manifested itself in the failure of the cumbersome Multilateral Nuclear Force concept for sharing control of nuclear weapons and in General Charles DeGaulle's 1966 decision to withdraw French forces from military participation in NATO. The Eastern European scene was also one of disarray, with the Rumanians in particular approaching the Chinese in their ostentatious demonstrations of independence from Moscow. Not surprisingly, both sides sought to profit from these trends. Johnson as early as 1964 had initiated a campaign to "build bridges" to Eastern Europe, a project endorsed with even greater enthusiasm by West Germany following the coming to power there of the Kiesinger-Brandt coalition in late 1966. The Russians responded by accelerating their own efforts to supplant NATO with an all-European security system, an idea they had first broached more than a decade earlier. Neither Washington nor Moscow could

---

[29] Ibid., pp. 487–491.

avoid noting, however, that the price of progress in either of these enterprises would likely be some attrition in the solidity of their own alliances.[30]

What the invasion of Czechoslovakia showed was that the West could more easily afford this price than could the Soviet Union. The Russians had made no effort to oppose the coming to power of Alexander Dubcek early in 1968, but as the new government in Prague began to move toward an abandonment of censorship, secret police rule, and restrictions on political activity by non-Communists, Moscow became alarmed. One can discount the official explanation the Russians gave for their decision to send Soviet and satellite forces into Czechoslovakia on the night of August 20–21: there is no evidence of NATO or West German collusion with the Dubcek regime; indeed the United States and its allies had gone out of their way to avoid any appearance of provocation during that spring and summer. What the Russians feared was rather the impact of "reform communism" on their long-range military position in Eastern Europe and, ultimately, on the security of the Soviet regime itself.[31] Because it served, to a greater extent than did NATO, the interests of a single dominant state, the Warsaw Pact simply could not accommodate the diversities of viewpoint, and hence of political systems, that characterized its Western counterpart.

Both Vietnam and Czechoslovakia represented efforts by the superpowers to secure what each had perceived to be an eroding power base; paradoxically, the effect of the actions each took was to accelerate that process of erosion. Far from enhancing the credibility of American commitments, the war in Vietnam raised widespread doubts regarding Washington's ability to wield power in a manner consistent with its own self-interest, world opinion, and sheer common sense. The war weakened NATO, fueled inflation, shattered a domestic consensus on foreign policy dating back to the 1940s, accelerated the Soviet achievement of strategic parity, and, ultimately, forced Johnson from the

---

[30] Wolfe, *Soviet Power and Europe*, pp. 312–313. See also Stebbins, *The U.S. in World Affairs, 1964*, pp. 36–37, 99–101; Richard P. Stebbins, *The United States in World Affairs, 1966* (New York: 1967), pp. 6–8, 115–133, 148–168; and Richard P. Stebbins, *The United States in World Affairs, 1967* (New York: 1968), pp. 143–151.
[31] Wolfe, *Soviet Power and Europe*, pp. 359–392.

presidency. The Soviet invasion of Czechoslovakia, far from eliminating the threat of "reform communism," actually strengthened that trend within Western European communist parties, especially after the Russians sought clumsily to legitimize their action through the "Brezhnev Doctrine," an assertion of Moscow's right to intervene in the affairs of any "socialist" country to suppress "counterrevolution." It also did much to repair the damage Vietnam had done to NATO, weakened the military potential of the Warsaw Pact forces, and tarnished overnight the image of moderation the new Soviet leadership had been trying to project since Khrushchev's downfall.[32]

Significantly, however neither Vietnam nor Czechoslovakia did lasting damage to the cause of detente. Both superpowers managed in time to swallow these repective insults in the interest of pursuing agreement on matters of mutual concern, notably arms control, trade, and the "management" of conflicts among third parties. Arguing from effect to intent, some critics, including the Chinese, even asserted that a tacit understanding had been reached between Washington and Moscow to perpetuate the international status quo.[33] This puts the matter too strongly, but what one can say accurately is that by 1969 both the United States and the Soviet Union had demonstrated a greater inclination than had previously been present to frame their relationship, not in terms of the instruments of diplomacy —alliances, weapons buildups, rhetorical posturing, quests for credibility—but in terms of its chief end—the resolution of outstanding differences. It was on this basis that the achievements of the next four years would rest.

III

Historians are likely to regard 1969 as a major turning point in the history of the Cold War, for it was in that year that the internal situation in each of the major countries involved simultaneously came to favor detente. During that year the Soviet Union achieved its long-sought goal of strategic parity with the United States; at the same time, however, hopes for economic

---

[32] See, on the impact of Czechoslovakia, ibid., pp. 383–385, 393–426.
[33] Lester A. Sobel, ed., *Kissinger & Detente* (New York: 1975), pp. 67–70.

parity receded with the realization that capitalist assistance would be necessary to solve Russia's industrial and agricultural problems. In China, the calculated irrationality known as the "Great Cultural Revolution" was coming to an end; meanwhile, fighting had broken out between Chinese and Soviet forces along the Ussuri River. In the United States, the slow process of disengagement from Vietnam had begun; there had also come to power in Washington an administration that could hardly be accused of "softness" toward communism and that therefore, in the odd logic of American politics, enjoyed greater latitude in negotiating with its ideological adversaries than had been available to its predecessors. This unusual juxtaposition of circumstances produced no overnight disappearance of Soviet-American tensions, but it did make possible, over the next three years, their considerable relaxation.

"After a period of confrontation, we are entering an era of negotiation."[34] It was an unexpected tone for Richard M. Nixon to take in his inaugural address, given his long record of hostility toward the communist world. One advantage of protracted ideological rigidity, though, is that by abandoning it one can enhance one's reputation for statesmanship; if this process alienates old supporters, then the influx of new found and pleasantly surprised allies will more than compensate for them. Another useful trait in a statesman is not to bear grudges: this characteristic (not often applied by Nixon in other situations, one must add) enabled the new president to obtain the services of Dr. Henry A. Kissinger as his assistant for national security affairs, despite the fact that the Harvard professor had only months before proclaimed the Republican nominee unfit to occupy the White House.[35] Students of diplomacy, politics, and human behavior will be arguing for years over the precise nature of this remarkable partnership; what is clear now is that Nixon and Kissinger grasped the significance of the moment at which they had come to power and were determined to use it to try to bring about an end to the Cold War.

---

[34] Richard P. Stebbins and Elaine P. Adam, eds., *Documents on American Foreign Relations, 1968–69* (New York: 1972), p. 41.

[35] Marvin Kalb and Bernard Kalb, *Kissinger* (Boston: 1974), pp. 15–16; Henry Brandon, *The Retreat of American Power* (Garden City, New York: 1973), pp. 24–25.

Their approach, as both men later described it, was to take advantage of uncertainties created by the Soviet achievement of strategic parity, economic difficulties within the USSR, and the fragmentation of the international communist movement to reinforce attitudes on the part of Kremlin leaders conducive to detente. As Nixon put it in 1972:

There were ambiguous tendencies in Soviet policy; the same factors that might lead the USSR toward greater hostility also suggested the opportunity for a relaxation of tension. The task of American policy was to recognize the persistence of this ambiguity and to take action to strengthen the more positive tendencies.

Kissinger described the same strategy in a slightly different manner two years later: "When Soviet policy moved toward conciliation we sought to turn what may have started as a tactical maneuver into a durable pattern of conduct."[36]

Because there exists no generally agreed-upon standard of strength in this field, it is difficult to say precisely when Soviet strategic power came to equal that of the United States. In numbers of land-based ICBMs, the Russians passed the Americans sometime in 1969; by the end of that year they had approximately 1200 such weapons, as compared to 1054 for the United States, a figure that had not changed since 1967. The Russians had also deployed by that time an ABM system of questionable reliability. The United States retained almost a three-to-one advantage in SLBMs, though (656 versus 230), and an even larger lead in long-range bombers (540 versus 150).[37] The Americans also led the Russians in missile accuracy and in numbers of warheads, an index of increasing significance with the perfection of MIRV (multiple independently-targetable re-entry vehicle) technology.

In the end, however, numbers and characteristics of weapons are not as significant as the attitudes of political leaders who control their use. In this respect, the turning point in the arms race may well have come with Nixon's first press conference as

---

[36] Richard M. Nixon, *U.S. Foreign Policy for the 1970's: The Emerging Structure of Peace: Report to the Congress, February 9, 1972* (Washington: 1972), p. 18; Kissinger statement before Senate Foreign Relations Committee, September 19, 1974, *Department of State Bulletin,* LXXI (October 14, 1974), 508.

[37] Institute for Strategic Studies, *Strategic Survey, 1969* (London: 1970), p. 27.

president, on January 27, 1969. In it, he explicitly renounced the goal of strategic "superiority," which he had strongly advocated during the campaign, in favor of "sufficiency," a concept Kissinger had supported. Nixon thereby served notice that he would not reverse the Johnson administration's tacit acquiescence in the Soviet attainment of strategic parity. The new chief executive had come to this decision for many of the same reasons his predecessor had: studies had shown that further increases in missile strength would provide little additional protection against a Soviet attack; such an effort would cost too much at a time when pressure was intensifying for cuts in the defense budget; and, finally, the Russians appeared capable of matching any new escalation of the arms race weapon for weapon.

Transforming a necessity into a virtue is easier, however, if one can avoid the appearance of having been pushed, and this Nixon and Kissinger skillfully did. The president coupled his blessing of "sufficiency" with the announcement that he would not proceed immediately into talks on the limitation of strategic weapons, stalled the previous year by the Soviet invasion of Czechoslovakia but now eagerly advocated both by the Russians and by former officials of the Johnson administration. He also announced, shortly thereafter, decisions to go ahead with construction of an American ABM system and to deploy MIRVs. The ABM program was almost certainly intended as a bargaining chip in future SALT negotiations: the costly system was untestable short of nuclear war and so provided little assurance of protection. MIRVs were far more reliable; moreover, Kissinger doubted whether they would ever be included in a SALT agreement, since verification would require on-site inspection, something the Russians had always resisted. Only after carefully establishing what arms control measures they could accept without violating the standard of "sufficiency" did Nixon and Kissinger, in October 1969, agree to begin SALT talks with the Russians the following month.[38]

Several things are noteworthy about Kissinger's approach to SALT. He appears to have viewed the early discussions as an

---

[38] Kahan, *Security in the Nuclear Age,* pp. 144–145, 172–177; Kalb and Kalb, *Kissinger,* pp. 100–115.

opportunity to "educate" the Russians, who at times demonstrated a surprising unfamiliarity with their own strategic weapons systems and the intricacies of arms control issues generally. He did all he could to avoid bureaucratic delays —especially useful in this regard were what he called "building blocks," a series of proposals, all cleared in advance, which the American delegation could put before the Russians in various combinations without consulting Washington on each change of position. During the latter stages of the talks Kissinger relied heavily on "back channel" contacts with Moscow, carried on independently of and at times without the knowledge of the SALT negotiators for the purpose of clarifying positions. And, possibly most important, Kissinger sought to circumvent the touchy issue of on-site inspection by focusing the talks on those weapons systems capable of being monitored by "national technical means"—a polite euphemism for satellite reconnaissance.[39]

It would be difficult to say who came out on top in the strategic arms limitation agreements Nixon and Brezhnev signed in Moscow in May 1972. On the one hand, the Russians, by agreeing to a mutual limitation of ABM deployments to two sites (one defending an ICBM emplacement, the other the national capital), in effect endorsed the long-standing American argument that stability in the nuclear arms race could best be attained by foregoing attempts to defend population centers. Approval of this "mutual assured destruction" concept (MAD) represented a significant change of attitude on the part of the security-conscious Soviet state. On the other hand, imposition of a freeze on existing numbers of land-based and submarine-launched ballistics missiles constituted not just an acknowledgment of Soviet parity—it actually left the United States with a substantial numerical inferiority in ICBMs (1618 versus 1054) and a smaller one in SLBMS (740 versus 656).[40]

Whether the Russians and the Americans would have done without SALT what they promised not to do under it is open to

[39] Ibid., pp. 116–117; Kahan, *Security in the Nuclear Age,* pp. 177–186; John Newhouse, *Cold Dawn: The Story of SALT* (New York: 1973), pp. 166–249.

[40] Ibid., pp. 3–4; Alton H. Quanbeck and Barry M. Blechman, *Strategic Forces: Issues for the Mid-Seventies* (Washington: 1973), pp. 13–15, 26.

question. The costly and unreliable characteristics of ABMs might have kept the Russians from deploying them on a large scale in any event; similarly the United States, convinced of the "sufficiency" of its deterrent, might never have matched Soviet increases in ICBMs and SLBMs. Certainly the SALT accords did little to forestall qualitative improvements in each side's strategic capabilities—satellite reconnaissance was of only limited use in determining a missile's range, accuracy, or the number of warheads it carried. Nor did the negotiations produce restrictions on manned bombers or cruise missiles, weapons systems with considerable actual and potential strategic implications. None of this is to say, however, that the agreements were without value.

The SALT I treaties should be evaluated, not in terms of whether they hastened or retarded the Soviet Union's emergence as the strategic equal of the United States, but in terms of the political context they created within which to deal with that probably unavoidable development. Predictions of what would happen when the Russians reached strategic parity had tended to range between two very different alternatives: either Moscow would use its new found strength to intimidate the West, as Khrushchev had tried to do a decade earlier, or the achievement of parity would give Kremlin leaders the self-confidence necessary to engage, for the first time, in meaningful negotiations to resolve outstanding issues.[41] It was the policy of the Nixon administration, through SALT, to encourage the latter over the former alternative.

The United States could have responded to the Soviet achievment of parity by embarking on a new arms buildup of its own, but such a decision would have required a major escalation of the Cold War in return for only transitory benefits. It could, alternatively, have lapsed into some combination of isolationism and appeasement, but the disadvantages here, too, were obvious. A third option, the one actually followed, was to explore with the Soviet Union opportunities for declaring "off limits" certain areas of strategic weapons competition, to the extent that this could be done without adversely affecting the

---

[41] Wolfe, *Soviet Power and Europe,* pp. 510–515; Horelick and Rush, *Strategic Power and Soviet Foreign Policy,* pp. 176–195.

military balance. There is no reason to believe that the agreements reached at Moscow threatened that equilibrium; in fact, they probably reinforced it by limiting the further deployment of Soviet ICBMs and SLBMs. Moreover, they set an important precedent for discussions on other issues. SALT may well have represented, then, the best of the available possibilities for coming to grips with the undeniable reality of Soviet strategic parity.

If detente was the product of Soviet self-confidence growing out of the attainment of strategic parity, however, it also developed in large part from anxieties generated by chronic economic difficulties. Such problems were, of course, nothing new—dislocations stemming from the effort to make economics fit ideology had long been a prominent feature of life in the USSR. What was new was the leadership's awareness that the economic gap between Russia and the West was growing, particularly in the areas of advanced technological and managerial skills, at a time when it confronted the twin necessities of maintaining Soviet military strength while satisfying growing internal demands for consumer goods. Prospects for resolving this dilemma through autarkic means appeared increasingly unpromising; it began to look as though the Soviet Union would not be able to compete with the West without help from the West, in the form of trade, investment, and, most important, technology transfers.[42]

As had been the case half a century earlier when the new Soviet state had sought to industrialize by importing foreign technology, Kremlin leaders counted on capitalist entrepreneurial instincts to override whatever political or strategic objections might exist to such exchanges. "The facts of contemporary reality," Soviet Foreign Trade Minister Nikolai Patolichev wrote in 1970, "confirm anew Lenin's thesis to the effect that objective economic interest is stronger than the policies of those imperialist powers who seek to hold back the development of business cooperation with the Socialist world."[43] On a superficial level, one could find some basis for Patolichev's assessment:

---

[42] Edmonds, *Soviet Foreign Policy*, pp. 84–86; Herbert S. Dinerstein, "The Soviet Outlook: America, Europe, and China," in Robert F. Osgood, ed., *Retreat From Empire: The First Nixon Administration* (Baltimore: 1973), pp. 113–117; Seyom Brown, *New Forces in World Politics* (Washington: 1974), pp. 67–69.

[43] Quoted in ibid., p. 69.

after all, the Nixon administration's sudden relaxation of restrictions on truck and machine tool exports to the Soviet Union in the summer of 1971 did coincide with the most severe balance of payments crisis since the end of World War II.

But the Soviet leadership's interest in expanding trade with the West stemmed as much from considerations of security as economics: riots over food prices in Poland the previous December had forced the resignation of Party Secretary Wladyslaw Gomulka and had very nearly provoked Soviet military intervention. This sobering demonstration of how internal discontent could shake the authority of the state was not lost on either Moscow or Washington: it was no accident that, three months later, the Twenty-Fourth Congress of the Soviet Communist Party endorsed a Five-Year Plan which, for the first time, emphasized raising consumer living standards over the needs of heavy industry. Nor was it fortuitous that, as early as January 1971, the Nixon administration had informed the Russians that it might be willing to loosen export restrictions in return for cooperation on outstanding political and military issues.[44]

Although overall trade turnover remained relatively small, considerable progress had been made by the end of 1972 in expanding Soviet-American economic ties. The Russians agreed to remedy an old grievance by making at least a token payment ($722 million over the next three decades) on their long-overdue World War II Lend-Lease debt; in return the Nixon administration promised to seek Export-Import Bank credits to finance Soviet purchases in the United States and the extension by Congress of "most-favored nation" treatment to imports from the USSR. Soviet buyers quietly placed orders for an astonishing 25% of the 1972 United States wheat crop—some 440 million bushels—to meet an unexpected shortfall in their own harvest. Several major American corporations, among them Pepsi-Cola and the Chase Manhattan Bank, made arrangements to open offices or manufacture their products in the Soviet Union; by mid-1973, even the First National City Bank, a prominent fixture of economic life in prerevolutionary Russia, had reopened its Moscow branch after an absence of fifty-one years. And in what may have been the most grandiose project of all, the Soviet

---

[44] Edmonds, *Soviet Foreign Policy*, pp. 89, 99–100; Kalb and Kalb, *Kissinger*, p. 213.

government had opened negotiations with the El Paso Natural Gas Company and the Occidental Petroleum Company (the latter headed by Armand Hammer, one of the few successful foreign concessionaires in Russia during the 1920s) for a $10 billion, seven-year plan to build pipelines and tankers with which to transport Siberian natural gas to Japan and the United States.[45]

The Nixon administration encouraged these trends on the assumption that a proliferation of economic relationships would render the Soviet Union dependent on American trade and technology and therby lessen the danger of war. "Our purpose," Secretary of Commerce Peter G. Peterson explained in August 1972,

is . . . to build in both countries a vested economic interest in the maintenance of an harmonious and enduring relationship. A nation's security is affected not only by its adversary's military capabilities but by the price which attends the use of those capabilities. If we can create a situation in which the use of military force would jeopardize a mutually profitable relationship, I think it can be argued that our security will have been enhanced.

Two years later, Kissinger, by that time secretary of state, described the same approach in even more succinct terms: "Over time, trade and investment may leaven the autarkic tendencies of the Soviet system, invite gradual association of the Soviet economy with the world economy, and foster a degree of interdependence that adds an element of stability to the political equation."[46]

Fissures within the international communist movement also provided the Nixon administration with opportunities to encourage movement toward detente. There had been earlier efforts to exploit such fragmentation to American advantage —Washington had long dealt with Yugoslavia as almost an ally, and the Johnson administration had made similar overtures toward Eastern Europe. No sustained attempt had been made to improve relations with the People's Republic of China, though,

---

[45] Brown, *New Forces in World Politics*, pp. 72–73; Sobel, ed., *Kissinger & Detente*, pp. 142–144.

[46] Peter G. Peterson, *U.S. - Soviet Commercial Relations in a New Era* (Washington: 1972), pp. 3–4; Kissinger statement of September 19, 1974, *Department of State Bulletin*, LXXI(October 14, 1974), 512.

in part because of that state's unremitting hostility toward the United States and in part because both Kennedy and Johnson had feared raising ghosts from the "who lost China" debates of the early 1950s. There is obvious irony in the fact that the president who made the breakthrough to Peking had himself led the attack on the Democrats' China policy two decades earlier; Nixon's views on the subject had never been as dogmatic as his public rhetoric indicated, however. As early as 1954, he had privately argued against keeping China indefinitely isolated; by 1967 he was saying much the same thing openly.[47] Nixon entered the White House at a delicate moment in the history of Sino-Soviet relations: during the summer of 1969 Soviet diplomats had begun sounding out American officials on what Washington's response would be to a preemptive strike by the USSR on Chinese nuclear installations, and in the course of the SALT talks the following summer, the Russians formally proposed what would have been in effect a Soviet-American alliance designed to discourage "provocative" actions by China.[48]

Far from encouraging such cooperation with Moscow against Peking, Nixon instead initiated a series of gestures aimed at bringing about a Sino-American reconciliation: these concluded with the surprise announcement in July 1971 that the president would visit China early the following year. Both Nixon and Kissinger were careful to deny that their "opening to Peking" was directed against the Russians, but there is little doubt that such considerations were present. "The worst thing that could happen for us," Nixon had told his staff in August 1969, "would be for the Soviet Union to gobble up Red China. . . . We're not doing this because we love the Chinese. We just have to see to it that the U. S. plays both sides." In addition to maintaining the global balance of power, such tactics might induce Soviet cooperation on other issues. "They haven't helped on Vietnam, on the Mideast, on the arms talks," Nixon added: "We've got to give them a reason to help us."[49]

---

[47] Brandon, *The Retreat of American Power*, pp. 181–182; Richard M. Nixon, "Asia After Vietnam," *Foreign Affairs*, XLVI(October, 1967), 121–123.
[48] Kalb and Kalb, *Kissinger*, pp. 225–226; Newhouse, *Cold Dawn*, pp. 164, 188–189.
[49] Quoted in William Safire, *Before the Fall: An Inside View of the Pre-Watergate White House* (New York: 1975), p. 370.

Nixon's strategy of "linkage" never produced the results he expected from it in those areas, partly because he publicized it too widely and partly because he exaggerated Moscow's ability to shape events in Cairo and Hanoi.[50] But there are convincing indications that the China initiative did cause the Russians to speed up efforts to reach agreements on SALT;[51] certainly it was responsible for the invitation, issued in October 1971, for Nixon to visit Moscow the following spring after his return from Peking. Brezhnev, in a speech delivered in March 1972, described the Sino-American rapprochement as a "natural" development, although he could not help wondering whether Nixon's talks with the Chinese had not gone "beyond the framework of bilateral relations between the USA and China. How else is one to understand, for instance, the statement made during the banquet in Shanghai that 'today our two peoples hold the future of the whole world in their hands'?"[52] It was the tone of a man resigned to relinquishing at last the luxury of having adversaries who despised each other more than they despised him.

"Linkage" did work in other ways, though. Attempts to solve the perennial German question had received a major boost in September 1969, with the victory of the Social Democrats in West Germany and the emergence, as chancellor, of Willy Brandt. Three separate series of negotiations with the Russians soon got underway, with progress on each linked to developments in the others: (1) discussions between West Germany, Poland, and the Soviet Union confirming existing boundaries in Eastern Europe, including the controversial Oder-Neisse frontier—Brandt signed treaties to this effect with the Russians in August 1970 and with the Poles the following December; (2) negotiations among the four powers occupying Berlin aimed at normalizing the position of that divided city—the resulting agreement, recognizing Western access rights there, was signed in September 1971; (3) contacts between representatives of NATO and the Warsaw Pact looking toward eventual talks on mutual and balanced force reductions (MBFR) and the Russians' long-

---

[50] Kalb and Kalb, *Kissinger*, pp. 102–106.

[51] See Newhouse, *Cold Dawn*, pp. 234–236.

[52] Leonid Brezhnev, *On the Policy of the Soviet Union and the International Situation* (Garden City, New York: 1973), p. 178.

sought Conference on Security and Cooperation in Europe (CSCE).

What emerged from these overlapping and interlocking negotiations was the outline of a European settlement based on tacit West German abandonment of reunification, Soviet recognition of the Western position on Berlin, a continued American military presence on the Continent, and a greater reliance than in the past on diplomacy as a means of resolving differences.[53] These agreements by no means removed Europe from the arena of Cold War rivalries, but they did represent an acknowledgement by the major powers of the status quo there. And since postwar Soviet policy in Europe can be explained as much by fear of the Germans as of anyone else, this was no insignificant achievement.

"Linkage" also proved to be an effective "crisis management" tool. Intelligence reports in September 1970 indicated that the Russians were building what appeared to be a nuclear submarine base in Cuba. Whatever its purpose, construction at the offending site soon stopped after Kissinger warned that such activity could impair prospects for detente. Another dangerous situation developed that same month in the Middle East, when Syrian tanks crossed into Jordan to aid Palestinian commandos in their struggle with King Hussein. "You and your client started it," Kissinger is said to have told a Soviet diplomat, "and you have to end it." Whether on Moscow's orders or not, the Syrians did turn back, but not before Kissinger had arranged for joint Israeli-Jordanian-American operations against both Syrian and Russian forces, if necessary. Fifteen months later, in December 1971, war broke out between India and Pakistan over the secession from the latter of Bangladesh. Concerned over rumors that the Indians, with Soviet encouragement, might dismember West Pakistan as well, Kissinger threatened to cancel the forthcoming Moscow summit unless the Russians induced New Delhi to show restraint.[54]

To what extent these crises actually reflected hostile intent on the part of the Soviet Union—or, alternatively, overreaction on

---

[53] Karl E. Birnbaum, *East and West Germany: A Modus Vivendi* (Lexington, Massachusetts: 1973), pp. 91–96.

[54] Kalb and Kalb, *Kissinger,* pp. 196–215, 257–263.

the part of the United States—is still not clear. Certainly Washington appears to have exaggerated Soviet responsibility for the India-Pakistan confrontation (although this may have been done by design to impress the pro-Pakistani Chinese). What these incidents do illustrate is the administration's conviction that the Russians needed detente badly enough to pay a substantial price for it—that they would pass up opportunities to exploit specific crises at the expense of the West in order to make progress toward a general relaxation of tensions. Moscow's response to the events of early May 1972 suggests that these were not entirely invalid assumptions.

On May 8, Nixon, acting in response to a large-scale North Vietnamese offensive against South Vietnam, ordered the mining of Haiphong and several other ports, together with an intensification of air strikes against Hanoi's overland supply lines. Closing North Vietnamese harbors had long been talked about in Washington, but the option had been rejected in the past for fear of provoking Chinese or even Soviet intervention.[55] Nixon now chose to act only two weeks before a long-planned meeting with Kremlin leaders in Moscow, at which final discussions were to take place on the normalization of economic relations and on the laboriously negotiated treaties limiting the deployment of offensive and defensive strategic weapons systems. For a moment, it appeared as though prospects for detente had been ruined. "What would happen," *Pravda* complained, "if the several states, whose legitimate interests . . . are threatened by the unilateral action of the USA, were to respond in the same manner?"[56] And yet, when Soviet Foreign Trade Minister Patolichev visited the White House three days after Nixon's announcement, he responded to newsmen's questions about the summit with bland reassurances: "We never had any doubts about it. I don't know why you asked this question. Have you any doubts?"[57] Two weeks later, Nixon and Brezhnev were toasting each other with champagne in the Kremlin.

Thanks to the Russians' eagerness to proceed, the May 22-29

[55] See Johnson, *The Vantage Point*, p. 369.

[56] *Pravda*, May 12, 1972, quoted in Kulski, *The Soviet Union in World Affairs*, pp. 439–440.

[57] *New York Times*, May 12, 1972.

summit more than lived up to its advance billing. The two delegations managed to keep agreements flowing roughly at the rate of one a day, on issues ranging from the avoidance of naval incidents at sea to health and environmental cooperation and plans for a joint Soviet-American space mission in 1975. No specific decisions were reached on economic issues, but a joint trade commission was established to facilitate future discussions on this point. The SALT I accords, limiting ABM and ICBM deployments, required hard bargaining and last-minute compromises, but the first major bilateral arms control agreement of modern times was finally signed late on the evening of May 26. Three days later, the conference wound up with a solemn declaration of "Basic Principles" jointly affirming the doctrine of "peaceful coexistence," undertaking to prevent the development "of situations capable of causing a dangerous exacerbation" of Soviet-American relations, and recognizing that "efforts to obtain unilateral advantage at the expense of the other, directly or indirectly, are inconsistent with these objectives."[58]

That the Haiphong decision did not produce the same effect as had the U-2 incident on the 1960 Paris summit, or the invasion of Czechoslovakia on Johnson's projected 1968 trip to Moscow, suggests that the Russians had developed an even greater stake in the improvement of Soviet-American relations than existed in Washington. Or so it was made to appear. The borderline between illusion and reality, like that between luck and skill, is an exceedingly fine one in diplomacy: clearly all of these qualities were present in the series of maneuvers that brought President Nixon and his protean assistant for national security affairs to Moscow in the spring of 1972.

No amount of adroit diplomacy could have produced the results achieved between 1969 and 1972 had not the circumstances been right—had not the Nixon administration had the good fortune to come to power at a time when the internal situations in the United States, the Soviet Union, and the People's Republic of China simultaneously favored detente. But auspicious circumstances are no guarantee of success in and of themselves; clumsy diplomacy has snatched failure from the jaws of triumph more than once. There was undeniably skill, as well as luck, in a

---

[58] *Department of State Bulletin*, LXVI(June 26, 1972), 898–899.

foreign policy that expanded American freedom of action in the world at a time when American strategic power, relative to that of the Soviet Union, was declining. There was wisdom, as well as expediency, in a course of action that reverted to the original concept of containment: the conviction that only Soviet expansionism, not international communism, possessed the capacity to threaten American security, and that the United States could effectively weaken the former phenomenon by exploiting strains which existed within the latter. The future of detente would, of course, be at the mercy of both men and circumstances; its prospects for survival, however, would depend in large measure on the extent to which the agreements reached at Moscow matched the interests of the states whose statesmen signed them.

IV

Curiously, few careful efforts were made, in either official or academic circles in the United States, to define "detente" until after that policy had been mutually endorsed by Nixon and Brezhnev at the 1972 Moscow summit. This lapse stemmed partly from the hope that there would be no substantive differences in the way in which Soviet and American leaders understood the term; partly too, one suspects, from fear that too close an investigation might contribute to just such differences. Once the belated exercise was carried out, it was discovered that while areas of congruence did exist, there were also important contradictions in the behavior each side expected of the other. Clarification of these by no means destroyed "detente", but it did lead to a scaling-down of expectations—to a realization that despite progress made, much remained to be done before the word could accurately be regarded as a synonym for "rapprochement."

In one sense, Brezhnev's concept of detente paralleled that of Nixon and Kissinger. Like the Americans, the Soviet leader saw contradictory tendencies shaping the other side's foreign policy and sought to reinforce those he considered desirable. "We are realists," Brezhnev proclaimed in December, 1972, and are well aware that influential circles in the imperialist world have not yet abandoned attempts to conduct policy "from positions of strength". . . . The Soviet Union will continue to work for detente and for consolidation of peace, persevering in its efforts to untie the knots of international tension, and working for stable good relations with countries with a differing social system. And if our policy evokes the appropriate response from them, then we shall say confidently that detente will become stable, and peaceful coexistence a universally accepted standard of inter-state relations.

But Brezhnev then added an important qualification:

The CPSU [Communist Party of the Soviet Union] has always held, and now holds, that the class struggle between the two systems—the capitalist and the socialist—in the economic and political, and also, of course, the ideological domains, will continue. That is to be expected since the world outlook and the class aims of socialism and capitalism are opposite and irreconcilable. But we shall strive to shift this historically inevitable struggle onto a path free from the perils of war, of dangerous conflicts, and an uncontrolled arms race. This will be a tremendous gain for world peace, for the interests of all peoples, of all states.[59]

This distinction between diplomatic and ideological goals was, of course, no new phenomenon in Soviet foreign policy, but it did call into question Brezhnev's acknowledgment, in the Moscow statement on "Basic Principles" six months earlier, of a "special responsibility" to ensure "that conflicts or situations will not arise which would serve to increase international tensions."[60]

It would, perhaps, have been too much to expect the general secretary of the Soviet Communist Party to disavow the class struggle, even in an era of detente, but there did exist in Washington the expectation that the Kremlin would continue to cooperate in "managing" crises generated by third parties in order to prevent escalation that might involve the superpowers. "The leaders of the Soviet Union are serious men," Nixon noted in May 1973: "Their willingness to commit themselves to certain

---

[59] Brezhnev, *On the Policy of the Soviet Union*, pp. 230–231.
[60] *Department of State Bulletin*, LXVI (June 26, 1972), 899.

principles for the future must be taken as a solemn obligation."[61] Within five months, this assumption would be seriously called into question.

There is no conclusive evidence that the Soviet Union instigated the October 6, 1973, attack on Israel by Egypt and Syria or the oil embargo against Israel's supporters in the West which the Organization of Arab Petroleum Exporting Countries (OPEC) imposed several days later. But Soviet behavior during this crisis was difficult to reconcile with the "code of conduct" Nixon and Brezhnev had agreed upon the previous year. Despite advance knowledge of the attack by at least 48 hours, the Russians did nothing to warn Washington. Nor did they seek to restrain the Egyptians and Syrians from initiating hostilities nor make any moves to encourage a cease-fire until it had become clear that the Israelis were going to win. Moscow welcomed the OPEC embargo, a tactic it had been advocating in broadcasts to the Arab world for some time. And, on October 24, angered by Israeli violations of a cease-fire that Kissinger and the Russians had arranged, Brezhnev, in a harsh note, proposed dispatching a Soviet-American peacekeeping force to the Middle East and threatened, if the United States did not cooperate, to act unilaterally there.[62]

Alarmed by this development and by intelligence reports of Soviet airborne troop movements, Nixon, late on the evening of October 24 authorized a worldwide Defense Condition 3 military alert (DefCon 1 is war), news of which had become public by the following morning. The president coupled this with a note to Brezhnev warning that unilateral action in the Middle East could threaten detente and suggesting instead the dispatch of a United Nations peacekeeping force from which the big powers would be excluded. Brezhnev denied plans for unilateral intervention and accused Nixon of fabricating the crisis, but as the Egyptian-Israeli cease-fire began to take hold, tensions eased

---

[61] Richard M. Nixon, *U.S. Foreign Policy for the 1970's: Shaping a Durable Peace: Report to the Congress, May 3, 1973* (Washington: 1973), pp. 37–38.

[62] Kalb and Kalb, *Kissinger*, pp. 489–490; Foy D. Kohler, Leon Gouré, and Mose L. Harvey, *The Soviet Union and the October 1973 Middle East War: Implications for Detente* (Miami: 1974), pp. 80–82, 87–92; Vladimir Petrov, *U.S.-Soviet Detente: Past and Future* (Washington: 1975), pp. 28–38.

and both sides reiterated their commitment to detente.[63] The episode had shown clearly, though, that Moscow's cooperation in managing third-party crises would extend only to preventing escalation to nuclear war, not to foregoing opportunities to exploit such developments at the expense of the West.[64]

This pattern of behavior showed up in other areas as well. Detente proved to be of little value in extricating the United States gracefully from the Vietnam War: while the Russians may have helped arrange the January 1973 cease-fire, they were either unwilling or unable to prevent the North Vietnamese from launching the series of offensives that finally overwhelmed South Vietnam and Cambodia in the spring of 1975. Nor could the Russians resist passing up opportunities created by the April 1974 revolution in Portugal: they not only funneled aid to Portuguese communists in their unsuccessful bid for power but also sought to fill the vacuum created by the resulting collapse of Portugal's African empire by supporting Marxist factions in Mozambique and Angola. The latter enterprise even involved the dispatch of Cuban mercenaries, a move Secretary of State Kissinger denounced in January 1976 as "counter to the crucial principles of avoidance of unilateral advantage and scrupulous concern for the interests of others which we have jointly enunciated."[65]

But Soviet officials, too, had reason to complain that detente had not met their expectations. To a greater extent than had been apparent in the West, they had looked to imports of food and technology from the United States to relieve their own overburdened economy, confronted as it was with the simultaneous necessities of improving living standards in a backward society while providing military security against two potential adversaries. As good Marxists, Kremlin leaders expected economic self-interest to ensure American cooperation; had such decisions been left to the business community alone, such might well have been the course of action taken. But Soviet

---

[63] Kalb and Kalb, *Kissinger,* pp. 492–493; Sobel, ed., *Kissinger & Detente,* pp. 158–159.

[64] Theodore Draper, "Detente," *Commentary,* LVII(June, 1974), 38–40.

[65] Kissinger press conference, January 14, 1976, *Department of State Bulletin,* LXXIV(February 2, 1976), 125.

analysts have shown a persistent tendency to underestimate the influence of noneconomic considerations on American foreign policy; they therefore failed to anticipate the extent to which the price of American economic assistance would come to hinge on considerations other than profit and loss.

Nixon had considered Soviet willingness to repay World War II Lend-Lease debts sufficient compensation for extending Export-Import Bank credits and "most-favored nation" tariff treatment (MFN), but Congress had to approve these moves and quickly made it clear that it considered the price too low. On October 4, 1972, Senator Henry M. Jackson of Washington introduced an amendment to the Trade Reform Act denying credits and MFN to "nonmarket economies" that taxed or restricted the emigration of their citizens.[66] It required little imagination to realize that this obliquely worded measure was aimed at Soviet practices regarding Jewish emigration or to conclude, from its list of seventy-two cosponsors, that it had excellent chances of passage. Administration officials spent much of the next two years in parallel negotiations, with the Russians to get them to raise emigration levels and with Jackson to get him to modify his amendment, on the grounds that the trade bill was an inappropriate instrument with which to try to reform Soviet society. Jackson was able to claim a major victory on October 18, 1974, when he announced that the Russians had agreed to allow at least 60,000 Jewish emigrants to leave the Soviet Union each year in return for Eximbank credits and MFN.[67]

The Senator spoke too soon, however, for on January 10, 1975, shortly after Congressional passage of the trade bill, the Russians abruptly rejected the entire economic package that had been under discussion since 1972—tariffs, credits, and Lend-Lease debts.[68] Soviet leaders took this action, one suspects, not so much from fear of relaxing emigration restrictions as from reluctance to yield to external pressure on a sensitive internal issue. The dangers of establishing such a precedent apparently outweighed the relatively marginal benefits promised by MFN and Eximbank credits, expecially after Congress in December

---

[66] *Congressional Record,* October 4, 1972, pp. 33658–33659.

[67] *New York Times,* October 19, 1974.

[68] Ibid., January 15, 1975.

cut the latter back to $300 million, a figure most experts regarded as unreasonably low. Jackson's effort to tie increased trade to increased emigration raised the price of the first commodity beyond what the Russians were willing to grant in terms of the second, with the result that neither side achieved either.

Oddly, no comparable efforts were made to use food as an instrument of reform, despite the Russians' obvious need for it to meet current agricultural shortfalls and despite the fact that they had few sources other than the United States to which to turn for it, something that was not the case in most other items of trade. Soviet purchasers had been allowed to buy wheat in 1972 at prices so low they failed to match resulting costs to American taxpayers in export subsidies and inflated prices for bread and flour; no political concessions were demanded in exchange. Three years later, Russian buyers again entered the American market on a large scale; this time the only demand made on them was that they sign a long-term purchasing agreement designed to cushion the impact of massive wheat sales on American consumers.[69] The most plausible explanation for this striking disparity in trading tactics is also, unfortunately, the least charitable one: Congress' solicitude regarding the plight of Soviet Jews did not exceed its unwillingness to alienate American farmers by restricting wheat exports. It was an illuminating commentary on the priorities of those who had sought to enlist detente in support of the cause of human rights.

The temptation to use economics as an instrument with which to reform the internal structure of the Russian state was, of course, an old one: as early as 1911, it had brought about abrogation of the Russian-American commercial treaty; similar considerations had entered into Roosevelt's negotiations with Litvinov over recognition in 1933 and discussions on the extension of credits after World War II. In each of those cases, Russian officials had refused to relax internal controls to obtain external benefits; domestic order, and the means to maintain it, occupied a higher priority in their minds than did the advantages to be derived from expanding trade with the West. Whether this was

---

[69] Sobel, ed., *Kissinger & Detente,* pp. 138–139, 190–191; see also Marshall I. Goldman, *Détente and Dollars: Doing Business with the Soviets* (New York: 1975), pp. 193–224.

still the case in the 1970s was open to question: certainly, internal stability in the Soviet Union had come to depend, to a greater extent than in the past, on economic contacts with the capitalist world; on the other hand it seems unlikely that the Kremlin would have been willing at any stage to risk Western intervention in Soviet domestic affairs to secure that assistance.[70] What is clear is that Congress blunted American bargaining potential by looking more to its own political priorities than to those of the Russians in deciding what price to place on the economic component of detente.

If detente is looked upon solely as a bargaining process, then evidence from the years 1972-1976 would tend to sustain the argument that the Russians handled themselves more shrewdly than did their American counterparts. Detente imposed no significant limitations on the Russians' ability to intervene by proxy in Third World areas, nor did rejection of the 1972 trade package deny them access to American agriculture or Western technology. Internally, the Soviet regime became less tolerant of dissent than before, with the result that such figures as Alexander Solzhenitsyn and Andrei Sakharov emerged as vigorous critics of detente. That policy produced no reduction in Soviet military expenditures, which have continued to rise relative to gross national product while by same standards American spending has declined.[71] And, at the Conference on Security and Cooperation in Europe, held in Helsinki on July 30-August 1, 1975, the Russians successfully capped a twenty-year campaign by securing the signatures of the United States and its NATO allies on a document affirming the "inviolability" of, and thereby appearing to legitimize, all existing boundaries in Europe.[72]

Meanwhile, American policy seemed paralyzed by indecision and self-doubt, products of the twin traumas of Vietnam and Watergate. Despite Israel's victory in the Middle East war, the United States found itself deferring respectfully to oil-rich sheiks and potentates suddenly possessed of the capacity to wreak havoc with its economy, not to mention those of its Euro-

---

[70] Ibid., pp. 69–70, 279–280. See also Alex Nove, "Can We Buy Détente?" *New York Times Magazine,* October 13, 1974, pp. 34, 89–93.

[71] Sobel, ed., *Kissinger & Detente,* p. 167.

[72] *Department of State Bulletin,* LXXIII(September 1, 1975), 324–325.

pean and Japanese allies. Proliferating scandals eroded the Nixon administration's credibility to the point that the October 1973 Defcon 3 alert was widely regarded as an artificially generated crisis, intended to distract attention from Watergate.[73] Nixon came to rely on his personal relationship with Brezhnev as a major justification for remaining in office, but the Russians uncharitably dropped the word "personal" from their translation of one of his speeches on the subject during the June 1974 Moscow summit and further added to the president's discomfiture by holding several of the sessions at a place called Yalta.[74] Continuing Congressional distrust kept the new administration of Gerald Ford from taking steps to save American clients in Southeast Asia or from opposing Soviet and Cuban efforts in Angola; Ford himself projected an image of appeasement by refusing to receive the now-exiled Solzhenitsyn at the White House in July 1975 and by abruptly firing Secretary of Defense James R. Schlesinger, a staunch critic of the Russians, at the end of October.

But these developments lay more in the realm of symbolism than of substance: it would be foolish to project from them generalizations regarding the long-term impact of detente on Soviet-American relations or on the configuration of power in the world at large. Things are not always what they seem in diplomacy: there is evidence that, thanks to Kissinger's "shuttle diplomacy," it was Soviet and not American influence that declined in the Middle East following the 1973 Arab-Israeli War; similar trends may yet emerge in southern Africa and possibly Southeast Asia as well. Vietnam and Watergate may come in time to be regarded as less than total losses for the United States: the first because it brought an end to indiscriminate globalism in American foreign policy; the second because it demonstrated, in a way few other countries could have managed, the supremacy of constitutional processes over individual leaders, however powerful.[75] The Helsinki declaration may seem important to future historians, not for its implied recognition of

---

[73] Kalb and Kalb, *Kissinger,* pp. 494–495.

[74] Sobel, ed., *Kissinger & Detente,* p. 168.

[75] See, on the above points, the analysis in International Institute for Strategic Studies, *Strategic Survey, 1975* (London: 1976), pp. 1–4.

Soviet hegemony in Eastern Europe, but for the standard its human rights provisions established against which to measure Moscow's treatment of its own citizens and those of its satellites. In short, the phenomenon of "unintended consequence," which has shaped so many aspects of Soviet-American relations, should be enough to give the responsible analyst pause before jumping to the conclusion that the Russians have surged far ahead in the great "game" of detente.

For the fact is that detente is not a game from which one side or the other must emerge victorious: it is rather a process by which the superpowers have agreed to *refrain* from competition in certain areas, while continuing it in others. Its durability depends on the extent to which agreements not to compete can be reconciled with perceived interests on each side and on the ability of the competitors, in areas where competition still perists, to keep it limited. It is not likely, in and of itself, to alter decisively existing power relationships in the world: by its very nature, detente rules out dramatic coups by one side at the expense of the other. Furthermore, to an increasing degree, influence in contemporary international relations is the product of circumstances only partly within the control of the superpowers. What detente can do is to lessen the danger of war by preventing competition in one area from producing escalation in another, while working simultaneously to identify and expand such congruities of interest as exist. As such, it represents progress toward the goal of "graduated reciprocation in tension reduction"; beyond that, however, not too much should be claimed.

CHAPTER X

Epilogue

S ECURITY IS, OF COURSE, A RELATIVE AND NOT AN ABSOLUTE
CONCEPT; much in international affairs depends on
how statesmen define it. The history of relations between the
United States and Russia can be written largely in terms of variations, within both countries, between what might be called
"universalist" and "particularist" approaches to the problem of
achieving security in the world.[1] The "universalist," equating
security with homogeneity, discounts the possibility of achieving that condition until the international environment has been
modified to resemble the nation; only then can there be assurance that nothing in that environment can pose a threat. The
"particularist" seeks to ensure that nothing in the international
environment can harm the nation, whether the environment
resembles the nation or not; security, from this perspective, requires diversity. The "universalist" sees harmony as a distant
but attainable prospect in world affairs, and thinks that security
ultimately depends on achieving it. The "particularist" regards
harmony as unlikely, but thinks that security can be obtained
nonetheless, through a careful balancing of power, interests,
and antagonisms.

Not surprisingly, periods of relative cordiality in Russian-
American relations have coincided with those periods in which
particularism has prevailed in both countries. Thus the long his-

---

[1] I have employed here, in a slightly different context, terminology used by
George F. Kennan in a 1948 Policy Planning Staff paper, PPS 23, "Review of
Current Trends, U. S. Foreign Policy," February 24, 1948, *FR: 1948*, I, 526–527.
See also Kennan, *The Realities of American Foreign Policy* (Princeton: 1954), pp.
15–16; and Charles Burton Marshall, *The Limits of Foreign Policy* (Baltimore: 1968),
pp. 38–39.

tory of amicable contacts during the nineteenth century grew out of the American government's restraint regarding European issues, and out of the fact that the Russians, while hardly particularist in dealing with their immediate neighbors, were so when it came to the affairs of the New World. This pattern of mutual forebearance broke down during the late nineteenth and early twentieth centuries, first as the result of a broadened American perception of vital interests in the world, then from the advent within Russia of an ideology possessed of global pretensions. Despite the competing universalist legacies of Wilson and Lenin, cooperation remained possible where interests coincided, as in the area of economic relations during the 1920s or military collaboration against the Axis in World War II. Even after that latter event had catapulted both powers into a contest for world leadership, reason dictated respect for certain "rules of the game," notably an inclination to avoid risks which might lead to nuclear war. In general, though, relations between Washington and Moscow in the twentieth century have reflected the suspicion universalism characteristically provokes: the conviction, on each side, that its rival will not rest until it has altered fundamentally the environment the other considers necessary for its security.

Neither Russians nor Americans are likely to abandon their respective ideological positions anytime soon. But ideologies do have a way of bending to accommodate circumstances, and one circumstance both Soviet and American leaders have to take into account is the fact that their ability to shape events in the world at large is declining. The two countries are approaching the point at which they will be able to project military power safely only by proxy: force may soon be a luxury allowed only to small, "unsophisticated" states—not because their "sophisticated" counterparts have any monopoly on wisdom, or even peaceful intent, but because the costs and risks of direct involvement have soared far beyond possible gains. And "influence," short of force, has proven to be a decidedly delicate commodity in what is now, more than ever, the "age of nationalism." Logic, it would appear, leaves Washington and Moscow little choice but to embrace particularism: to learn to live with a diverse world.

Unfortunately, international relations do not always proceed in a logical manner. Foreign policy ultimately reflects the internal structure of the states it serves; accommodation to diversity requires not just a rational assessment of the international situation but a favorable domestic climate as well. There is reason to wonder whether a state like the Soviet Union, whose self-confidence is so fragile as to be shaken by the issuance of a dissident manifesto, or by the surreptitious circulation of an unpublished novel, can ever find security in a diverse external environment.[2] Nor, as the presidential campaign of 1976 vividly demonstrated, have those aspiring to high office in the United States outgrown the temptation to place foreign policy at the mercy of domestic politics. The future of detente will depend, more than anything else, on the extent to which a particularist view of the world can be reconciled with the exigencies of wielding power inside both the United States and the Soviet Union.

Whether Soviet-American relations assume universalist or particularist overtones during the remainder of this century may be a less important question than we are apt to think, however, providing of course that rationality prevails to the extent of inhibiting a nuclear exchange. New issues have emerged which overshadow in significance traditional sources of antagonism between Washington and Moscow; new determinants of power have arisen not susceptible to control from either capital. As a consequence, it may soon be possible to say, with greater assurance than seems warranted today, that the Cold War is in fact over. But whether Russians or Americans will take much comfort in that development is another matter: given the intractability of these new problems they may well find themselves looking back with a certain amount of nostalgia, some years hence, to the "good old days" of the Cold War, when all the world had to worry about was the prospect of mutual, instantaneous annihilation.

---

[2] See, on this point, Hedrick Smith, *The Russians* (New York: 1976), pp. 439–463; and Robert G. Kaiser, *Russia: The People and the Power* (New York: 1976), pp. 400–450.

Bibliographical Essay

F OR A BOOK BURDENED WITH THE NUMBER OF FOOTNOTES
THIS ONE HAS, an extended bibliographical essay
could only be an exercise in redundancy. What follows, rather,
is an attempt to identify and evaluate the basic body of literature
with which students of Russian-American relations should be
familiar. I have also ventured some suggestions as to where
more work needs to be done.

First, a word about primary sources. From the American side,
the most important single source is the Department of State's
documentary series, *Foreign Relations of the United States*, which
begins in 1861 and has, as of this writing, reached 1950. Published documentary sources for the pre-1861 period exist, but the
most reliable approach is to work through the documents themselves, which are conveniently available on microfilm from the
National Archives for the period 1781–1929. Because *Foreign Relations* is selective, especially for the pre-World War I period,
these microfilmed records provide a valuable supplement even
for the years covered by that series. Diplomatic records from
1929 through 1949 are available at the National Archives, though
not yet on microfilm. For the period since 1949, one is generally
limited to public documents, which are accessible through the
series *Documents on American Foreign Relations* (Boston:
1938–1953; New York: 1953–   ), the *Department of State Bulletin,*
or the *Public Papers of the Presidents of the United States* (Washington: 1960–   ).

Russian documents, as might be expected, are much less accessible. Except in selected areas, Russian archives are not open
to Western historians, nor are Soviet documentary publications
as complete as their American counterparts. Students with a

knowledge of Russian can derive some benefit, however, from two series published by the Soviet Ministry of Foreign Affairs, *Vneshnaia politika Rossii XIX i nachala XX veka* [*Russian Foreign Policy in the 19th and the Beginning of the 20th Centuries*] (Moscow: 1960–   ), which at present covers only the early 19th century, and *Dokumenty vneshnei politiki SSSR* [*Documents on the Foreign Policy of the U.S.S.R.*] (Moscow: 1957–   ), which begins with 1917 and has reached the late 1930s. A collection of reports from Russian ministers in Washington between 1818 and 1823 was published in the *American Historical Review*, XVIII(1913), 309–345, 537–562; also useful is Frank A. Golder, *Guide to Materials for American History in Russian Archives* (Washington: 1917, 1937). For Soviet public documents on foreign policy up to World War II, the standard source is Jane Degras, ed., *Soviet Documents on Foreign Policy, 1917–41* (London: 1951–1953), 3 volumes; for later periods this can be supplemented by the series *Documents on International Affairs* (London: 1929–   ).

There are three general surveys of Russian-American relations, all now badly out of date. Foster Rhea Dulles' *The Road to Teheran: The Story of Russia and America, 1781–1943* (Princeton: 1944) is a competent discussion, but reflects the period of wartime cooperation during which it was written. Thomas A. Bailey's *America Faces Russia: Russian-American Relations From Early Times to Our Own Day* (Ithaca: 1950) is vigorous and anecdotal but also much influenced by the atmosphere in which it was composed. The most complete survey is William A. Williams, *American-Russian Relations, 1781–1947* (New York: 1952), a pioneering work in its anticipation of New Left revisionism but not always persuasive in its conclusions.

Among surveys of Soviet-American relations since the Revolution the most eloquent account (though heavily weighted toward the 1917–1921 period) is George F. Kennan's *Russia and the West under Lenin and Stalin* (Boston: 1961). Two works covering the entire history of Soviet-American relations but with emphasis on the Cold War are André Fontaine, *History of the Cold War* (New York: 1968–1969), 2 volumes, and D. F. Fleming, *The Cold War and Its Origins, 1917–1960* (Garden City, New York: 1961), 2 volumes, an early revisionist account. The most comprehensive discussion of Soviet-American relations from the Revolution to the present can be found in Adam B. Ulam's authoritative *Expansion and Coexistence: The History of Soviet Foreign Policy, 1917–73*, Second Edition (New York: 1974). Two important memoirs covering much of the history of Soviet-American relations are George F. Kennan, *Memoirs* (Boston: 1967, 1972), 2 volumes, and Charles E. Bohlen, *Witness to History: 1929–1969* (New York: 1973). For a revealing Soviet perspective on these events, see B. Ponomaryov, A. Gromyko, and V. Khvostov, eds., *History of Soviet Foreign Policy, 1917–1970* (Moscow: 1969, 1974), 2 volumes.

Soviet scholars have been active in studying the early history of Russian-American relations, most notably N. N. Bolkhovitinov, whose *The Beginnings of Russian-American Relations, 1775–1815*, translated by Elena Levin (Cambridge, Massachusetts: 1975), is now the definitive account. Bolkhovitinov can be supplemented with two much older studies: John C. Hildt, *Early Diplomatic Relations of the United States with Russia* (Baltimore: 1906), and Benjamin Platt Thomas, *Russo-American Relations, 1815–1867* (Baltimore: 1930). Also valuable for the particular topics with which they deal are Alfred W. Crosby, Jr., *America, Russia, Hemp and Napoleon: American Trade with Russia and the Baltic, 1783–1812* (Columbus: 1965); Alan Dowty, *The Limits of American Isolationism: The United States and the Crimean War* (New York: 1971); and Max Laserson, *The American Impact on Russia–Diplomatic and Ideological–1784-1917* (New York: 1950). Generally, though, the student of early Russian-American relations must rely on such original sources as are available and on periodical literature. In this latter connection, the articles of Frank A. Golder, David M. Griffiths, Norman E. Saul and Irby C. Nichols, Jr., cited in the notes to Chapter I, are of particular value.

One topic from the early history of Russian-American relations which has been well covered is the Alaska Purchase and the events leading up to it. Two recent complementary accounts are Howard I. Kushner, *Conflict on the Northwest Coast: American-Russian Rivalry in the Pacific Northwest, 1790–1867* (Westport, Connecticut: 1975), and Ronald J. Jensen, *The Alaska Purchase and Russian American Relations* (Seattle: 1975). See also Victor J. Farrar, *The Annexation of Russian America to the United States* (Washington: 1937), and Hector Chevigny, *Russian America: The Great Alaskan Venture, 1741–1867* (New York: 1965).

Despite great interest in this problem today, there is no comprehensive account of American concern regarding Russian persecution of Jews and dissidents in the late nineteenth and early twentieth centuries. Cyrus Adler and Aaron Margalith, *With Firmness in the Right: American Diplomatic Action Affecting Jews, 1840–1945* (New York: 1946) is little more than a list of American initiatives on this subject. Some attention is paid to the problem in David Hecht, *Russian Radicals Look to America, 1825–1894* (Cambridge, Massachusetts: 1947), and in Arthur W. Thompson and Robert W. Hart, *The Uncertain Crusade: America and the Russian Revolution of 1905* (Amherst, Massachusetts: 1970), but neither is a satisfactory account. There is a useful discussion of the issue in Taylor Stults, "Imperial Russia Through American Eyes, 1894–1904" (Ph. D. Dissertation, University of Missouri, 1970); see also the periodical literature cited in the notes to Chapter II, notably the articles of Stults, Naomi Cohen, Clifford Egan, and Philip Schoenberg.

Russian-American antagonism in the Far East during this period has been thoroughly covered. The most satisfactory single account is still Edward H. Zabriskie, *American-Russian Rivalry in the Far East: A Study in Diplomacy and Power Politics, 1895–1914* (Philadelphia: 1946). Pauline Tompkins, *American-Russian Relations in the Far East* (New York: 1949), treats the subject within a broader chronological framework. Other works which address this topic in varying degrees of detail are Howard K. Beale, *Theodore Roosevelt and the Rise of America to World Power* (Baltimore: 1956); Tyler Dennett, *Roosevelt and the Russo-Japanese War* (Garden City, New York: 1925); Raymond A. Esthus, *Theodore Roosevelt and Japan* (Seattle: 1966); Michael H. Hunt, *Frontier Defense and the Open Door: Manchuria in Chinese-American Relations; 1895–1911* (New Haven: 1973); Charles Neu, *An Uncertain Friendship: Theodore Roosevelt and Japan, 1906–1909* (Cambridge, Massachusetts: 1967); Walter V. and Marie V. Scholes, *The Foreign Policies of the Taft Administration* (Columbia, Missouri: 1970); Eugene P. Trani, *The Treaty of Portsmouth: An Adventure in American Diplomacy* (Lexington: 1969); John A. White, *The Diplomacy of the Russo-Japanese War* (Princeton: 1964); Marilyn Blatt Young, *The Rhetoric of Empire: American China Policy, 1895–1901* (Cambridge, Massachusetts: 1968); and a Soviet account, L. I.

Zubok, *Ekspansionistskaia politika SShA v nachale XX veka* [*Expansionist Policies of the USA at the Beginning of the 20th Century*] (Moscow: 1969).

Secondary sources are virtually nonexistent for Russian-American economic relations prior to World War I. Two dated but still valuable unpublished dissertations are George S. Queen, "The United States and the Material Advance in Russia, 1887–1906" (University of Illinois, 1942), and Gilbert C. Kohlenberg, "Russian-American Economic Relations, 1906–1917" (University of Illinois, 1951). The most detailed treatment of Russian-American relations immediately prior to American entry into World War I is R. Sh. Ganelin, *Rossiia i SShA, 1914–1917* [*Russia and the USA, 1914–1917*] (Leningrad: 1969).

The definitive work on the United States and the Bolshevik Revolution is, of course, George F. Kennan's magisterial *Soviet-American Relations, 1917–1920* (Princeton: 1956, 1958), 2 volumes. Kennan's account should be supplemented, however, with Arno Mayer's *Political Origins of the New Diplomacy, 1917–1918* (New Haven: 1958), and *The Politics and Diplomacy of Peacemaking: Containment and Counterrevolution at Versailles, 1918–1919* (New York: 1967), and with N. Gordon Levin, *Woodrow Wilson and World Politics* (New York: 1968). For a comprehensive Soviet account, see L. A. Gvishiani, *Sovetskaia Rossiia i SShA, 1917–1920g.* [*Soviet Russia and the USA, 1917–1920*] (Moscow: 1970).

There is no comprehensive account of American relations with the Provisional Government, but two helpful dissertations are Harry H. Savage, "Official Policies and Relations of the United States with the Provisional Government of Russia, March-November, 1917" (University of Minnesota, 1971), and Alton Earl Ingrams, "The Root Mission to Russia, 1917" (Louisiana State University, 1970). Other useful treatments of special topics relating to Russian-American relations during the Revolution are Beatrice Farnsworth, *William C. Bullitt and the Soviet Union* (Bloomington: 1967); David F. Trask, *The United States in the Supreme War Council: American War Aims and Inter-Allied Strategy, 1917–1918* (Middletown, Connecticut: 1961), and W. B. Fowler, *British-American Relations, 1917–1918: The Role of Sir William Wiseman* (Princeton: 1969), good on the role of coalition diplomacy in the decision to intervene; William S. Graves, *America's Siberian Adventure: 1918–1920* (New York: 1931), an absorbing account by the commander of United States forces in Siberia; Christopher Lasch, *American Liberals and the Russian Revolution* (New York: 1962), and Robert K. Murray, *Red Scare: A Study in National Hysteria, 1919–1920* (Minneapolis: 1955), both good on the ideological impact of the Revolution in the United States; three books by Leonid I. Strakhovsky, *American Opinion About Russia: 1917–1920* (Toronto: 1961), *The Origins of American Intervention in North Russia, 1918* (Princeton: 1937), and *Intervention at Archangel* (Princeton: 1944); John A. White, *The Siberian Intervention* (Princeton: 1950); Betty M. Unterberger, *America's Siberian Expedition, 1918–1920* (Durham: 1956); Robert D. Warth, *The Allies and the Russian Revolution From the Fall of the Monarchy to the Peace of Brest-Litovsk* (Durham: 1954); John M. Thompson, *Russia, Bolshevism, and the Versailles Peace* (Princeton: 1966); and William A. Williams, *American-Russian Relations, 1781–1947* (New York: 1952), good on the role of Raymond Robins.

Soviet-American relations during the years of nonrecognition have been surprisingly well covered. Two persuasive and methodologically sophisticated treatments are Peter G. Filene, *Americans and the Soviet Experiment: 1917–1933* (Cambridge, Massachusetts: 1967), and Joan Hoff Wilson, *Ideology and Economics: United States Relations with the Soviet Union, 1918–1933* (Columbia, Missouri: 1974). Frederick L. Schuman, *American Policy Toward Russia Since 1917* (New York: 1928), is an early but still useful account, while Edward M. Bennett, *Recognition of Russia: An American Foreign Policy Dilemma* (Waltham, Masachusetts: 1970), covers the period from the perspective of the recognition issue.

Valuable treatments of particular topics include Daniel M. Smith, *Aftermath of War: Bainbridge Colby and Wilsonian Diplomacy, 1920–1921* (Philadelphia 1970); Benjamin M. Weissman, *Herbert Hoover and Famine Relief to Soviet Russia, 1921–1923* (Stanford: 1974); Theodore Draper, *American Communism and Soviet Russia: The Formative Years* (New York: 1960); Floyd J. Fithian, "Soviet-American Economic Relations, 1918–1933: American Business in Russia during the Period of Non-Recognition," (Ph. D. Dissertation, University of Nebraska, 1964); Anthony C. Sutton, *Western Technology and Soviet Economic Development, 1917 to 1930* (Stanford: 1968); Meno Lovenstein, *American Opinion of*

Soviet Russia (Washington: 1941); Sylvia R. Margulies, *The Pilgrimage to Russia: The Soviet Union and the Treatment of Foreigners, 1924–1937* (Madison: 1968); and James K. Libbey, "Alexander Gumberg and Soviet-American Relations, 1917–33," (Ph. D. Dissertation, University of Kentucky, 1976).

On the decision to recognize the Soviet Union, in addition to works on the subject already mentioned, see Robert Paul Browder, *The Origins of Soviet-American Diplomacy* (Princeton: 1953), and Donald G. Bishop, *The Roosevelt-Litvinov Agreements: The American View* (Syracuse: 1965), which concentrates on the implementation of the recognition agreement. Except for the question of recognition, Soviet-American relations during the 1930s have been curiously neglected. The most comprehensive account is an as yet unpublished manuscript, Thomas R. Maddux, "Years of Estrangement: American Relations with the Soviet Union, 1933–1941," the revision of a 1969 University of Michigan dissertation. Orville H. Bullitt, ed., *For the President: Personal and Secret: Correspondence Between Franklin D. Roosevelt and William C. Bullitt* (Boston: 1972), provides a detailed glimpse of Soviet-American relations between 1933 and 1936; it should be balanced with the breathless and deliberately selective account of Bullitt's successor as ambassador to the Soviet Union, Joseph E. Davies, *Mission to Moscow* (New York: 1941). Two useful dissertations are Keith David Eagles, "Ambassador Joseph E. Davies and American-Soviet Relations, 1937–1941," (University of Washington, 1966), and Joseph E. O'Connor, "Laurence A. Steinhardt and American Policy Toward the Soviet Union, 1939–1941," (University of Virginia, 1968). There is some discussion of economic issues in Lloyd C. Gardner, *Economic Aspects of New Deal Diplomacy* (Madison: 1964), and Frederick C. Adams, *Economic Diplomacy: The Export-Import Bank and American Foreign Policy* (Columbia, Missouri: 1976).

On the series of events leading up to World War II, the most complete account is still William L. Langer and S. Everett Gleason, *The Challenge to Isolation: The World Crisis of 1937–1940 and American Foreign Policy* (New York: 1952), and *The Undeclared War, 1940–1941* (New York: 1953), but these volumes should be supplemented with Franz Knipping, *Die Amerikanische Russlandpolitik in der Zeit des Hitler-Stalin-Pakts, 1939–1941* (Tübingen: 1974); Andrew J. Schwartz, *America and the Russo-Finnish War*

(Washington: 1960); Robert Sobel, *The Origins of Interventionism: The United States and the Russo-Finnish War* (New York: 1960); and Raymond H. Dawson's excellent *The Decision to Aid Russia, 1941* (Chapel Hill: 1959).

For World War II, William H. McNeill, *America, Britain and Russia: Their Cooperation and Conflict, 1941–1946* (New York: 1953), remains, despite its age, an extraordinarily perceptive account. Herbert Feis, *Churchill, Roosevelt, Stalin: The War They Waged and the Peace They Sought* (Princeton: 1957), is long on detail, short on analysis. Two briefer but perceptive surveys are Gaddis Smith, *American Diplomacy During the Second World War, 1941–1945* (New York: 1965), and William L. Neumann, *After Victory: Churchill, Roosevelt, Stalin and the Making of the Peace* (New York: 1965). My own book, *The United States and the Origins of the Cold War, 1941–1947* (New York: 1972), examines tensions within the wartime alliance and the events which led to its breakup. For a relentlessly New Left analysis, see Gabriel Kolko, *The Politics of War: The World and United States Foreign Policy, 1943–1945* (New York: 1968).

Views of well-placed observers can be traced in William H. Standley and Arthur H. Ageton, *Admiral Ambassador to Russia* (Chicago: 1955); John R. Deane, *The Strange Alliance: The Story of Our Efforts at Wartime Cooperation with Russia* (New York: 1947); and W. Averell Harriman and Elie Abel, *Special Envoy to Churchill and Stalin, 1941–1945* (New York: 1975). These accounts should be balanced with the extraordinary diary of Henry A. Wallace, accessible in John Morton Blum, ed., *The Price of Vision: The Diary of Henry A. Wallace, 1942–1946* (Boston: 1973).

Accounts of special topics include: Robert Beitzell, *The Uneasy Alliance: America, Britain and Russia, 1941–1943* (New York: 1972), and Richard W. Steele, *The First Offensive, 1942: Roosevelt, Marshall and the Making of American Strategy* (Bloomington: 1973), for the second front question; Lynn Etheridge Davis, *The Cold War Begins: Soviet-American Conflict Over Eastern Europe* (Princeton: 1974), and Geir Lundestad, *The American Non-Policy Towards Eastern Europe, 1943–1947* (New York: 1975), for Eastern Europe; George C. Herring, Jr., *Aid to Russia, 1941–1946: Strategy, Politics, the Origins of the Cold War* (New York: 1973), and Robert Huhn Jones, *The Roads to Russia: United States Lend Lease to the Soviet Union* (Norman: 1969), for Lend-Lease; Ralph B. Levering,

American Opinion and the Russian Alliance, 1939–1945 (Chapel Hill: 1976), a sophisticated study of public opinion; and Lisle A. Rose, *Dubious Victory: The United States and the End of World War II* (Kent, Ohio: 1973), covering the events of 1945.

There is no comprehensive study of the Teheran Conference; for Yalta, see Diane Clemens, *Yalta* (New York: 1970), and for Potsdam, Herbert Feis, *Between War and Peace: The Potsdam Conference* (Princeton: 1960) and Charles L. Mee, Jr., *Meeting at Potsdam* (New York: 1975), an oversimplified account. Gar Alperovitz, *Atomic Diplomacy: Hiroshima and Potsdam* (New York: 1965), is a misleading account of the decision to use the atomic bomb; more reliable are Herbert Feis, *The Atomic Bomb and the End of World War II* (Princeton: 1966); Walter Smith Schoenberger, *Decision of Destiny* (Athens, Ohio: 1969); and Martin J. Sherwin, *A World Destroyed: The Atomic Bomb and the Grand Alliance* (New York: 1975).

Soviet diplomacy during World War II has yet to receive a comprehensive treatment, although Vojtech Mastny is preparing one. In the meantime, one can consult Alexander Werth, *Russia at War, 1941–1945* (New York: 1964), and the appropriate chapters in Adam B. Ulam, *Stalin: The Man and His Era* (New York: 1973). Also useful on this subject is Frederick C. Barghoorn, *The Soviet Image of the United States* (New York: 1950).

The debate over the origins of the Cold War has been both protracted and bitter. The most satisfactory introduction to it is Thomas G. Paterson, ed., *The Origins of the Cold War,* Second Edition (Lexington, Massachusetts: 1974). The orthodox point of view can be traced in W. W. Rostow, *The United States in the World Arena: An Essay in Recent History* (New York: 1960); John Wheeler-Bennett and Anthony Nicols, *The Semblance of Peace* (London: 1972); Herbert Feis, *From Trust to Terror: The Onset of the Cold War, 1945–1950* (New York: 1970); John W. Spanier, *American Foreign Policy Since World War II,* Fourth Revised Edition (New York: 1971); Paul Y. Hammond, *Cold War and Detente: The American Foreign Policy Process Since 1945* (New York: 1975); Lisle A. Rose, *After Yalta: America and the Origins of the Cold War* (New York: 1973); and, in many ways, the most satisfactory orthodox accounts, Louis J. Halle, *The Cold War as History* (New York: 1967), and Adam B. Ulam, *The Rivals: America and Russia Since World War II* (New York: 1971).

Representative revisionist accounts include Lloyd C. Gardner, *Architects of Illusion: Men and Ideas in American Foreign Policy, 1941–1949* (Chicago: 1970); Thomas G. Paterson, *Soviet-American Confrontation: Postwar Reconstruction and the Origins of the Cold War* (Baltimore: 1973); Walter LaFeber, *America, Russia and the Cold War, 1945–1975,* Third Edition (New York: 1976); and, most thoroughly, Joyce and Gabriel Kolko, *The Limits of Power: The World and United States Foreign Policy, 1945–1954* (New York: 1972). The only revisionist account written with emphasis on Soviet policy is Alexander Werth, *Russia: The Postwar Years* (New York: 1971). For an eloquent and balanced synthesis, combining elements of the revisionist and orthodox points of view, see Daniel Yergin, *Shattered Peace: The Origins of the Cold War and the National Security State* (Boston: 1977).

Specialized accounts of value are Walter Millis, ed., *The Forrestal Diaries* (New York: 1951); Walter Bedell Smith, *My Three Years in Moscow* (Philadelphia: 1950); Joseph M. Jones, *The Fifteen Weeks (February 21–June 5, 1947)* (New York: 1955), for the origins of the Truman Doctrine and the Marshall Plan; Gaddis Smith, *Dean Acheson* (New York: 1972); David S. McLellan, *Dean Acheson: The State Department Years* (New York: 1976); Harry S. Truman, *Memoirs* (Garden City, New York: 1955, 1956), 2 volumes; Warner R. Schilling, Paul Y. Hammond, and Glenn H. Snyder, *Strategy, Politics and Defense Budgets* (New York: 1962); Robert E. Osgood, *NATO: The Entangling Alliance* (Chicago: 1962); and, for Soviet policy during the early years of the Cold War, Marshall Shulman, *Stalin's Foreign Policy Reappraised* (Cambridge, Massachusetts: 1963). McCarthyism is best covered in Earl Latham, *The Communist Controversy in Washington* (Cambridge, Massachusetts: 1966), and in Richard M. Fried, *Men Against McCarthy* (New York: 1976).

The best general account of the Korean War is David Rees, *Korea: The Limited War* (New York: 1964), but this should be supplemented with Glenn Paige, *The Korean Decision: June 24–30, 1950* (New York: 1968); John W. Spanier, *The Truman-MacArthur Controversy and the Korean War* (New York: 1965); and an important new explanation of the war's origins, Robert R. Simmons, *The Strained Alliance: Peking, Pyongyang, Moscow and the Politics of the Korean Civil War* (New York: 1975).

For the Eisenhower period, the most useful general accounts

are Herbert Parmet, *Eisenhower and the American Crusades* (New York: 1972); Peter Lyons, *Eisenhower: Portrait of the Hero* (Boston: 1974); Dwight D. Eisenhower, *The White House Years* (Garden City, New York: 1963, 1965), 2 volumes; Townsend Hoopes, *The Devil and John Foster Dulles* (Boston: 1973); Michael A. Guhin, *John Foster Dulles; A Statesman and His Time* (New York: 1972); and Charles C. Alexander, *Holding the Line: The Eisenhower Era, 1952–61* (Bloomington: 1975). Of special interest are Coral Bell, *Negotiation from Strength: A Study in the Politics of Power* (New York: 1963), a critique of the early diplomacy of the Eisenhower period; Alexander George and Richard L. Smoke, *Deterrence in American Foreign Policy: Theory and Practice* (New York: 1974), a theoretical approach based on an informative series of case studies; and Richard A. Aliano, *American Defense Policy from Eisenhower to Kennedy* (Athens, Ohio: 1975), an insightful discussion of the debate over defense spending in the late 1950s.

Soviet foreign policy has been surprisingly well documented for this period. The most important single source now that its authenticity has been confirmed is Nikita S. Khrushchev, *Khrushchev Remembers* (Boston: 1970; and *Khrushchev Remembers: The Last Testament* (Boston: 1974), an account as revealing about decision making within the Soviet Union as about its colorful author. Scholarly studies of importance include Thomas W. Wolfe, *Soviet Power and Europe: 1945–1970* (Baltimore: 1970), a book of broader scope than its title indicates; Arnold L. Horelick and Myron C. Rush, *Strategic Power and Soviet Foreign Policy* (Chicago: 1966), a cogent account of the Soviet practice of "strategic deception," Michel Tatu, *Power in the Kremlin: From Khrushchev to Kosygin* (New York: 1969), good on Khrushchev's later years in power; and William Zimmerman, *Soviet Perspectives on International Relations, 1956–1967* (Princeton: 1969), a study of the changing view of international relations within the Soviet Union. A somewhat comparable study from the American side is William Welch, *American Images of Soviet Foreign Policy* (New Haven: 1970).

The Cuban missile crisis has already generated a vast body of literature, portions of which can be sampled in Robert A. Divine, ed., *The Cuban Missile Crisis* (Chicago: 1971). The best account of the origins of the crisis is Herbert S. Dinerstein, *The Making of a Missile Crisis: October, 1962* (Baltimore: 1976). Graham

T. Allison, *Essence of Decision: Explaining the Cuban Missile Crisis* (Boston: 1971), is the definitive account of the crisis itself, as well as a methodological breakthrough in the study of bureaucracies and foreign policy. A popular but sound account is Elie Abel, *The Missile Crisis* (New York: 1966). A strong defense of Kennedy's handling of the crisis can be found in Theodore C. Sorensen, *Kennedy* (New York: 1965). More recent but less favorable assessments include Richard J. Walton, *Cold War and Counterrevolution: The Foreign Policy of John F. Kennedy* (New York: 1972); Louise FitzSimons, *The Kennedy Doctrine* (New York: 1972); and Bruce Miroff, *Pragmatic Illusions: The Presidential Politics of John F. Kennedy* (New York: 1976). Soviet accounts of the crisis are virtually nonexistent—one exception is Anatolii A. Gromyko, "Karibskii Krizis," *Voprosy Istorii* [*Problems of History*], 1971, no. 7, pp. 135–144, and no. 8, pp. 121–129.

For the period after the Cuban missile crisis, the secondary literature rapidly thins out. The best account of Soviet policy during the period is Robin Edmonds, *Soviet Foreign Policy, 1962–1973: The Paradox of Super-Power* (London: 1975). The strategic arms race is relatively well documented in George H. Quester, *Nuclear Diplomacy: The First Twenty-Five Years* (New York: 1973); Harland B. Moulton, *From Superiority to Parity: The United States and the Strategic Arms Race, 1961–1971* (Westport, Connecticut: 1973); Jerome H. Kahan, *Security in the Nuclear Age: Developing U.S. Strategic Arms Policy* (New York: 1975); and John Newhouse, *Cold Dawn: The Story of SALT* (New York: 1973). Soviet-American relations during the Johnson administration—particularly as affected by Vietnam—have hardly been touched, although there is some useful material in Robert E. Osgood, ed., *America and the World: From the Truman Doctrine to Vietnam* (Baltimore: 1970); and Seyom Brown, *The Faces of Power: Constancy and Change in United States Foreign Policy from Truman to Johnson* (New York: 1968). Johnson's own viewpoint can be obtained from Lyndon B. Johnson, *The Vantage Point: Perspectives on the Presidency, 1963–1969* (New York: 1971).

Documentation is somewhat better, though hardly definitive, for the Nixon years. Two good books with which to start are Henry Brandon, *The Retreat of American Power* (New York: 1973), and Marvin and Bernard Kalb, *Kissinger* (Boston: 1974). Also valuable are Robert E. Osgood, ed., *Retreat From Empire: The First Nixon Administration* (Baltimore: 1973); Seyom Brown, *New Forces in World Politics* (Washington: 1974); Marshall I. Goldman, *Detente and Dollars: Doing Business with the Soviets* (New York: 1975); and Vladimir Petrov, *U.S.-Soviet Detente: Past and Future* (Washington: 1975). Lester A Sobel, ed., *Kissinger & Detente* (New York: 1975), provides a useful chronology of recent developments.

The official Soviet view of detente can be conveniently sampled in Leonid Brezhnev, *On the Policy of the Soviet Union and the International Situation* (Garden City, New York: 1973). Two vivid and well-informed accounts of current conditions inside the Soviet Union, with significant implications for the future of the Soviet-American relationship, are Hedrick Smith, *The Russians* (New York: 1976), and Robert G. Kaiser, *Russia: The People and the Power* (New York: 1976).

Index

J